P9-DMV-151

THE BREWER'S APPRENTICE

BEVERLY MASSACHUSETTS

QUARRY BOOKS

AN INSIDER'S GUIDE TO THE ART AND CRAFT OF BEER BREWING, TAUGHT BY THE MASTERS

THE BREWER'S APPRENTICE

GREG KOCH AND MATT ALLYN

First published in the United States of America in 2011 by
Quarry Books, a member of
Quayside Publishing Group
100 Cummings Center
Suite 406-L
Beverly, Massachusetts 01915-6101
Telephone: (978) 282-9590
Fax: (978) 283-2742
www.quarrybooks.com

10 9 8 7 6

ISBN: 978-1-59253-731-0

Digital edition published in 2011
978-1-61058-159-2

Library of Congress Cataloging-in-Publication Data is available

Design: Paul Burgess: Burge Agency
Artwork: Pete Usher: Burge Agency
Front cover: istockphoto.com, except for bottom right: Foodcollection/Getty Images
Back Cover: Belgian Tourist Office, John Bollwitt (johnbollwitt.com), and istockphoto.com

Printed in China

Thanks to my family, friends, colleagues, fellow brewers (pro and amateur), and everyone else generous with advice, insight, and a fresh beer.

—Matt Allyn

To all the great brewers who have provided me with their liquid inspiration, and who showed me many years ago that "beer" was so very much more than the insipid nonsense of the TV commercials. Today, Craft and Artisanal brewing is alive and well...and growing in nearly every brewing culture. Here's to adding one more log to that fire, as well as another log to the funeral pyre of the notion that beer should be reduced down to nothing more than a cheap, flavorless, commodified fizzy yellow liquid!

—Greg Koch

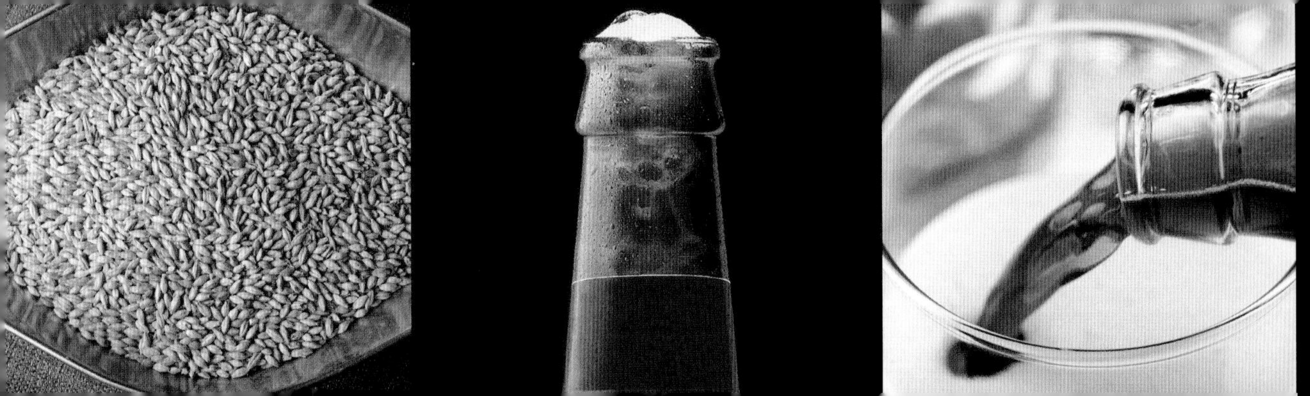

CONTENTS

Introduction 8

Brewing Basics 10

1: Mashing and Lautering: Eric Harper, Summit Brewing Co., U.S. 14

2: Bittering Hops: Vinnie Cilurzo, Russian River Brewing Co., U.S. 24

3: Aroma Hops: Nick Floyd, Three Floyds Brewing Co., U.S. 34

4: Lager Brewing: Bill Covaleski, Victory Brewing Co., U.S. 42

5: Water Chemistry: Mitch Steele, Stone Brewing Co., U.S. 52

6: Brewing Like a Belgian: Tomme Arthur, The Lost Abbey, U.S. 64

7: Wheat Beer: Hans-Peter Drexler, Weissbierbrauerei G. Schneider & Sohn, Germany 74

8: English Ales: John Keeling, Fuller, Smith & Turner, England 82

9: Lambic Brewing: Jean Van Roy, Brasserie Cantillon, Belgium 90

10: Brewing with Fruit and More: Sam Calagione, Dogfish Head Craft Brewery, U.S. 100

11: Brewing Big Beer: James Watt, BrewDog Ltd., Scotland 110

12: Barrel Aging: Scott Vaccaro, Captain Lawrence Brewing Co., U.S. 120

13: Organic Brewing: Ted Vivatson, Eel River Brewing Company, U.S. 128

14: Tasting and Evaluating Beer: Ray Daniels, Cicerone Certification Program, U.S. 140

15: Making Beautiful Beer: Ken Grossman, Sierra Nevada Brewing Co., U.S. 150

16: Mead: Bob Liptrot, Tugwell Creek Meadery, Canada 158

17: Hard Cider: James Kohn, Wandering Aengus Ciderworks, U.S. 166

18: Traditional Cider: Jérôme Dupont, Domaine Familial Louis Dupont, France 176

Brewer's Glossary 184

Contributors 186

Resources 187

Index 188

Photo Credits 191

About the Authors 192

TO OTHER CRAFT BEER ENTHUSIASTS, OUR WILLINGNESS TO ENGAGE IN NEAR-CONSTANT DIALOGUE ON OUR FAVORITE SUBJECT OFTEN CONFOUNDS THOSE WHO HAVEN'T CHOSEN TO LIVE A LIFE OF SUCH SUDSY IMMERSION. TO BE HONEST, THEY CONFOUND US, TOO. WHEN YOU TAKE A MOMENT TO TRULY CONTEMPLATE GREAT BEER, THE PATH IS CLEAR... AND COMPELLING, REWARDING, ENRICHING, SATISFYING.

I COULD GO ON.

QUITE WILLINGLY.

INTRODUCTION

And as such, this book has been born. Although it pays homage to the time-honored traditions of our favorite beverage, it is not just a repackaging of the solid, classic brewing tomes. As valid, important, and necessary, as they are, *The Brewer's Apprentice* offers a more picturesque view into our favorite subject.

In the writing of this book, we have had the great privilege of taking many educational sightseeing excursions along the great road-trip that is a brewing life. Although this book could certainly be read in a straight-line fashion, and is organized so it follows the steps of the brewing process, I invite you to bounce around as you wish. Interested in a deep-dive into malt? Turn to chapter 1 and be our guest. Eager to get a brewer's-eye-perspective on traditional Bavarian-style hefeweizens? Skip ahead to chapter 7, and learn from the best! Fancy a snifter of imperial stout while curled by the fire reading tales of conquest and woe at the hands of buggers such as *Pedio*, *Brett*, and *Lactobacillus*? Turn gingerly to chapter 9 on spontaneous fermentation.

I once heard, and have since oft repeated, what has become a favorite saying: "Buy a man a beer, waste an hour. Teach a man to brew, waste a lifetime." While I've known some who take offense to the saying, I feel that it is nothing but complimentary. "Wasting an hour" suggests a temporary yet rewarding pause from an otherwise hectic and go-go-go life. However, "wasting a lifetime" is not a true "waste," but instead, a diversion from the rat race into one of life's nobler pursuits: the art of brewing.

"Buy a man a beer, waste an hour. Teach a man to brew, waste a lifetime." While I've known some who take offense to the saying, I feel that it is nothing but complimentary.

As noble as brewing is (and as just about anyone would attest if they were anywhere past the half-pint mark), a junior executive might scoff at brewing, instead preferring to pursue upward mobility. He can have his upward mobility, as I don't care much for it.

Not to say that I don't crave forward movement and progress. I admit, I do. Does this pose a conflict? Joyfully, no. The world of craft beer and brewing has afforded me all of life's rewards that I could wish for: satisfaction from a job well done, respect of my friends and peers, standing in the community, access to the world's best culinary experiences, friends and comrades-in-arms around the world, an endless opportunity for creative flow, and yes, the proverbial food on the table.

And then there's the beer. And the opportunity to work with co-author Matt Allyn to bring you front-row and behind-the-scenes access to the greatest minds and talents in the brewing world.

The world of home brewing is both stuck in old-world tradition (in the best of senses) and simultaneously rocketing forward into new and barely charted territories. We've had the privilege of consulting, cajoling, and cavorting with both old friends and new to bring you unique access into the insights of those who live and breathe the art of brewing. Many of the names you'll hear in this book are familiar, and we're excited to bring you their insights. Other names will be new, and this introduction invites further discovery, as you will no doubt be inspired to seek out their fine work in order to back up the veracity of their studied opinions.

You might expect a portion of this book to be dedicated to the straightforward how-to of home brewing, or a starter's guide to professional brewing. A novice brewer might feel that omitting the basics of brewing might leave one with little orientation, as though the steering wheel, speedometer, tachometer, and shift column were completely omitted in favor of an on-board computer system and the automatic window controls. After a brief introduction to the brewing process and a glossary of equipment and ingredients, the book focuses on the technical, diverse, and the spectacular. And a spectacular view it is.

So, pull the owner's manual out of the glove compartment when you must review the operational basics of brewing—there are many great ones out there, and most likely you already have a trusted, well-worn, perhaps even wort-stained one on your shelf. Leave this book on the coffee table to peruse when you want to think about brewing (but not necessarily while you're brewing).

A great beer in hand is optional, but it's always in good taste.

— Greg Koch

BREWERS USE ONLY FOUR INGREDIENTS TO MAKE A BASIC BEER—WATER, BARLEY, HOPS, AND YEAST. EACH PART IS IRREPLACEABLE AND ESSENTIAL TO THE PROCESS, SO UNDERSTANDING ITS ROLE AND WHAT IT BRINGS TEACHES YOU HOW TO MODIFY, TWEAK, AND USE THE INGREDIENTS TO CREATE NEARLY ANY BEER, WILD OR MILD, YOU CAN DREAM UP.

BREWING BASICS

INGREDIENTS

WATER

Water constitutes 90 to 95 percent of a beer, so always use a clean source for brewing. Most tap water is acceptable as long as it's run through a carbon filter prior to brewing. Advanced brewers learn to adjust their water to suit their beer (see chapter 5 for how to modify your water).

MALT

Malted grains bring color, aroma, and flavor to a beer, but most importantly, they are the fuel for creating alcohol. Malt houses let grains such as barley and wheat germinate and begin to grow, creating starch. Then they dry the grains and stop the process, leaving a large amount of starch. The majority of any beer will use a pale malt (called base malt). Darker beer adds "specialty grains" that are roasted to different temperatures and impart various flavors and color.

New brewers often use liquid or dried malt extract to simplify the brewing process. This provides the same maltose (sugar) grains impart for brewing. While extracts are just as fermentable, their flavors can be inconsistent and lack the subtlety and complexity of true barley or wheat.

HOPS

These dried green flowers contribute bitterness, aroma, and flavor to a beer. A 5-gallon (19 L) batch of homebrew might need only an ounce of dried hop pellets to balance a sweeter amber ale, while a hop-centric India pale ale could use up to 8 ounces (227 g) or more.

YEAST

This microorganism is the engine behind beer. It consumes sugar derived from the malt starch to make alcohol. There are hundreds of different brewing yeast strains, each working at different temperatures and producing varying flavors. German wheat beers (hefeweizens), for example, owe much of their spicy character to their specialized yeast.

SUPPLIES

These are the supplies necessary to brew beer from grain to glass like a pro. Beginners should feel no shame in skipping the mash and lauter by adding malt extract to the kettle, but these are the tools of the trade for homebrewers ready to emulate their favorite brewmasters.

Pictured from left to right: gypsum, crushed crystal malt, malt extract, Cluster hop pellets, Northern Brewer hop pellets, molasses, brown sugar, Belgium candy, Irish moss, Kent Golding Hops, yeast, maple syrup, and priming sugar.

MASH TUN

Your crushed grains and hot water are combined in the mash tun to produce sugar during the first step of homebrewing. The two most common options are insulated coolers and metal mash kettles. Coolers, like the ones in which you would store beer at a party, hold the mash at a constant temperature with minimal work, but it's difficult to raise the mash temperature if needed. Mash kettles are heavy-duty pots, usually fitted with a spigot and false bottom for lautering.

LAUTER TUN

Often the mash and lauter tun are the same thing. A lauter tun is a large container with a screen or false bottom under the grains that allows the wort to drain out.

BREW KETTLE

Any large metal stock pot will do—copper, stainless steel or aluminum—as long as it's big enough. Your brew kettle should have one to two gallons (4 to 8 L) more capacity than the liquid in it. Extract brewers uses 5-gallon (19 L) pots, and all-grain brewers use at least 7-gallon (26 L) pots.

WORT CHILLERS

These copper or stainless coils have an inlet (and outlet) for tap water to run through the coil. When placed in hot wort, the water-cooled coil quickly drops the wort temperature.

FERMENTOR

Brewers need a primary fermentor, usually a food-grade plastic bucket, and then a secondary fermentor, typically a glass carboy for aging. The bucket is easy to use and clean, but it is also porous, letting small amounts of oxygen in, making it a bad candidate for aging beer.

BOTTLING BUCKET

This plastic bucket with a spigot allows you to mix your beer with priming sugar and then easily dispense into bottles.

CAPPER

This simple device crimps bottle caps and seals your beer.

AUTOSIPHON

It's not a necessity, but this makes transferring beer from one container to another a breeze.

HYDROMETER AND REFRACTOMETER

These devices will tell you how much sugar is in your beer, indicating how much can be fermented, and later, how much has been fermented out.

A stout is pitch black, but only uses a small percentage of black roasted malt. Use black roasted barley for five to ten percent of the total grains to get the color and flavor.

The brew deck at the Firestone Walker Brewer looks endlessly complicated but follows nearly all the same processes as a 5-gallon home brewery.

UNDERSTANDING GRAVITY, CALCULATING ABV

When the sugars from your mash dissolve into the hot water, the liquid (your wort) becomes denser. As yeast ferments that sugar out, converting it to alcohol, the beer becomes less dense. By subtracting the second, third, or final gravity reading from the first, and then accounting for the density of alcohol (multiply by 1.31), you can easily calculate a beer's alcohol content.

Starting gravity – final gravity x 1.31 x 100 = alcohol by volume

THE BREWING PROCESS: AN OVERVIEW

Brewing is a simple process that's easily complicated. And this book assumes a basic understanding of the principles that turn barley starch and hop flowers into pale ales and porters. These steps provide a basic reference for the steps to reach a finished (and delicious) beer, but for a more in-depth look at brewing fundamentals, read Charlie Papazian's *The Complete Joy of Homebrewing* and John Palmer's *How to Brew.*

STEP 1. MASH AND LAUTER THE GRAINS

The first step on the road to homebrewing is mashing the malted grains. You need sugar to ferment beer, and this is where you create it. The mash is a mixture of crushed grains and hot water that converts the starch in barley, wheat, or other grains into sugar (which yeast will turn into alcohol). Barley has two enzymes (proteins that encourage chemical reactions) that break starch down into sugar when they're within particular temperature ranges. Home brewers typically mix their grains with hot water and hold their mash between 145°F and 158°F (63°C and 70°C) for at least 20 minutes.

STEP 2. LAUTER
Once enzymes have converted most of the starch to sugar, drain the liquid out in a process called "lautering." Add additional hot water (around 170°F [77°C]) to help flush out the sugar. The first couple gallons of liquid drained out should be gently poured back over the grains. Water clarity should improve, and small bits of husk will stop coming out. This recirculation creates a filter to keep grain out of the wort. In total, you should have 5.5 to 6 gallons (20 to 23 L) of wort to create a five-gallon (19 L) batch of beer.

STEP 3. BOIL
Boiling wort sanitizes the liquid and absorbs bitter acids from the hops. The longer hops are boiled, the more bitterness they add. The later they're added, the more flavor and aroma they infuse. After 60 minutes, cool the wort as quickly as possible to prevent infection by wild bacteria. Homebrew stores sell wort chillers that cool batches to room temperature in 20 minutes or less, but placing the kettle in an ice bath for 30 to 60 minutes also works.

STEP 4. INOCULATION
When the wort is at least below 100°F (38°C)—higher temperatures kill brewing yeast—you'll mix in oxygen and add the yeast. The easiest way to aerate and add oxygen is by pouring the wort back and forth between the fermentor and kettle until there's a tall head of foam. You can also transfer the wort to the fermentor, seal the top, and shake it for 45 seconds. Before you add the yeast and seal the fermentor, measure the gravity (density) of your beer with a hydrometer or refractometer. This tells us how much sugar is in the wort. For reference, a beer that is aiming to hit 5 percent alcohol by volume (ABV) will have a starting gravity around 1.052. Finally, add the yeast and close the top of the fermentor. Use an airlock to allow CO_2, a byproduct of fermentation, to escape.

STEP 5. FERMENTATION
Every yeast has a particular temperature range for its ideal fermentation, but most beers ferment well at room temperature. After ten days, most of the sugar will have been converted into alcohol. You can take a second gravity reading to see how much sugar has fermented. Beer yeast leaves about a quarter of the total sugar behind (unlike a dry wine, for example). A common beer will have a final gravity around 1.012 to 1.016.

STEP 6. CONDITION
Conditioning acts like a filter. After the first (primary) fermentation, almost all the alcohol has been created, but letting the beer sit for at least two weeks will allow the yeast to stay active and literally clean itself up. With a siphon, transfer the beer to a conditioning fermentor, leaving the layer of yeast behind in the bottom of the primary. Tiny hops, barley, and yeast particles will also slowly sink to the bottom of the conditioning fermentor, clarifying the appearance and further improving the flavor.

STEP 7. BOTTLING
After your beer is fermented, conditioned, and tasting satisfactory (that one's up to you), the final step is to bottle. By adding a little (about an ounce per gallon [7 g per liter]) sugar to your beer and sealing it, the yeast will create both a small amount of alcohol and enough CO_2 to carbonate the brew.

Five gallons (19 L) of beer needs about two cases of bottles, plus a six-pack (54 total), but don't be surprised if you lost beer along the way when transferring from the kettle and then again to the conditioning fermentor. To bottle, boil the priming sugar in a cup of water for 15 minutes to sanitize it, then cool the liquid and add it to the beer. Then either siphon each beer individually into bottles, or transfer to a bottling bucket with a spigot near the bottom. Cap the beer, let it sit at room temperature for two weeks, and then enjoy. Congratulations, you've made beer.

BARLEY TO BEER, SIMPLIFIED

- **Select your grains and crush them (most homebrew shops will do this for you).**
- **For every pound of grain, mix in 1 to 2 quarts of hot water (2 to 4 liters per kilogram), creating the mash.**
- **Hold the mash at a temperature between 145°F and 158°F (63°C and 70°C) for 30 to 60 minutes.**
- **Add sparge water and drain out the liquid (now called the wort).**
- **Heat the wort to a boil and hold there for 60 minutes.**
- **Add hops: 1) at the start of the boil for bitterness, or 2) within the final 30 minutes for aroma and flavor.**
- **Cool the wort to below 80°F (27°C) and transfer to the fermentor.**
- **Shake the closed fermentor vigorously, then add yeast. Ferment the wort for 10 days as it becomes beer.**
- **Siphon the beer to a second fermentor and age it for at least two weeks.**
- **Add priming sugar (0.5 to 1 ounce per gallon [4 to 7 grams per liter]), then bottle the beer.**
- **Let the beer carbonate for two weeks, then enjoy.**

AN ALL-GRAIN MASH SEPARATES THE NOVICES FROM EXPERT HOMEBREWERS. YES, MALT EXTRACT IS A GOOD START FOR SMALL KITCHENS AND SIMPLE BREWING, BUT ONCE YOU'RE MASHING, YOU'RE PLAYING ON THE SAME FIELD AS PROFESSIONALS.

CHAPTER 1: MASHING AND LAUTERING

The basic process is simple enough. Add hot water to grain, wait while the malt starch converts to sugar, and drain out the newly created sugar water to boil. Aside from being a necessary brewing step, it's an opportunity to shape and mold your beer. By adjusting the water temperature, you can make beer with the feel of a featherweight Belgian, or the viscous body of a sticky imperial stout.

Perhaps a bit of the magic of beer is that it transforms itself before our eyes. And the ultimate sleight of hand on the road to beer happens in the mash tun. Microscopic enzymes attack the barley's starch, converting it into sugars that will eventually become alcohol.

INTRODUCTION TO MASHING

Mashing is the first big step on the trip from grain to glass. By turning the barley starch into sugar, you've created not only fuel for your yeast to create alcohol but the base of your flavor. Here are the basic steps:

STEP 1: SELECT AND GRIND BREWING GRAINS

While malted barley is the most commonly used grain, portions of wheat, oats, and rye can be added to create different tastes and mouthfeels. Most homebrewing shops will be happy to grind your brewing grains.

STEP 2: MASH IN

Most simple beers only need a single infusion of hot water for the grains. By soaking the grains and holding them at around 153°F (67°C), enzymes on the barley will break starch down into sugar.

STEP 3: LAUTER

After most of the starch has converted, lauter, or drain, the grains from the sugar solution.

STEP 4: SPARGE

To assist the lautering, additional hot water (around 170°F [77°C]) is added to help rinse out the sugar and reach the desired brewing volume.

In this chapter, you'll learn:

- **How the grinding of grains affects beer**
- **The different temperature steps of mashing**
- **How to mash, lauter, and sparge**
- **How to perform a decoction mash**

For mashing and lautering, you need:

- **Malted grains**
- **5-gallon (19 L) or larger stockpot**
- **Water**
- **Stove or burner**
- **Mash tun, such as a cooler with at least a 5-gallon (19 L) capacity**
- **90 minutes**

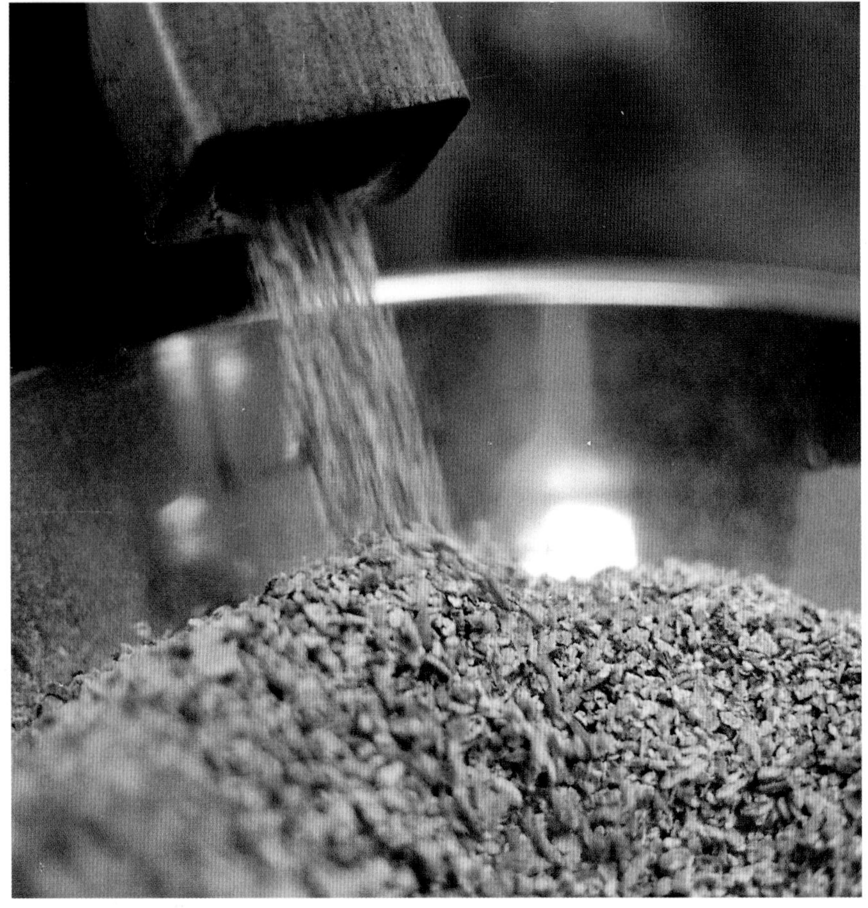

GRIST

The grind of your grain and the amount of water in the mash can further complicate your mash. Keeping a consistent grind and water-to-grain ratio will save you considerable headaches. If you mill your grain at home, know that too coarse of a grind will prevent the starch from getting wet while also insulating it from the hot mash water. If you grind too fine and have a mix of dust in your grist, you risk clogging your mash and extracting tannins from the grain.

For your water-to-grain ratio, 1 quart (0.9 L) to 1 pound (455 g) of grain is considered thick and 2 quarts (1.9 L) to 1 pound (455 g) is thin. A thicker mash protects those enzymes from degrading, allowing them to work longer. If you use a thinner mash, your extract is more soluble and washes out of the grain better. A ratio of 1¼ quarts (1.2 L) per 1 pound (455 g) is considered a safe, efficient middle-ground ratio.

MASHING STEPS

Your average homebrewed beer gets all the diastolic conversion power (enzyme activity) it needs from an hour-long mash somewhere between 146°F and 158°F (63°C and 70°C). For a thinner beer, such as a Belgian ale, aim for the lower end of the scale. For a chewy beer with less fermentable sugar, mash hotter, and for something like an everyday pale ale, shoot for 153°F or 154°F (67°C or 68°C).

Brewing tradition calls for additional steps to lower pH, increase starch solubility, and break down proteins and beta-glucan. However, today's base malt is packed full of enzymes and bred for lower protein levels. Furthermore, not being constrained within the restraints of Reinheitsgebot, Germany's restrictive brewing purity law, lowering the mash pH is as easy as dropping a teaspoon of lactic acid into the mash tun. If you feel like going the extra mile for the sake of tradition, look at the table to the right.

Note: For most brewing purposes, the only additional step worth noting is the beta-glucan rest at 98°F to 113°F (37°C to 45°C) for 20 minutes. If you're using large amounts of rye, oatmeal, or unmalted grains, this rest breaks down the gummy beta-glucan molecules that would otherwise create a stuck mash.

MASH AND LAUTER TUNS

Professional brewers use insulated copper and stainless steel vessels, complete with stirring rakes and steam heat. Homebrew mash tuns, while decidedly less glamorous, are just as effective. The most common option for homebrewers is an insulated cooler with a false bottom or screen filter to drain out the wort. This cooler works as a combination mash and lauter tun, saving you the hassle and mess of transferring the hot, sticky grains to a second vessel to sparge.

When you mash in a cooler, your only challenge is hitting the mash temperature. You can preheat your cooler with a quart (0.9 L) of hot water, but because your grains are at room temperature, they'll lower your strike water temperature as much as 20°F (11°C) depending on how much water you add. A thick mash on a cold day will need that extra 20°F (11°C), but a thin mash might only need an extra 10°F (6°C). Typically, though, a thick mash needs about 16°F (9°C) from the strike water.

Brewing software, such as BeerSmith and many online calculators, can give you a better estimate of strike water temperatures to begin, but it is best to take notes on how your mash tun reacts so you can calibrate future batches. Should you miss your target mash temperature, don't fret. Adding cold water to the tun or leaving the tun lid open will drop the temperature, while adding a quart (946 ml) of boiling water will raise it. Monitor the mash temperature closely with an instant-read thermometer.

ADDITIONAL REST STEPS

Rest	Temperature	Time (Minutes)	Benefit
Dough In	95°F to 113°F (35°C to 45°C)	20	This initial step mixes the starches, enzymes, and water. It raises efficiency by a few points. To lower the pH, extend this rest to at least two hours.
Protein	113°F to 131°F (45°C to 55°C)	20 to 30	If you have poorly modified malt or a large share of unmalted grain, this will break down protein that would otherwise add a haze and additional body to the beer.
Beta-Glucan	95°F to 113°F (35°C to 45°C)	15 to 20	This breaks down the sticky beta-glucans that come with rye, oatmeal, and unmalted grains.
Beta-Amylase	131°F to 150°F (55°C to 66°C)	15 to 60	Beta-amylase produces maltose and is the main contributor in starch conversion.
Alpha-Amylase	154°F to 162°F (68°C to 72°C)	20 to 30	Some maltose is created, but so are unfermentable sugars.
Mash Out	170°F to 175°F (77°C to 79°C)	5 to 20	This final step ends the enzymatic activity.

BREWING TERM: REINHEITSGEBOT

In 1516, the Bavarian government created strict standards for brewing beer to maintain quality, as well as protect wheat and rye demand for bakers. The Reinheitsgebot famously limited beer to three ingredients—water, the barley, and hops (yeast was centuries away from being identified). The law was later adopted by all of Germany. It is still followed by brewers today. Some see it as a statement of purity; adventurous brewers see it as an archaic and unnecessary restriction.

LAUTER AND SPARGE

Lautering is the process of removing liquid from the grains. The sparge is a step in lautering that flushes converted sugars out of the grains and into the brew kettle. Further, you don't mash with the final amount of water that you'll boil. The sparge water will fill the gap to reach your desired batch size (usually 5 gallons, or 19 L).

Preheat your sparge water to 168°F to 180°F (76°C to 82°C) to stop the diastolic conversion of your mash and optimize wort flow without extracting astringent tannins from the grain husks. Plan to use a lower temperature, however, if you want to continue the starch conversion throughout the lautering. Stop once you've hit your boil volume or a specific gravity of 1.012 (3 Plato) with your runoff.

A MASH FOR THE AGES: DECOCTION

If you want to make a truly old-school brew, start with a decoction mash. This age-old European brewing technique predates thermometers yet achieves the same processes of a modern multiple-step mash. Instead of adding hot water or heating the entire mash up to the next rest, brewers pull off and boil up to a third of the mash in a second vessel. Boiling aided with starch breakdown, and when the boiled mash was returned to the main vessel, it raised the overall temperature to the next rest.

The boiling caramelizes sugars and combines sugars and amino acids to create sweet melanoidins, flavors lost with a step mash. For this reason many German brewers still swear by a full four-step triple decoction. Fortunately, you can get similar results at home from a single decoction.

MASH

Begin with a standard mash at 148°F to 158°F (64°C to 70°C) to convert your starch for at least 30 minutes.

PULL

Remove a third of the mash to a pot and gradually heat to a boilover 10 to 15 minutes.

STIR

As you reach a boil, stir the mash often and don't leave it unattended. You need to keep the decoction at a boil, but not scorch grains on the bottom of the pot.

MASH OUT

After boiling for 15 to 30 minutes, return the decoction to the mash. It should raise the temperature to about 167°F (75°C) and end the enzymatic activity.

INTERVIEW WITH:
ERIC HARPER: BREWER, SUMMIT BREWING CO., ST. PAUL, MINNESOTA, U.S.

GROWING UP IN THE SHADOW OF SHEBOYGAN, WISCONSIN'S MALTING HOUSE, ERIC HAD HIS HANDS IN A MASH TUN BEFORE LEAVING HIGH SCHOOL. AFTER BREWING SCHOOL, HE HONED HIS CRAFT AT NEW GLARUS, ONE OF THE MIDWEST'S MOST REVERED CRAFT BREWERIES, AND IS NOW A BREWER AT MINNESOTA'S CRAFT BEER BEACON, SUMMIT BREWING.

LET'S GO BACK TO THE BEGINNING. DO YOU REMEMBER YOUR FIRST ALL-GRAIN MASH?

I was somewhere in Milwaukee [Wisconsin] at a friend's place, and it was a pale ale. We had a 5-gallon (19 L) cooler with a piece of braided cable in the bottom for my false bottom. I actually bought the cooler and the valves to build my mash and lauter tun. I stopped at three Home Depots on the way to my friend's house to get all the pieces. We were building it on the fly and would realize we needed another hose clamp.

DID YOU HAVE A BREWING PARTNER?

Yes, but I basically did all the work and they listened to me because I was the "expert." I made sure the mash temperatures were good, then we'd let it sit and walk down the street to a bar.

YOU FELT CONFIDENT ENOUGH TO GO DOWN THE STREET FOR A BEER?

It was literally at the end of the block, it was this tiki bar called the Foundation. Maybe my friends weren't all that interested in homebrewing, but that was my first all-grain.

HOW'D IT TURN OUT?

I think the wort turned out really well, but the end result was definitely undercarbonated. Not a stellar effort.

HOW DID YOU MOVE FROM A WISCONSIN-ONLY BREWERY TO A LARGER REGIONAL BREWERY LIKE SUMMIT?

Well, I married a girl from St. Paul, Minnesota and she wanted to move back. Summit had an opening. I'm one of seven brewers and we all do brewhouse, cellaring, and filtration, rotating on a monthly schedule.

HARPER
SUMMIT
BREWING CO.

Eric checks the mash tun volume.

It's funny how efficient a little homebrewery can be compared to a big brewery. You can get a lot of extract out of our malt with limited resources.

HOW DOES THAT ROTATION WORK OUT? IS IT A CHALLENGE?

It's definitely a benefit—we have a diverse team, but everyone has professional training and a lot of experience. This gets fresh eyes on your work. You don't get complacent and let things slide 'til something breaks.

MOST HOMEBREWERS SINGLE-STEP MASH. WHY WOULD YOU DO THE MULTISTEP?

If you have a lot of beta-glucan in your malt, you'll want to mash in at a lower temperature, in the 45°C to 50°C (113°F to 122°F) range, to break that up for lautering and clarity.

I brewed a Belgian beer here this spring, and one of the things I really wanted to avoid was phenolic characteristics later on. Ferulic acid is a precursor to phenolic flavor. When you're mashing, if you avoid a low range of 43°C to 44°C (109°F to 111°F), then you prevent producing these phenolic precursors. Some people mash in to knock out the beta-glucans, but then have phenol problems down the line. It's a tradeoff.

IS A PROTEIN REST STILL NECESSARY?

Today, so much of the malt we get is well-modified with a lot of enzymes, so it's not an issue. Unless you're using a high amount of adjunct or raw barley and need to break down protein there, a protein rest is not necessary. But in homebrewing, if you want to add adjunct, flakes are a good option. You can get pregelatinized barley or corn, or flaked oats. Then the starch has already been broken down.

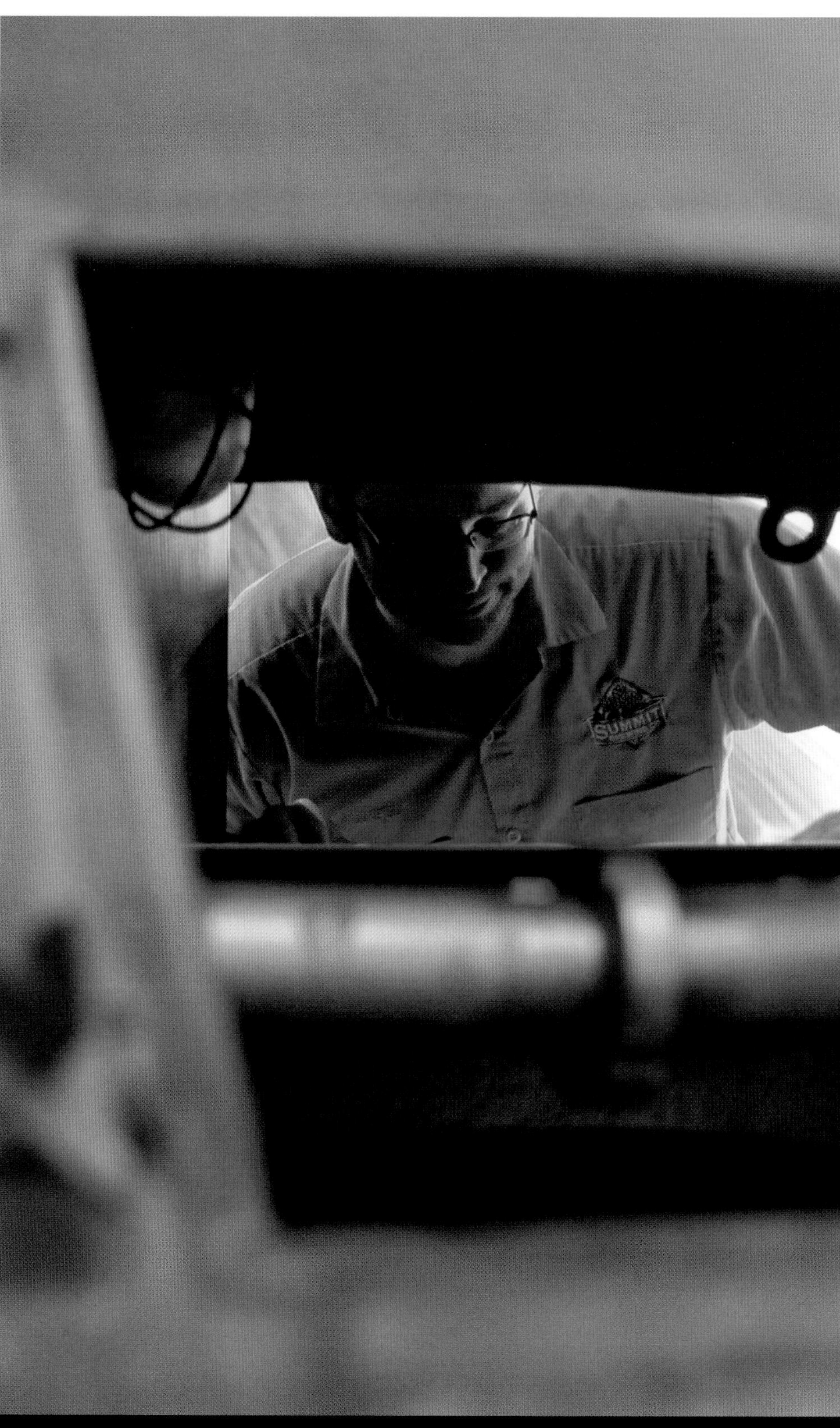

Eric Harper examines the mash for a batch of Summit Extra Pale Ale.

BREWING TERM: PHENOL

Phenol is a flavor and aroma compound created by yeast from the ferulic acid in malt, and to a small extent, from hops. Most yeast strains are bred to avoid phenol production, but wheat beer and some Belgian strains create it on purpose. When phenol unexpectedly occurs in beer, it can be a sign of wild yeast contamination.

WHAT CHALLENGES DO OTHER GRAINS LIKE WHEAT OR OATS PRESENT?

Unlike barley malt, wheat doesn't have a husk to help strain and filter the lauter bed. If you did an all-wheat mash, you'd have a stuck mash. With rye and oats, you're going to have a lot of beta-glucan, but a 45°C to 50°C (113°F to 122°F) rest for 20 minutes will break it up. An alternative is to use rice hulls and throw those into your mash—it shouldn't affect flavor.

WHAT DO YOU DO WITH A STUCK MASH?

It doesn't have to be a lost cause. The big breweries use rakes to fluff up the grain bed. At home, turn off your flow and decompact that grain. It doesn't have to be sterile; a big salad fork works. This happened at Davis [Brewing School] once on the pilot system. We'd gotten a kernel of grain stuck in the run-off valve, so we hooked it up to an air line to pump it backwards. In the brewery we call that an underlet.

HOW DO YOU CHECK THAT YOUR GRAINS ARE PROPERLY GROUND?

At Summit, we do a sieve analysis where you put a sample of the grist through a series of sieves with the coarsest on top. You take a sample of known weight, shake the sieve, and when you're done, you weigh the amount on each sieve to compare how well your grain mill is working.

CAN THAT WORK FOR HOMEBREWERS?

Sure, just buy a coarse sieve for a single limit. If you know your grind, shake a given amount of your malt through, then weigh the remains. Now you have a control weight to test against future grists.

WHAT DOES A GOOD GRIND LOOK LIKE?

It should be a mix of pieces, but no powder or huge chunks—a third of a chunk of barley is too big. Even a quarter piece is big.

TELL US ABOUT YOUR KEY STEPS IN THE MASHING AND LAUTERING PROCESS.

I'd say from the start of the mash, you have your strike water temperature. Too hot, around 169°F (76°C), and you'll kill off your enzymes and you can't convert your sugars. Sure, you can cool it down, but if you've killed the enzymes, you can't make beer. After stirring in the grains and water, check your temperature and take note of whether it's on or off.

[In lautering] I run off the wort until the grain bed just starts showing, then I sparge. And then there's how you sparge. At home, I always liked poking holes in the bottom of a milk jug, because you get a nice dispersal, but there are also inexpensive rotating sparge arms like you see in a brewery.

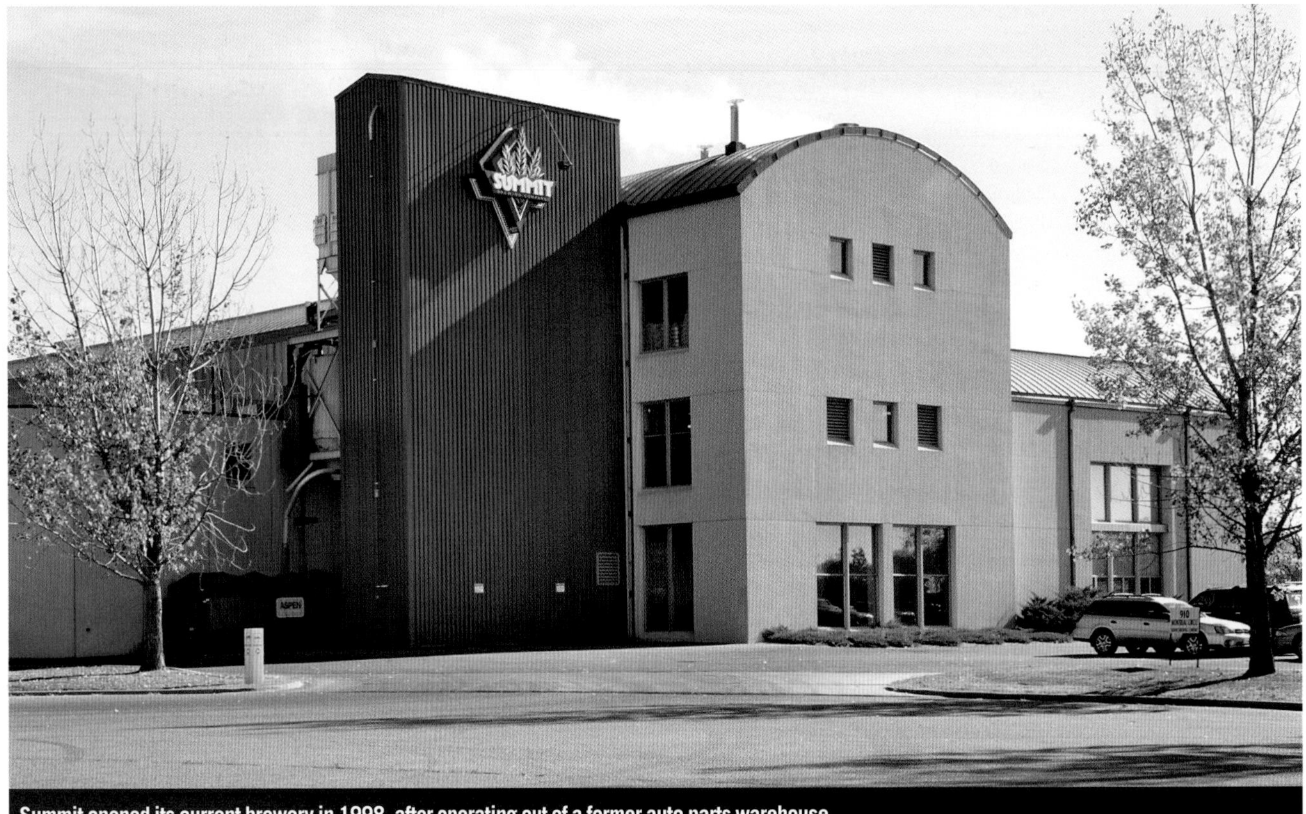

Summit opened its current brewery in 1998, after operating out of a former auto parts warehouse.

The clear tube and faucet allow brewers at Summit to observe wort clarity and pull test samples.

SPARGE WATER IS HEATED TO STOP ENZYMES, BUT WHAT HAPPENS WHEN IT'S TOO HOT?

If you get it too hot, you extract things you don't want, like tannins, undegraded starch, and silicates, and there is a potential for haze formation. I think 76°C (169°F) is a good temperature number for sparge water temp.

AND WHAT ABOUT WHEN YOU DO A MULTISTEP MASH?

Look at what rate you're heating the grains and water (we raise the temperature 1°C [1.8°F] per minute). If you're heating slowly, you give your enzymes more time. More importantly, always heat the same way to recreate a beer. Be consistent.

HOW IMPORTANT IS PH? HOW DO YOU CONTROL IT?

If your pH is off, the enzymes are not going to be happy. A mash pH of 5.3 or lower is typically good for the enzymes. You want to look at your water composition. Getting a pH meter is a good step for a homebrewer. If you mash in at 5.4, that's okay. If you get down into the upper-fours, that's also good. The enzymes will be more active.

HOW DO YOU ADJUST YOUR PH?

An interesting way is to create a sour wort to dose your mash. That's a natural tool that goes back to Reinheitsgebot and the Germans. The *Lactobacillus* is actually living on barley. Take a cheesecloth or container and fill it with grain. Dunk it in your wort and keep it warm. You'll get a soured wort overnight, and that's an effective and fun way to acidify your mash.

ANY FAVORITE MALTS? ARE YOU A PILSNER MALT GUY OR A PALE MALT GUY?

Yeah, I like German pilsner malt. It's easy to use in the brewhouse, and the kernels just seem to look so much nicer than American two-row malt. They're bigger, plumper, rounder. They taste good when you chew them, and they make better-tasting worts.

For specialty grains, I like to use Victory. It's really nutty and biscuity, a really toasty malt. It tastes and smells good—kind of dusty—but it's a neat product. Munich has a similar toasty character, but this is a lot nuttier. I'm also interested in making beer with flaked corn, or some kind of whiskey mash. Have you heard of the Kentucky Common style? They take partially what's like distiller's mash—about 50 percent corn and 50 percent distillers malt—and then blend that with brewers malt and have it be a sour mash and then ferment it with an American ale yeast.

Hops awaiting the fall harvest.

HOPS ARE THE BALANCING WEIGHTS IN BEER. UNLIKE CIDER, MEAD, OR WINE, ALES AND LAGERS DON'T FERMENT DRY. THE RESIDUAL SUGAR LEFT BEHIND WOULD TURN EVERY PINT INTO A SWEET, MALTY DESSERT WITHOUT THE ADDITION OF BITTERING HOPS FOR BALANCE.

CHAPTER 2: BITTERING HOPS

INTRODUCTION TO HOPS

After mashing, lautering, and sparging, brewers heat up their kettles of wort. Once the wort reaches a boil, they add hops to create bitterness in a beer. The longer hops are boiled, the more bitterness is added. Hops boiled for more than 30 minutes will contribute little flavor or aroma; however, the variety of hops used for bittering can change how the bitterness feels and how much is contributed. Just like some apples are more tart, with higher acid levels, hops with higher levels of bittering acids provide more kick.

In this chapter, you'll learn:

- **The history of hops**
- **The chemicals that define their bitterness**
- **How that bitterness is quantified**
- **What varieties to use**

A BRIEF HISTORY OF HOPS

The green, sticky harbingers of bitterness are a relatively recent addition to beer when you consider the beverage dates back to the dawn of civilization. The first records of hops cultivation come from Germany's Hallertau region in the year 736. Monastery (where else?) statutes from the eighth century appear to be the first records of using hops for beer. Until hops were adopted worldwide in the nineteenth century, brewers often used a mix of bitter herbs, such as bog myrtle, ground ivy, mugwort, and yarrow—called gruit—to balance the malt sweetness. Not only did most drinkers prefer the taste of hops, but the antibacterial nature of hops helped brewers ward off beer spoilage.

Hop bines fresh from the field in Yakima Valley, Washington.

Like most agricultural commodities, today's hops have been bred and farmed to the point where they barely resemble those used even a century ago. The alpha acid contents of even the weakest hops today are many times more potent than both their wild and farmed ancestors. The last several decades have seen an explosion in the number of hop varieties thanks in large part to university research farms. So now whether you're a megabrewer looking for an efficient, super high-alpha acid hop, or a homebrewer in search of a spicy, fruity American-European hybrid, there's a hop for you.

ALPHA ACIDS AND UTILIZATION

Within the hop flower (technically called a catkin) are small yellow sacks of oils. Much like barley has starch hidden within the husk, hops have alpha acids. In short, this is the good stuff.

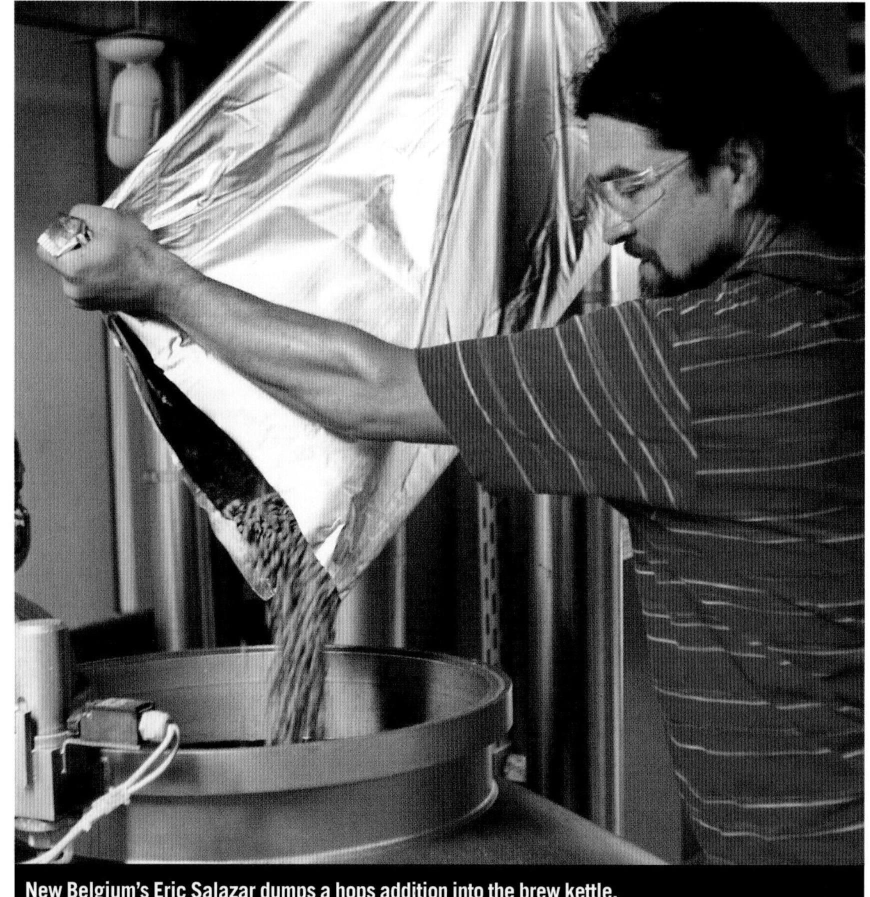

New Belgium's Eric Salazar dumps a hops addition into the brew kettle.

The amount of these bitter acids you can extract from hops is a balance of boil time and wort sugar content. The greater the gravity of your wort, the less alpha acid in your beer. And the longer you boil, the more acids pull out. The alpha acids in hops isomerize during the boil, meaning the molecular shape changes, and they become water-soluble, sticking to your wort.

Your average beer (specific gravity [SG] 1.040 to 1.060) will be able to utilize between 20 and 25 percent of the alpha acids over a 60-minute boil. Bumping up to 90 minutes will only increase the utilization by a point or two. Using hop plug or whole-leaf hops in place of the standard pelletized hops will also lower your overall utilization by about 10 percent due to the decreased surface area compared to a dissolved pellet.

COHUMULONE

There are three different alpha acids in hops: humulone, adhumulone, and cohumulone. It's unclear what humulone and adhumulone contribute beyond bitterness, but cohumulone levels control the type of bitterness. A beer hopped with low cohumulone-level hops will have a clean bitterness, while hops with a high level have harsher, biting bitterness.

When picking hops, look beyond the alpha acids percentage when considering the bitterness of your final product. If you want a tongue-ripping bitterness in your pale ale, pick bittering hops with at least a 30 percent cohumulone share of the alpha acids.

INTERNATIONAL BITTERING UNITS

IBUs represent the proportion of iso-alpha acids in a beer. In a lab, a single IBU equals a milligram of isomerized alpha acid in one liter of wort. A high IBU number, however, does not guarantee a bitter beer. The perceived bitterness is a result of the balance between residual (unfermented) sugar and hops. Big, thick beers, including stouts and barleywines, require a high IBU level simply to achieve a level of balance. At the same time, a drier pale ale with the same IBU level would feel more bitter simply because there's less sweet barley sugar to begin with.

IBU LEVELS FOR POPULAR STYLES OF BEER PER THE BEER JUDGE CERTIFICATION PROGRAM STYLE GUIDELINES

Add as much or as littler bitterness as you please—it's your beer after all—but knowing the bitterness ranges for classic beer styles can help you connect what you're tasting in your beer aisle to your homebrewery.

Style	IBU
Light American Lager	8 to 12
Classic Bohemian Pilsner	35 to 45
German Weissbier	8 to 15
English Pale Ale	30 to 50
American IPA	40 to 70+
Belgian Tripel	20 to 40
German Bock	20 to 27
American Stout	35 to 75
American Double IPA	70 to 100+

FIRST WORT HOPPING

If you're curious enough to try something different, use first wort hopping on your next batch of hoppy beer. This old, somewhat forgotten, German technique calls for an addition of hops while the wort collects in the kettle.

The results of scientific studies on first wort hopping found slight increases in IBUs and flavor and aroma, with the theory that different chemical reactions happen to the hops as they steep in the roughly 140°F to 160°F (60°C to 71°C) wort. If you want to try this on your next pale ale, they recommend adding at least 30 percent of your hops to the first wort addition to notice a difference.

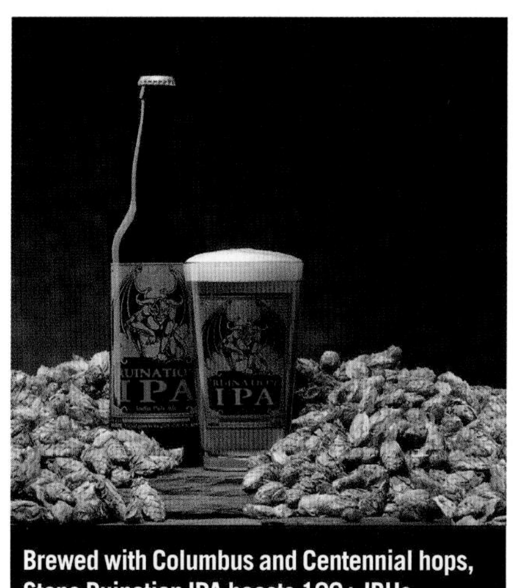

Brewed with Columbus and Centennial hops, Stone Ruination IPA boasts 100+ IBUs.

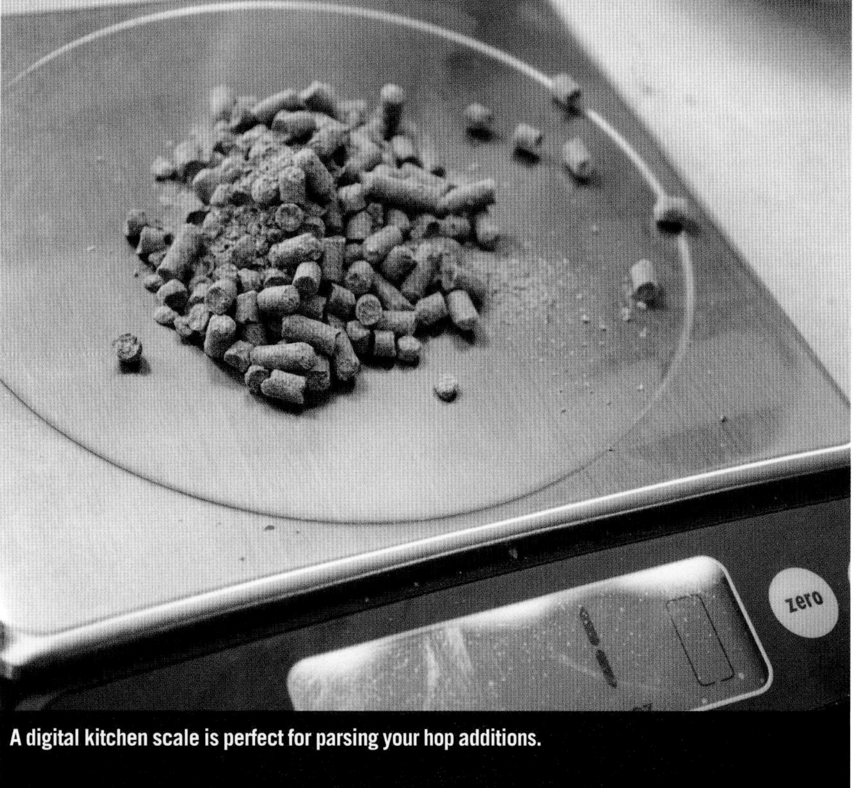

A digital kitchen scale is perfect for parsing your hop additions.

KNOW YOUR BITTERING HOPS

Creating a beer with low or high IBUs and smooth or harsh bitterness comes down to the type of hops you use. Keep in mind that hops experience some variation every year based on growing conditions. Use these tables as a guide when formulating a recipe and then find out the precise numbers from your homebrew supply store.

Clean Bittering Hops	Alpha Acids (%)	Cohumulone (% of AA)
U.S. Horizon	11 to 13	16 to 19
U.S. Simcoe	12 to 14	15 to 20
UK Challenger	6.5 to 8.5	20 to 25
Amarillo	8 to 11	21 to 24
U.S. Crystal	3.5 to 5.5	20 to 26
U.S. Glacier	5.5	11 to 13
U.S. Golding	4 to 5	20 to 25
U.S. Hallertau	3.5 to 5.5	18 to 24
U.S. Mt. Hood	5 to 8	22 to 23
U.S. Northern Brewer	8 to 10	20 to 30
U.S. Nugget	12 to 14	20 to 30
U.S. Santiam	5 to 7	22 to 24
U.S. Tettnang	4 to 5	20 to 25
U.S. Vanguard	5.5 to 6	14 to 16
German Hallertau	3.5 to 5.5	17 to 24
German Hersbrucker	3 to 5.5	19 to 25
German Magnum	12 to 14	24 to 25
German Select	4 to 6	21 to 25
UK Kent Golding	4 to 5.5	20 to 25

Medium Bittering Hops	Alpha Acids (%)	Cohumulone (% of AA)
U.S. Ahtanum	5.7 to 6.3	30 to 35
U.S. Centennial	9.5 to 11.5	29 to 30
U.S. Chinook	12 to 14	29 to 34
U.S. Columbus	14 to 16	30 to 35
U.S. Fuggle	4 to 5.5	25 to 32
U.S. Liberty	3 to 5	24 to 30
U.S. Magnum	12 to 14	24 to 28
U.S. Millennium	15.5	30
U.S. Perle	7 to 9.5	27 to 32
U.S./Czech Saaz	3 to 4.5	24 to 28
U.S. Sterling	6 to 9	22 to 28
U.S. Warrior	15 to 17	24
U.S. Willamette	4 to 6	30 to 35
French Strisselspalt	3 to 5	20 to 25
German Northern Brewer	7 to 10	28 to 33
German Perle	6 to 8	25 to 32
German Spalt	4 to 5	23 to 28
German Tettnang	3.5 to 5.5	23 to 29
German Tradition	5 to 7	26 to 29
Styrian Golding	4.5 to 6	25 to 30
UK First Gold	6.5 to 8.5	31 to 36
UK Fuggle	4 to 5.5	23 to 30
UK Northdown	7.5 to 9.5	24 to 30
UK Progress	5 to 7	25 to 30
UK Target	9.5 to 12.5	29 to 35

Harsh Bittering Hops	Alpha Acids (%)	Cohumulone (% of AA)
U.S. Brewer's Gold	8 to 10	40 to 48
U.S. Cascade	4.5 to 7	33 to 40
U.S. Cluster	5.5 to 8.5	36 to 42
U.S. Galena	12 to 14	38 to 42
U.S. Newport	13.5 to 17	36 to 38
German Brewer's Gold	5.5 to 6.5	40 to 48
NZ Hallertau	7 to 9	35
NZ Pacific Gem	14 to 16	39
AU Pride of Ringwood	7 to 10	33 to 39

INTERVIEW WITH: VINNIE CILURZO: OWNER, RUSSIAN RIVER BREWING CO., SANTA ROSA, CALIFORNIA, U.S.

HOPHEADS AND IPA LOVERS CAN THANK VINNIE FOR NOT ONLY BREWING THE WORLD'S FIRST DOUBLE INDIA PALE ALE, BUT ALSO SIMPLY PRODUCING BIG HOPPY BEER WHETHER PEOPLE WANTED IT OR NOT. CREATED BACK WHEN YOUR AVERAGE PALE ALE WAS STILL TOO BITTER FOR CRAFT BEER LOVERS, VINNIE'S RUSSIAN RIVER BREWING COMPANY CELEBRATES HIS DEVOTION TO HOPS AND NOW PRODUCES SEVERAL OF THE WORLD'S MOST-SOUGHT-AFTER IPAs.

YOUR FAMILY HAS A HISTORY IN THE BUSINESS OF FERMENTATION, BUT WITH WINE. WHY BEER?

After high school, I moved to San Diego and started homebrewing with my roommates. Even though the first batch was terrible, probably near undrinkable, I knew I wanted to continue on. And I liked the idea of being able to turn a batch in, say, three weeks instead of wine, which can take a year or two or even more. I loved that if you didn't get it quite right, you had another opportunity to brew and knock out another batch. Things weren't being dictated by season.

Eventually, I moved back to the winery and started working, and that's when I really got into homebrewing, in 1989. Down in the basement of the winery was where I did most of my early experimentation that still carried on into what we do today.

SO THAT LED TO OPENING YOUR OWN BREWERY, THE BLIND PIG.

Yes, that was in 1994. I had two other business partners, but I was the brewing side. I was there three years, then ducked out. They kept going a couple more years before they shut it down.

In 1997, [my wife] Natalie and I came up to Santa Rosa. Neither of us had jobs or a place to stay. We had a couple of leads and that was it. We got hired by Korbel to start Russian River Brewery in 1997. In 2003, they decided to get out of the beer business, so we bought the name and the brewery, closed for a year, and then reopened as a brewpub.

The Pizza Port still serves up its influential Swamis IPA.

BREWING LEGEND: PIZZA PORT

In 1987, siblings Vince and Gina Marsaglia bought up a struggling restaurant outside San Diego called Pizza Port. Vince began homebrewing in their extra storage space and began commercially brewing in 1992. With a passion for hops long before consumers would catch on, Vince helped define Southern California as the home of American IPA. The brewpub has since expanded to three additional locations along with purchasing Stone Brewing's original facility, allowing Port to launch its Lost Abbey family of Belgian-style beers.

LET ME GO BACK TO THE BLIND PIG DAYS. YOU MAY HAVE BREWED THE FIRST DOUBLE IPA ON THE PLANET.

The Blind Pig IPA was definitely a straight-up IPA and there weren't a lot of IPAs being made at the time, particularly in bottles. Rubicon was making one at their pub. Vince and Gina Marsaglia were making their first IPA at their Pizza Port brewpub.

THE SWAMIS IPA.

Yeah, and as a bright-eyed, fell-off-the-turnip-truck homebrewer turning pro, I didn't know how to bump a recipe up or take a homebrew from a 5-gallon (19 L) batch and turn it into seven barrels. I still remember Vince just giving me their entire recipe for the Swamis to use as a reference. That sort of thing still shines through to how our industry is today. The "high tide floats all boats" mind-set.

Master of the hops Vinnie Cilurzo

BUT YOU BREWED THE FIRST DOUBLE IPA AT BLIND PIG.

It was the first beer we made at Blind Pig, called Inaugural Ale. We took what was going to be our regular IPA recipe and literally doubled the hops on it and brought the alcohol up a little bit. Everything was all-malt at the time—we didn't use any sugar—which is something we use a lot of now in our double IPAs.

We actually let it dry-hop for a year and then released it. Our second year, we started brewing it on the spot.

Back then, those beers were way more bitter than they are now, comparing what I remember the anniversary beers to be, compared to our Pliny The Elder beer. It's got more roundness to it, more malt foundation, a little more balance.

I thought we should take our regular IPA recipe, double the hops on it, and the idea was not only would we get this super, over-the-top hoppy beer, but also that hops act as a natural preservative. Really, I didn't know any better, but that's still how we all operate.

I REMEMBER THE ANNIVERSARY IPA HAD SOME HARSHER BITTERNESS.

As someone put it, it was like licking the rust off a tin can. That definitely was very true of those beers. One of these days, I'm going to have to break out the recipes and rebrew it. I think a part of those beers at Blind Pig can never be recreated because of the equipment we were using.

YEAH, YOU HAVE TO GET YOURSELF SOME PLASTIC FERMENTERS.

Well, that too, but the kettle was so inefficient, and then the utilization was so poor, that you'd have to pour gobs of hops in to achieve any sort of bitterness. When you did that, you were obviously also extracting all sorts of flavor from the hops.

THERE HAD TO BE MORE TO THE VISION THAN SEEING VINCE'S SWAMIS RECIPE. WHAT ON EARTH CAUSED YOU TO MAKE A BEER THAT IS JUST SO HUGELY BITTER?

I was homebrewing our Blind Pig IPA recipe for a long time, taking it to the homebrew club in Temecula and the SoCal Homebrewers Festival. I was getting a lot of great remarks for it. When we looked at the market, there were pale ales, but we kind of wanted to do something different and the IPA was the flavor we liked.

For the anniversary beer, the double IPA—that was purely because we thought the equipment and the plastic fermenters might not yield something that was sellable on the first batch. So I thought we should take our regular IPA recipe, double the hops on it, and the idea was not only would we get this super, over-the-top hoppy beer, but also that hops act as a natural preservative. Really, I didn't know any better, but that's still how we all operate.

CAN I QUOTE YOU ON THAT? THAT YOU MADE A BIG HOPPY BEER BECAUSE YOU DIDN'T KNOW ANY BETTER?

It's true. Think with all the beers [we] put out—it's not like we're out doing market studies. We're putting beers out because we like them. And we've convinced the consumer to drink our style of beer, not the other way around.

LET'S GET INTO TECHNICALITIES. WHEN WE'RE TALKING ABOUT BITTERING HOPS, HOW LONG OF A BOIL DO YOU RECOMMEND?

I know a lot of brewers will cut to a 60-minute boil, but we use a 90-minute boil for blowing off all the dimethyl sulfide (DMS) that might be there in the malt. We typically have three hop additions, sometimes four. Now that we're all-steam at both our breweries, we're getting a ripping

A beacon to hopheads, Vinnie and Natalie's Russian River Brewing Company.

INDIA PALE ALE

No style has captured the taste and excitement of American craft beer like the American IPA (and American Double IPA). At its essence, it's a beer overloaded with hops and propped with more malts than usual. A great IPA requires proper bittering and aroma hops.

A beer sampler at the Russian River Brewing Co. Brewpub includes Vinnie's Blind Pig IPA (far left).

boil. The efficiencies are much higher. I know Blind Pig IPA was somewhere around 92 IBUs. Compared to how many hops it takes now on a per-barrel basis, we were probably using one and a half times as many hops back then, but in doing so we captured just a ton of hop flavor.

WHEN YOU CONSIDER YOUR BITTERING HOPS, DO YOU LOOK AT THEIR COHUMULONE CONTENT?

When I started, I didn't really think about cohumulone. A textbook will tell you that you have to use a low-cohumulone hop or you'll get a harsh bitterness. I think an IPA or double IPA benefits from a hop like Chinook, which we use as the bittering hop in Blind Pig, and the Columbus/Tomahawk/Zeus (CTZ), also used as bittering hops. These aren't low cohumulone hops, and I like them because they add a bit of an edge to a beer and a little more personality, as opposed to only using a hop like Magnum, Warrior, or Horizon, which have a superlow cohumulone and translate to a really nice, clean bitterness.

ARE THERE ANY NEW HOP VARIETIES YOU'RE EXCITED ABOUT?

I travel to Yakima once a year and often I'll be fortunate enough to rub some new varieties that are in their experimental phase. The hop growers, through a couple of different research groups, are always looking to breed new varieties. But, it takes about ten years for a hop variety to go from its first planting to commercial availability. In most cases, each year each hop breeding program will start with at least 20,000 plants, but most often they will only have less than a dozen that might have a chance of making it.

DO YOU THINK THERE'S A LIMIT TO HOW MUCH BITTERNESS WE CAN PERCEIVE? AS IN, IS THERE A RELATIVE LEVEL OF IBU AFTER WHICH YOU'RE WASTING HOPS?

Yes, there is a point where you can't taste the bitterness and it becomes unpleasant. We have this thing at our brewery that we call the Lupulin Threshold Shift. This is the idea that as a person drinks more and more hoppy beers, their palate craves more hop flavor and more hop bitterness. So someone who started out drinking a pale ale might eventually move to an IPA and eventually move to a double IPA, and so on.

We have this thing at our brewery that we call the Lupulin Threshold Shift. This is the idea that as a person drinks more and more hoppy beers, their palate craves more hop flavor and more hop bitterness.

Dried and pressed hop flowers waiting for brew day.

YOU CAN NO MORE BLAME CRAFT BEER DRINKERS FOR RAISING THE IPA ABOVE ALL OTHERS THAN YOU CAN BLAME HOPS FOR TASTING AND SMELLING TENACIOUSLY GOOD. WHEN THE CARBONATION AND ESSENTIAL HOP OILS ARE JUST RIGHT, A BEER'S AROMA CAN BURST FORTH UPON HITTING YOUR GLASS, ONLY FURTHER WHETTING YOUR APPETITE. YOU MIGHT EVEN SAY THAT A FINE HOPPY BEER IS A TEASE.

CHAPTER 3: AROMA HOPS

INTRODUCTION TO AROMA HOPS

Aroma hops are added to the boil after bittering hops. Despite the name, they contribute both aroma and flavor. By adding them later in the boil, the aroma and flavor compounds are retained. The closer to the end of the boil the hops are added, the brighter and more crisp they'll be while also contributing more to aroma. Any hop variety can be used for aroma and bittering, but certain types have been bred for one or the other.

In this chapter, you'll learn:

- **The different types of hops**
- **Recommended hop blends**
- **When to add hops**
- **Hop flavor compounds**

AMERICAN HOPS

American pale ales owe their hoppy beginnings to Cascade, which in 1972 became the first widely accepted American aroma hop. Innovation was slow for that generation of homebrewers, as most modern varieties didn't appear until the 1990s.

Today, about thirty American varieties are available with aromas ranging from pungent citrus to delicate floral spice. Hops defy concrete characterization, and to a degree are like grapes, with good and bad years. However, the more established a variety, the steadier it becomes year after year. Reliable standbys, such as Cascade and Centennial hops, are bedrocks of consistent brewing.

Weyerbacher Brewing's Double Simcoe IPA is one of few single-hop double IPAs.

SUGGESTED HOP BLENDS

For lesser-known hops, most postharvest descriptions from distributors leave much to be desired. How helpful is it to know a new variety's aroma is "mild and pleasant"? To help supplement your own batch-to-batch hopping experiments, try some of these hop mixes for flavor and aroma.

Varieties	Blend Ratio	Character
Amarillo and Simcoe	1:1	Tropical fruit and pine
Crystal (or Mt. Hood) and Simcoe	3:1	Pine with herbal and floral hints
Amarillo and Centennial	1:1	Tropical fruit, lemon, grapefruit, and mango
Centennial, Amarillo, and Simcoe	1:1:1	Fruity, pine, and citrus
Goldings and Target	4:1	For English ales; earthy and spicy with hints of tangerine
Saaz and Hallertau	3:1	Pepper and floral
Strisselspalt and Crystal (or Mt. Hood)	1:1	Floral and citrus

Blends courtesy of Stone Brewing Co.'s Head Brewer, Mitch Steele

Farmers in Tettnang, Germany, celebrate their harvest with a Hops Queen.

EUROPEAN HOPS

The classic hop fields in Kent, England, or Hallertau, Germany, grow beautiful, wonderfully subtle hops. Where American hops tend toward the big and bold citrus flavor, many German and English hops hold a more delicate spicy character. If blending both types of hops, and you should try it at some point, be wary of overpowering the milder hops.

If you're recreating classic European styles, strictly traditional hops aren't always necessary. Going back more than one hundred years, British brewers were known to employ American hops when the prices were right. Today, German brewers import about a third of their hops from the United States.

HOP TERRIOR

Hop distributors largely sell hop varieties as a commodity, with only a country of origin to distinguish them. Just like vintners might have a favorite hillside of grapes, brewers make appointments with growers to find the perfect crop and place orders for the year.

Homebrewers can't always have the luxury of rubbing fresh cones between their fingers, but smaller independent growers may sell direct to brewers online in small quantities for homebrewing. Each farm's soil, climate, and tending bring a slight, but unique, character to hops.

The fall hop harvest in Washington state's Yakima Valley, the largest hop-growing region in the United States

HOP BURSTING

Hoppy doesn't always equate to bitter beer. In fact, by pulling your IBUs from aroma and flavor additions (the final 30 minutes of a boil), you can create a smoother bitterness that lets the malt stand up for itself in the final beer character.

The name "hop bursting" was given by homebrewers, and the technique calls for adding a large charge of hops near the end of the boil. Some brewers prefer to distribute the hops over the final half hour their wort is on the heat. Others drop their hops in for the final 5 minutes. The essential rule to follow is that at least half of the IBUs should be drawn from the aroma and flavor additions.

POSTBOIL ADDITIONS

Once the heat is off, there are two popular spots to boost the hop aroma. In both cases, about 2 ounces (57 g) of hops will have a noticeable effect in a 5-gallon (19 L) batch of IPA.

HOPBACK

Immediately out of the kettle, before the wort even cools, brewers will pump the hot liquid through a hopback. Think of it as adding back hop aromas and oil lost to the boil. The device goes back at least a couple hundred years in brewing history and is essentially a sealed container with a filter that allows wort to pass through the hops, absorbing the fragrant oils. The wort would then be cooled and retain the aromatic compounds.

Some hopback advocates claim exposing the hops to hop wort is more sanitary, but hops have their own aseptic properties, and infection through hops is rarely, if ever, an issue.

DRY-HOPPING

This simple, but slow, process can potentially add a crisper, more pungent hop aroma than a hopback. Brewers typically add the hops for the last five to fourteen days of conditioning, but if that's all the time your beer will mature, rack the batch onto the hops. Unless added to a sterile, weighted hop bag, your addition may float on top of the beer, not maximizing contact area. This is more a problem for whole-leaf hops.

Hop pellets spill over the top of a container during a dry-hop addition.

For an extra hop punch, try the technique of double dry-hopping. Split your dry hops into two equal charges. Then if, for example, you're dry-hopping for ten days, add the first charge with ten days remaining and the second with five days remaining. The two levels of dry-hopping will add depth to your aroma.

HOP CHEMISTRY

Homebrewers can create more interesting beer if they understand the roles of the chemicals that make up those delicious alpha acids.

MYRCENE

Alpha acids and cohumulone help us understand bitterness (see chapter 2 for more), but myrcene is an easy indicator of pungent citrus and pine character. It's one of four essential oils that contribute to flavor and aroma. Hop distributors will list the share of myrcene just like alpha acids. The classic noble hops of Europe are low in myrcene (about 20 percent of the oils), while stereotypically rich American hops, such as Amarillo, Simcoe, and Cascade, are higher in myrcene (about 60 percent).

HUMULENE

Humulene represents a spicy, herbal central European character. Hops that are particularly strong in this sense, such as Fuggle, Saaz, and Hallertau, will have one to two times more humulene than myrcene.

SPOTLIGHT: HOW NEW HOPS ARE BORN

Every year, one or, if we're lucky, two new hops varieties are planted en masse and make their way to your local homebrew store. These low numbers aren't for a lack of effort. Every spring in the largest hop-growing region in the United States, the Yakima Valley, about 100,000 new varieties are bred through cross-pollination and planted with the hope that in ten years one of these plants will produce strong, pleasing, and consistent hops.

Over the first year, about half the breeds will simply die, while others are quickly eliminated for reasons such as poor disease resistance, weak cone structure, and bad yield. The following year, about one hundred potential varieties remain and the planting expands so farmers can begin to predict how they'll act if widely planted. Some will develop strong onion or garlic aromas while others lack consistency. After five or six years, growers begin letting brewers experiment. If the feedback is positive, the next Simcoe or Amarillo may be born.

INTERVIEW WITH:
NICK FLOYD: OWNER, THREE FLOYDS BREWING CO., MUNSTER, INDIANA, U.S.

KNOWN AS THE "ALPHA KING," NICK AND HIS MASTERY OF HOPS STARTED AT AN UNLIKELY BREWERY. BUT OVER THE LAST DECADE, HE DEVELOPED A CULT FOLLOWING FOR BEERS THAT ARE ALMOST BAWDY IN THEIR HOPPINESS.

WHAT WAS YOUR FIRST BREWING JOB?
The first job I could get was in Auburndale, Florida, alligator country, at the Florida Brewery, which made Falstaff, Gator Lager, Malta, and even Hatuey, the Cuban brand.

WOW, MALTA.
Yeah, unfermented [expletive] porter. You'll put that in your book?

I MAY HAVE TO NOW.
And we were brewing with old cast-iron equipment.

I DIDN'T KNOW THERE WAS CAST-IRON BREWING EQUIPMENT.
Oh yeah, these guys didn't care. The mash mixer, where you mash in, and the kettle were cast iron with direct steam injection. Metallic was the house character.

THAT THING MUST HAVE BEEN A LOCOMOTIVE.
I was 21, so sometimes I'd goof off and leave the kettle. Boilovers would shoot off a 20-foot rainbow of wort.

SO YOU MAY NOT HAVE TAKEN THE MOST PRIDE IN YOUR PRODUCTS?
When you went in the offices, you'd see 300 different cans of beer brands, but 200 of them were the same lager. And we brewed for ABC Liquors, a big chain down there. They had a light, an ale, a lager, and a malt liquor, but the ale and the lager were the same and the malt liquor had a handful of Melomalt added to give it a slight golden color. It's hard to believe, but it's a good experience when you're 21.

I EXPECT THIS NEXT QUESTION WILL GET SOME CHUCKLES OUT OF YOU—HOW WERE HOPS REGARDED THERE?
I think we had two different kinds. Nugget hops and Saaz for special lagers like Hatuey. All I knew about hops was that there was a bittering kind and an aroma kind.

WHAT TURNED YOU ON TO HOPPY BEER?
Part of it was brewing all that crap in Florida. I had a Sierra Nevada in Tampa and I was amazed, then I started liking fresh German hoppy stuff.

LIMIT 6 bottles Per Person
ALPHA KING
PRIDE + JOY
ROBERT THE BRUCE
RABBID RABBIT 22oz $10 bottle $100 case
BEHEMOTH 22oz $15 bottle $150 case
BRIAN BORU 22oz $7 bottle $70 case
DREADNAUGHT 22oz $10 bottle $100 case
CASH ONLY
THANKS

IT SOUNDS LIKE IT GOT YOUR ATTENTION AND IMAGINATION. THEN WHAT?

This uptight German dude in Chicago had a job available at the Weinkeller Brewery. I'm like, you have all stainless equipment and I can make whatever I want? Ja.

I started bringing in all the Cascade, Centennial, or whatever freak-show new American hops we could get our hands on. But the German guy was so tightly wound he must have fired half of Chicago, and the place didn't last long.

LET'S TALK ABOUT EXPERIMENTING WITH NEW HOP VARIETIES.

For professional brewers, it's really important to go to the hops harvest in Yakima. Set up appointments, rub and smell all the hops, find out what field you like, what growing region you like, what variety. Find out which farms are growing experimental hops.

In 2010, we were one of eight breweries to get El Dorado hops. We used a control beer, like a pale ale or German altbier for a single-varietal batch to test it. We'll do several batches like that a year with different and new varieties. Whenever we find a new hop we like, we jump on it and start making new stuff.

VARIETIES CHANGE CHARACTER EVERY YEAR.

I think Amarillo hops aren't as good as they used to be; we're phasing them out. Summit, in my opinion, used to be great when it was grown as a dwarf; now it tastes to me like onions if you go to a hop field. Centennial and Cascade are always solid, and more varieties are becoming more reliable every year. But you start by adjusting your hop blends to mimic the aroma and flavor you want, maybe mix in a hop like Warrior or Simcoe.

LET'S SAY YOU'VE GOT A HANDFUL OF HOPS, BUT THEY DON'T NECESSARILY SMELL LIKE WHAT THEY'LL BRING TO THE BEER...

They don't, but for us, when we smell the hops we can visualize it. Any hint of dirt, onions, or bad aromas will be picked up later if you dry-hop. Not so much with kettle hops. The way we do it is hand to nose to kettle.

DO YOU HAVE CURRENT FAVORITE HOP VARIETIES AND OLD STANDBYS?

Our big three are Centennial, Cascade, and Warrior. We mix different high-alpha American hops to emulate what we want, basically.

ISOMETRIZED HOP EXTRACT: WHERE DOES THAT FIT IN?

You might look at it as an abomination by big breweries, 'cause they use gallons of that. But I think it's a secret weapon for making double IPAs and giant IBUs without having the vegetable matter you'd otherwise need. It has its benefits.

I KNOW OF ONE HIGHLY SOUGHT-AFTER IPA THAT USES IT. DO YOU?

All our double IPAs. I think they have a place, but it's an art to using them. I say why not try it out for anything over 80 IBUs.

IS THERE A LIMIT TO HOP AROMA? CAN YOU OVER-DRY-HOP?

Not to me. Yeah, I'm sure when you spend a lot of money making four kegs of beer, that might be a limit. It tastes the same as XYZ IPA, but you can brag about it on your menu and charge more at bars. The hop aroma wars are like World War II tanks: The Germans came out with a new panzer, and then suddenly the Russians have their new tank. I think the war's ended, but some brewers are still going. I guess we've been there, done that, and know where our limit is.

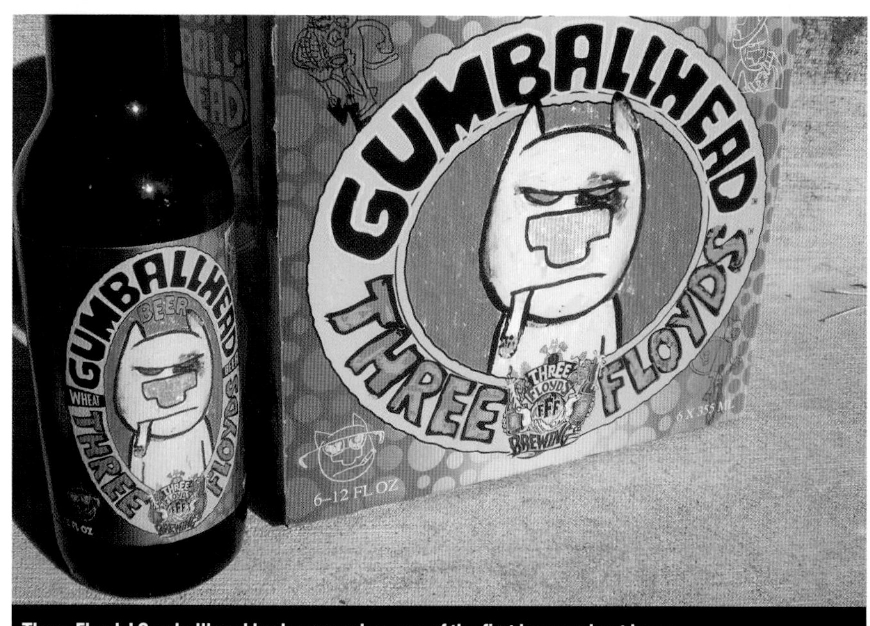

Three Floyds' Gumballhead broke ground as one of the first hoppy wheat beers thanks to its use of Amarillos.

It's no surprise that the Three Floyds brewpub is swathed in hop plants.

ALL THIS EXTREME BREWING HAS CERTAINLY PUSHED A LOT OF THRESHOLDS AND FRONTIERS. ARE THERE ANY LEFT?

Now the rush is to go back and make extremely sessionable, amazing quality beers like a helles lager. Not many people are doing that. I think most extremes have been met. Now I'm more happy to make a kickass lager and put it in a can.

WHAT DO YOU THINK ABOUT IDEAL WINDOWS FOR IPA OR PALE ALE, ABOUT HOW FAST HOPS DETERIORATE?

It's a big issue for double IPAs. All these beer geeks want to drink it at two weeks old and say it's garbage at five weeks. It kills me because real IPAs took three or four months to get to India and then they were mellow and rounded.

YOU DON'T MIND A LITTLE TIME ON YOUR BEERS?

I like Alpha King when it's three months old, but to the new extreme geeks, that's past its prime. They're not looking for any other nuances besides getting kicked in the nostril by a pinecone. Even our double IPA at eight months, people say it's crap. Me personally, I like stuff that's aged a bit more.

SO WHERE DO YOU PUT AGING LIMITS?

I'd go by IBUs. A day for every IBU, if it's bottled clean to begin with.

IS THERE A THRESHOLD AFTER THAT?

I think anything over 90 IBUs you can give at least half a year or a year. And don't call it a drain-pour, just 'cause hops have mellowed a bit; it's still a good, clean, bitter, bright IPA. Look for the other nuances in the beer.

DO YOU HAVE A PREFERENCE BETWEEN WHOLE-LEAF HOPS AND PELLETS?

We choose pellets for their stability. If we were closer to growers, we might favor whole-leaf. But for shipping and storing, pellets make more sense. Some of the greatest microbreweries out there use pelletized hops, so I don't think there's a disadvantage.

YOU'RE KNOWN MORE FOR NEW AMERICAN HOP VARIETIES THAN TRADITIONAL EUROPEANS. CAN EUROPEAN VARIETIES BE USED IN NONTRADITIONAL WAYS?

Oh yeah. We now make Blackheart, an English version of Dreadnaught Imperial IPA with Styrian Golding and East Kent Golding hops. What prevented us before is that European hops have been so expensive and iffy on consistency. But once you have a stable of American-hopped beers, why not go back and experiment with European and noble hops?

WHAT'S A BLEND OF AMERICAN AND EUROPEAN HOPS YOU ENJOY?

I'd use a small amount of Warrior for bitterness and then large amounts of English aroma varieties.

Schwaben Bräu
wilhelmer`s
HWABEN ELT
Das Leben ein Fest
Schwaben Bräu
wilhelmer`s
SCHWABEN ELT
Das Leben ein Fest

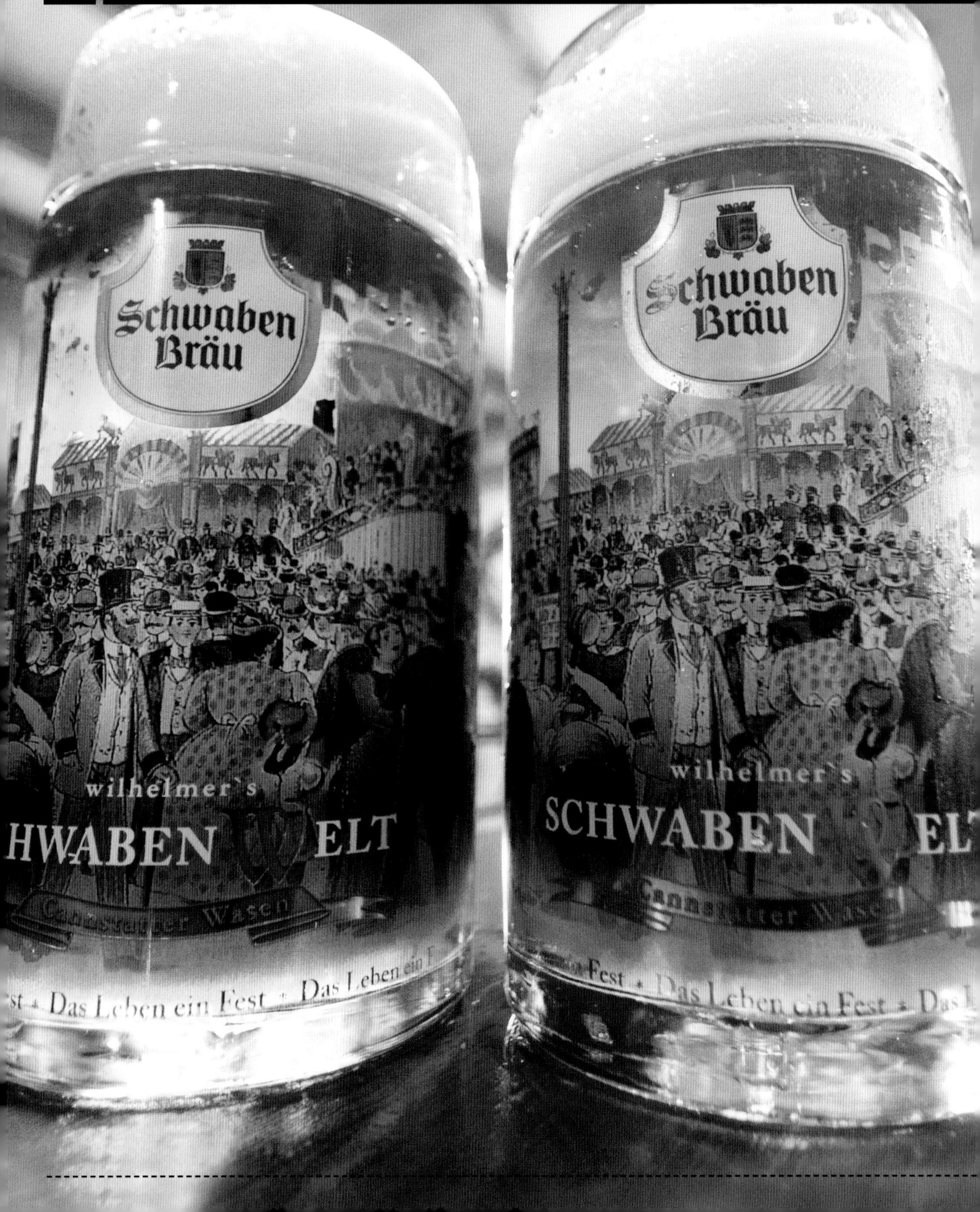

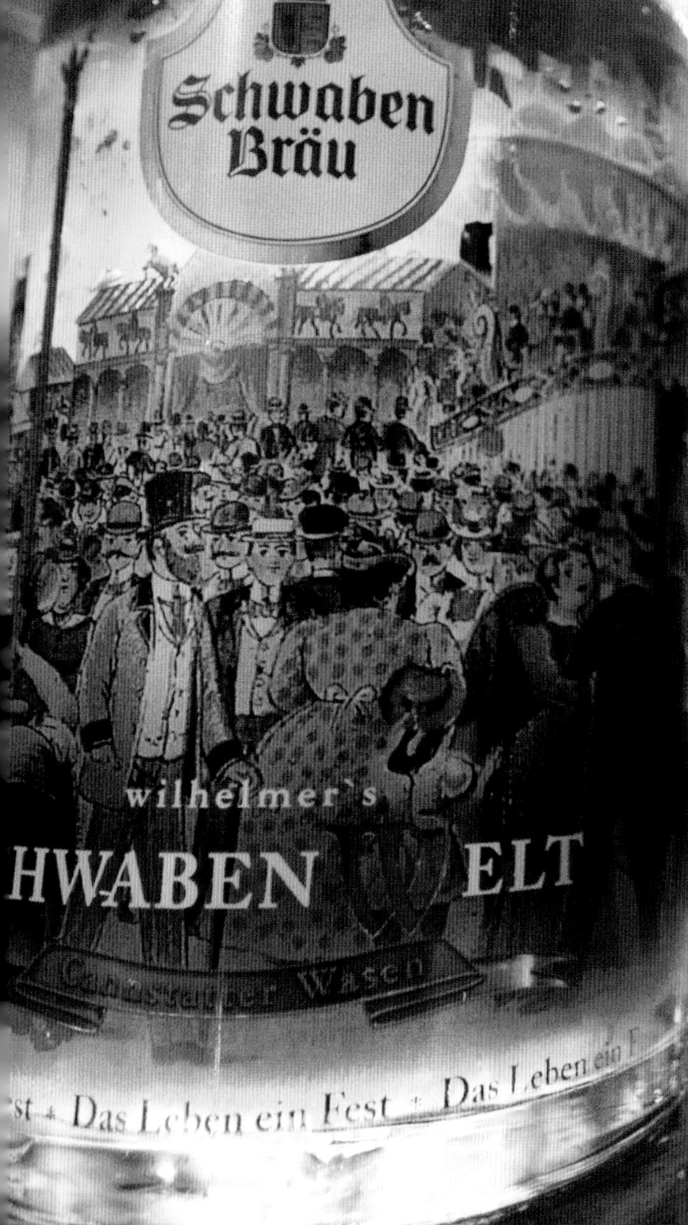

Schwaben Bräu Festbier at the Stuttgart Oktoberfest. Like a traditional Oktoberfest beer, it's lighter in color than the amber lagers that are exported.

COLD-FERMENTED BEERS DATE BACK ABOUT 500 YEARS, BUT IT WASN'T UNTIL 1883 THAT A SCIENTIST AT THE CARLSBERG BREWERY IDENTIFIED AND SEPARATED LAGER YEAST. ALONG WITH THE PRODUCTION OF PALE BARLEY MALT A FEW DECADES EARLIER, LAGERS HAVE INFAMOUSLY COME TO DOMINATE THE WORLD'S BEER-DRINKING POPULATION—ALBEIT WITH WATERY CORRUPTIONS OF FORMERLY GREAT BEERS. BUT UNLESS YOU WANT TO BREW SUCH A BEER PURELY FOR THE TECHNICAL CHALLENGE—A LIGHT LAGER REQUIRES GREAT SKILL TO TASTE SO BLAND—LOOKING TO THE FULL-FLAVORED LAGERS, INCLUDING GERMAN PILSNERS, VIENNA LAGERS, OR SCHWARZBIER, IS A PALATE-SATISFYING ENDEAVOR.

CHAPTER 4: LAGER BREWING

INTRODUCTION TO LAGERS

Lagers are defined by their use of lager yeast, also called bottom-fermenting yeast. While the vast majority (volumetrically) of the world's beer is lager, most homebrewers make ales with top-fermenting ale yeast because it ferments at room temperature. Lager yeast requires colder conditions, usually around 50°F (10°C). This temperature also slows down the yeast, requiring a longer fermentation and maturation period.

In this chapter, you'll learn:

- **Lagering equipment**
- **Lager yeast strains**
- **Lager fermentation and conditioning**
- **Ingredients for traditional lager styles**

LAGERING EQUIPMENT

If you're not blessed with a consistently cool cellar, or cave if you're old-school, you'll need new equipment to chill your beer and keep it cold throughout the fermentation and conditioning. Professional brewers use glycol-filled heating and cooling jackets around their fermenters to control their beer temperatures. The homebrewers' solution, however, is less elegant.

Instead of attaching a cooling apparatus to your fermenter, the common strategy is to modify a chest freezer or refrigerator with more precise temperature controls. While a chest freezer is the most efficient use of space, old refrigerators are easier to come by. For temperature control, you'll need a digital temperature control and probe to automatically kick the refrigeration compressor into gear as the fermenter (if you attach the probe to it) or air heats up.

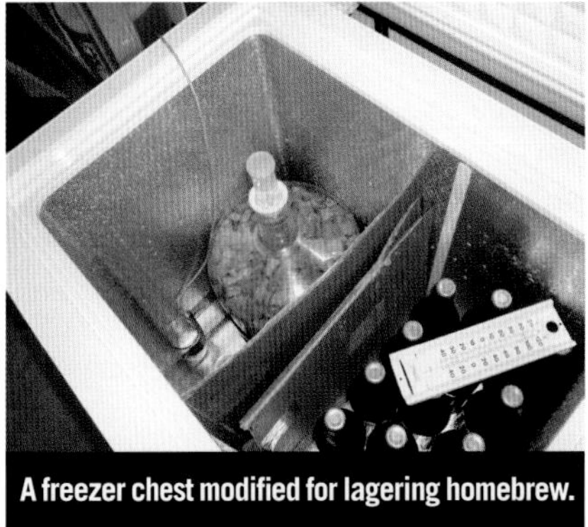

A freezer chest modified for lagering homebrew.

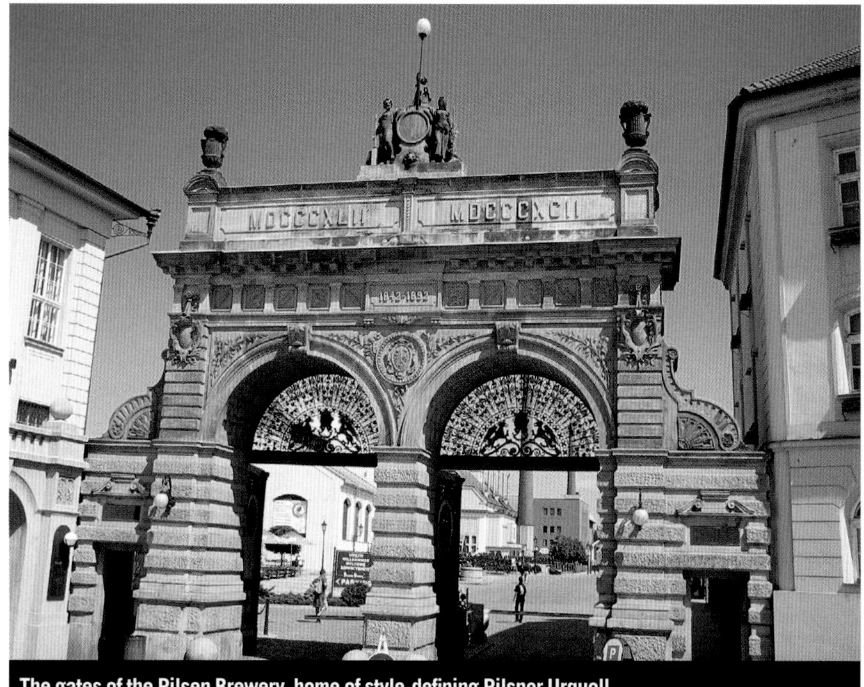

The gates of the Pilsen Brewery, home of style-defining Pilsner Urquell

LAGER YEAST

Conventional wisdom states that lager yeasts are a clean, cold-fermenting type of *Saccharomyces*. But to think of them as simple strains does a disservice to their potential. Like ale yeast, certain strains can accentuate the malt or hops while bringing their own distinctive signature notes.

LAGER STRAINS

The lager yeasts available don't number nearly as great as ale strains, but there's still a fine variety for fermenting any lager imaginable. Though this simplifies the selection, picking a geographical yeast region is a first step in building your next beer.

GERMAN

Emphasizes malt character. South German or Bavarian strains may produce more diacetyl. Oktoberfest-oriented strain makes exceptional malt-forward beers.

CZECH

Dry, but still malty and may produce more esters. The Pilsen strain tends toward cleaner profile and is the Chico equivalent of lager yeast.

SWISS

High-attenuating and designed to take on high-gravity lagers with potential alcohol levels greater than 11 percent.

AMERICAN

Dry and clean, but not without character. Slight fruit, some would say green apple, is characteristic.

LAGER FERMENTATION

Primary lager fermentation is not much colder than ale fermentation, but it's below room temperature. The general temperature target is around 50°F (10°C), though a smart brewer will check the yeast specifications. This stage requires refrigeration.

The colder temperature creates two differences beyond needing refrigeration. First, even though the yeast is bred for the brisk conditions, expect to pitch twice as many yeast cells. For a 5-gallon (19 L) batch, that's two White Labs vials or Wyeast smack packs. Second, lager yeast ferments slowly, with a ten- to fourteen-day primary fermentation being typical.

FERMENTER SHAPE

Stylistically, lagers share little with British and Belgian ales except using open fermenters in the recent past. Today, the open process is used by some German-style wheat brewers, but even the best craft brewers use cylindroconical fermenters. The theory behind wide open fermenters is that the reduced air pressure encourages richer and more complex flavor.

If you have a knack for sanitation, you can compare the differences yourself: Split a batch of beer into open and closed vessels.

For your open vessel, use a normal fermenter or stainless steel pot, and place a loose-fitting lid over the top. Aluminum foil can also serve as a lid; you simply want to prevent larger contaminants like pet hair and dirt from falling in. Ferment for the normal amount of time and age in a closed conditioning tank as usual.

CONDITIONING

Here's where your beer gets chilly. The notion of a lager is rooted in the act of conditioning. Historically, German lagers were stored in cool caves over the summer. The beer was named after this process, as lager in German means to stock or store something.

During lagering, flavors blend with off-tasting compounds including diacetyl, sulfur, and aldehyde—a chemical that gives some mainstream beers a tart apple flavor.

A good rule is to condition your standard lager for four weeks at just-above freezing temperatures (33°F to 34°F, or 0.6°C to 1°C).

Stronger beers, of course, benefit from extended aging. Giving a 9 percent doppelbock three to six months to mellow and develop is reasonable if you have the patience and space.

BREWING TERM: PITCH
To pitch yeast means to add your brewing yeast to cooled wort, thus inoculating it.

WARM PITCHING
To help counter the reduced capacity of cold yeast, some brewers will pitch their lager yeast warm (around 65°F, or 18°C) for the early stages of fermentation. This allows the cells to multiply before they begin converting sugar in earnest. Once activity begins, slowly drop the beer temperature by about 1°F (0.6°C) every hour.

Though this may allow you to ferment completely with the same amount of yeast as an ale, the warmer temperatures will create undesirable off-flavors from ester and diacetyl in the beer. A compromise is to still pitch double the yeast, but at 60°F (18°C) before lowering.

INGREDIENTS

MALTS

There's no right or wrong base malt for a lager. Traditionally, brewers mash in six-row barley, and if you're recreating a specific style of lager, you can use the traditional malt. Even the lightest pilsner malts have a lighter, grainier flavor profile that sets it apart from the popular ale malt, two-row barley. If you're used to brewing with two-row, expect up to 5 percent less extract as six-row has a larger husk and less starch.

Your attention should be on tailoring your ingredients to the malts and beer you've envisioned. Homebrew shops always keep German six-row pilsner malt on hand, but if you're interested in a Czech-style lager, look for Moravian malt. Or if the rich malty bocks are calling out to you, pick a malt-centric yeast such as an Oktoberfest strain.

HOPS

It is no coincidence your beer aisle is devoid of anything resembling an imperial India pale lager. (I challenge you to try brewing one, of course.) By nature, longer fermentation and conditioning time mellows hop character. And unlike British ale, there is no convention of Czech or German brewers adding hops postboil. Big hoppy lagers are absolutely possible, but if you're chasing IBUs and alpha acids, ales are more accommodating.

Noble hops produce a reliably classic (and tasty) lager. The list of noble hops is up for some debate, but Saaz, Hallertauer, Spalt, and Tettnanger safely fall into the group. There is small, but significant, variation between these varieties, but they're known for a spicy, herbal, and floral character.

German hops in Schwabhausen, Bavaria, wait to be picked and dried.

INTERVIEW WITH:
BILL COVALESKI: VICTORY BREWING CO., DOWNINGTOWN, PENNSYLVANIA, U.S.

WHILE SOME CRAFT BREWERS RACE TOWARD THE EXTREME, BILL AND RON STEERED VICTORY BREWING TOWARD MASTERING AND THEN IMPROVING UPON CLASSIC STYLES. THE BREWERY'S LINE OF GERMAN-INSPIRED LAGERS SETS THE STANDARD FOR WHAT BREWERS CAN ACCOMPLISH OUTSIDE OF A BEER'S MOTHERLAND.

HOW DID YOU AND YOUR COFOUNDER, RON BARCHET, GET INTO CRAFT BREWING?

We all started by drinking a beer that tasted different than the crap we were drinking the day before. In my case that could probably be traced to a bottle of Henry Weinhard's in 1984. My dad was also homebrewing and was getting pretty good at (believe it or not) a Heineken clone.

CAN YOU GET GOOD AT THAT?

Okay, to my sensibilities in 1985, he was pretty good at it. And it wasn't just because it was free. It encouraged me to try my hand at brewing. As a recently graduated arts student, I thought it was all about ingredients and how cool the label was going to look. Naturally, I overlooked some critical aspects of sanitation and process and had a couple failures off the bat, which got me to study the science behind it. That's when I [discovered] the rich culture of brewing.

YOU BREW A LINE OF HOPPED-UP PILSNERS LIKE OTHER BREWERS WOULD WITH PALE ALES. WHAT WAS THE INSPIRATION?

Ron and I brewed at a German-centric brewery starting in 1989 for him, and 1990 for me. Their most impactful beer was an unfiltered pilsner that was really firmly hopped. It was unlike other pilsners floating around Europe and the U.S. We've been keen on pilsner flavors since and developed Prima Pils.

But there were still these great hops we wanted to experiment with, so in 2000, we initiated the Braumeister Pils series. Instead of the four noble hops we use in Prima Pils, we focus on one variety. The results inform our brewing decisions down the road.

Prima Pils is bursting with Saaz, Hallertauer, Spalt, and Tettnanger hops, but it does not use a dry-hop addition.

My recipe for a märzen is probably like 80 percent of the others out there. So there's no secret. But where I am sourcing my ingredients, how I use their primary characteristics, and how I achieve the flavors in my head make the difference.

WHAT HAVE YOU LEARNED?

We've learned a lot of what we liked and very little of what we disliked. Say, how Tettnanger hops at a certain point become minerally and metallic. Saaz at a certain threshold is lemony and bright.

This has helped us when we're creating other lager beers and looking for specific hop profiles. We know how they react to German malt at a low fermentation temperature. We know what hop to use if we make a schwarz pils.

SCHWARZ PILS, LIKE A BLACK PILS?

Yes, it's more of a deep chestnut, but it still has roast flavor to it.

CAN YOU REALLY CALL THAT A PILS?

I'm talking to the guy who should know the answer to that question. All I can say is we have one, so they do exist. [Laughs.]

WHAT ARE SOME OF YOUR FAVORITE HOP VARIETIES FOR LAGERS?

It became taboo to use Hallertau Mittlefrueh after Sam Adams Boston Lager came out because it was such a signature flavor for that beer. That's been in a lot of our beers, however. After we started a relationship with our grower in Tettnang, Germany, Tettnang became a little more prominent in the overall mix of things because of the quality we're able to get.

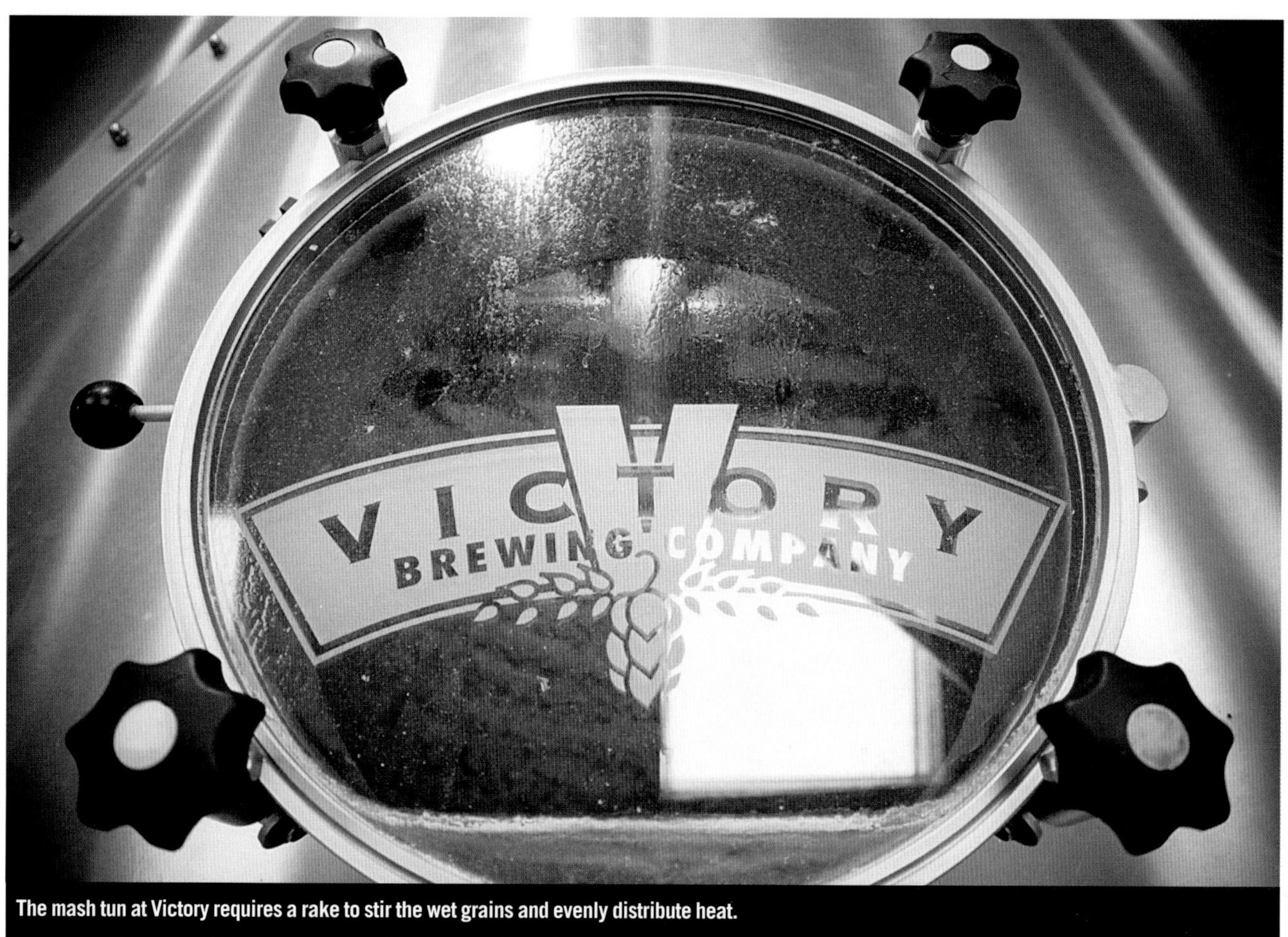

The mash tun at Victory requires a rake to stir the wet grains and evenly distribute heat.

HAVE ANY FAVORITE COMMERCIAL LAGERS INFLUENCED YOUR BEERS?

No, but there were milestones along the way that informed what I think lagers should be. Way back in my drinking history, I know Ron and I were both fond of Beck's. And in 1987 on our first tour of Germany, we drank Waldhaus Pils and Rothaus Pils. They were really stand-out beers.

I HAD A ROTHAUS PILS NOT TOO LONG AGO. I'D WAGER IT WAS BETTER WHEN YOU TRIED IT. IT SEEMS GERMAN BREWERS HAVE BEEN ON A TEAR TOWARD COST CONSCIOUSNESS.

It's sad to hear, but not surprising. You know in Germany, beer has a cost [threshold], and if you exceed that cost, people don't buy you. Most breweries are self-limiting and refuse to keep the IBUs up there in order to hit a certain price point.

IS DRY-HOPPING TRADITIONAL IN LAGER BREWING?

We do very little dry-hopping in this brewery at all.

I RECENTLY HEARD DRY-HOPPING ISN'T ALLOWED BY REINHEITSGEBOT IN GERMANY.

I haven't encountered German brewers that dry-hop, but hops are part of the process—come on people, lighten up. [U.S.] craft brewing has brought a lot of things into question. But all their nontraditional things aren't killing or poisoning people. Quite the opposite—it's making people very happy.

Bill and cofounder Ron Barchet

The aspiring homebrewer needs to focus on process more than having friends exclaim it's the coolest, most kickass beer they've had.

WHAT'S YOUR TYPICAL LAGER FERMENTATION?

We ferment straight through at 43°F (6°C). We need a larger cell count that's going to perform at that. We have a total of three yeast propagators around the brewery now.

THERE'S ALL THE TALK OF DECOCTION MASHING AND SO ON: WHAT'S THE RELATIVE IMPORTANCE?

When Ron and I started, we questioned whether we'd have capability to do decoction mashing. It was a big decision because it meant real money. And we arrived at yes by talking about our favorite German beers and recognizing that most of them were decoction-brewed. That said, we've got a decoction kettle and we only use it in 6 percent of our beers. So it's there for the right reasons, but it doesn't apply to everything.

HOW DO YOU DETERMINE WHEN IT DOES AND DOESN'T APPLY?

The beer styles really indicate that. Our largest-selling decoction beer is Festbier. In order to create that round, well-developed body and the protein structure necessary to achieve that, a decoction is important for that beer. We tried decoction mashing our Moonglow Weizenbock, because we do decoction-mash our bock beers, and we got nothing but a lauter tun of gum we had to scratch out over six hours.

ARE THERE ANY MALT VARIETIES BETTER SUITED TO COLD FERMENTATION AND CONDITIONING TIME?

Great question. It's a decision driven by recipe and outcome more than pairing malt to a fermentation profile. I love to talk about this with people. They think my recipes must be special or precious, but there's so much else that goes into it. My recipe for a märzen is probably like 80 percent of the others out there. So there's no secret. But where I am sourcing my ingredients, how I use their primary characteristics, and how I achieve the flavors in my head makes the difference.

SO ARE YOU SUGGESTING YOU MIGHT BE LESS A PIONEER THAN SOME PERCEIVE?

That could be inferred. What we've brought to the table is a holistic perspective of "Maybe we've got a traditional märzen recipe, but we're going to use it as a means to bring something new to the market." It's subtle, and it's not just better because it's different, but because specific improvements in depth of malt flavor or whatever improvement we want to see in an existing style. I don't think we're necessarily huge innovators. We've paired German Munich malt with American whole-flower hops for Hop Devil and that might be the most dramatic thing we've brought to the table. I think there are far more subtle successes for us.

WHAT ADVICE WOULD YOU HAVE FOR THE BURGEONING LAGER HOMEBREWER?

For home lager brewing, temperature control is a hill to climb unless you're an HVAC guy or a true geek. The other thing, too, is don't expect to make the most sensational lager, because that in itself is an impossible goal. They're sensational in their subtlety. The aspiring homebrewer needs to focus on process more than having friends exclaim it's the coolest, most kickass beer they've had.

I GUESS BY NATURE LAGERS AREN'T POISED TO BE OUTRAGEOUS.

The lagering process is almost dampening your bandwidth. You've got all these bright brassy flavors out of the fermenter, and then you take them down a few notches.

CA REDEMPTION VALUE
BREWED & BOTTLED BY THE STONE BREWING CO., ESCONDIDO, NORTH COUNTY SAN DIEGO, CA
STO
Emper
INDIA
8.9% Alc/Vol

ONE
erial IPA
PALE ALE
1 Pt. 6 Fl.Oz.

Stone adds gypsum, a brewing salt, to their Stone 14th Anniversary Emperial IPA to mimic the famous Burton-On-Trent water character and enhance the bitterness.

TODAY WE HAVE THE ADVANTAGE OF BREWING CHEMISTRY TO ALLOW ANY BREWER TO TWEAK HIS LIQUOR (THE BREWING TERM FOR WATER) TO MIMIC THE PROFILES OF FAMOUS BREWING CITIES. HOWEVER, THE REASON CITIES DEVELOPED TRADEMARK STYLES, SUCH AS THE PILSEN PILSNER, IRISH STOUT IN DUBLIN, OR HOPPY ALES FROM BURTON, ENGLAND, IS BECAUSE BEFORE BREWING HAD ADVANCED TO THE POINT OF RADICAL WATER ADJUSTMENT, BEERS WERE BREWED AROUND THE AVAILABLE WATER SOURCES.

CHAPTER 5: WATER CHEMISTRY

Of the four basic parts of beer, water is the most easily forgotten. It's understandable. Despite water being the greatest ingredient in good beer, good beer can be produced without much thought to the water. Details like this make the difference between good and great brewers.

INTRODUCTION TO BREWING WATER

Many new homebrewers will forget to think about their brewing water, but as it constitutes roughly 95 percent of a beer, you should never overlook it. Ideal brewing water has small amounts of minerals and minimal chlorine. Basic filtered water, though not mineral-free distilled water, will work. But closer attention to your water chemistry can optimize your brewing process and significantly affect flavor and bitterness.

In this chapter, you'll learn about:

- **Hard water**
- **Water reports**
- **Brewing salts**
- **How much water to use**

WHAT IS HARD WATER?

Hardness is a measure of the calcium and magnesium content in your water. If you're familiar with water softener salt from your house, this is the same characteristic we're talking about. For homebrewing, moderately hard water accentuates hop character, making for a rich and bitter taste. Conversely, soft water encourages a subtle and less biting hop flavor associated with many lager styles.

UNDERSTAND YOUR WATER REPORT

All cities make their water reports available to the public and most can be found on municipal government websites. Look for a water resources or management section; there will usually be a yearly water quality report for download. Home test kits are inexpensive, but also imprecise. If a report is not readily available online, call and request a water quality report from your municipal source.

Water reports aren't often easy to decipher. For brewing, the key is to look for the levels of permanent hardness. Again, this is the measure of calcium (Ca) and magnesium (Mg).

The report will also tell temporary hardness, represented by alkalinity, which is calcium carbonate ($CaCO_4$). Temporary hardness is less important as the $CaCO_4$ will drop out of solution when boiled. In large concentrations, without Ca or Mg to balance it out, $CaCO_4$ raises your pH. Regions known for their dark beers, such as Dublin, often had high temporary hardness levels. Roasted grains are more acidic and lowered the mash pH. When brewers with these conditions tried to brew pale lagers or ales, they would be met with a too-high, inefficient mash pH that extracted unpleasant tannins and phenols.

In addition to hardness and pH, the report will also likely show the sulfates and sodium.

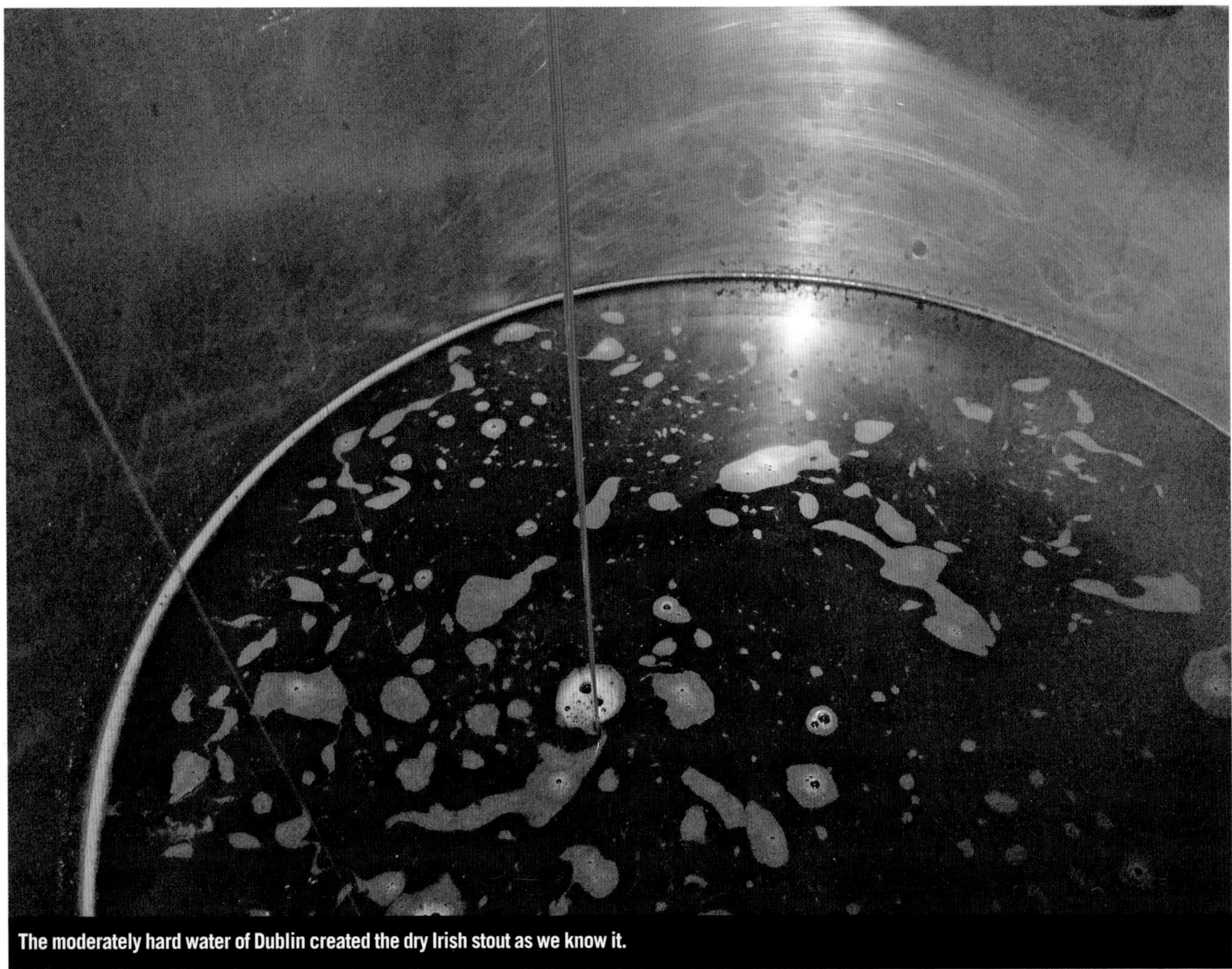

The moderately hard water of Dublin created the dry Irish stout as we know it.

WATER PH

Tap water from your faucet will typically have a pH around 7.5. A good mash needs to be at a pH of 5.3, but just adding your grains will automatically lower the acidity near the range of 5.0 to 5.5.

Aside from stocking brewing salts, homebrew shops will often carry lactic acid. Or for a classic approach, use acidulated malt. This extra-low pH malt was developed by Reinheitsgebot-bound German brewers looking to lower mash pH.

FILTERING WATER

If you do nothing else to your water, filter it before brewing. A basic carbon filter in the form of a pitcher, faucet attachment, or countertop filter will remove unpleasant flavors and chlorine. Some volatiles, such as chlorine, can also be driven off by boiling your strike water and then letting it cool down to mash in.

After filtering their water, some brewers will use reverse-osmosis filters for a portion of their brewing water. This distills a portion of the liquor, making it devoid of minerals, so it can lower the overall hardness of the water. Even without a reverse-osmosis filter, you can get the same effect from blending distilled water purchased at a grocery store. Keep in mind that distilled water contains none of the nutrients (zinc, copper, iron, etc.) that yeast requires for healthy growth and fermentation.

SOFT WATER

Most beer styles are brewed using moderately hard water (calcium levels from 100 to 120 ppm), but for subtler beer styles such as the Czech pilsner, brewing with soft water is a must. The town of Pilsen's incredibly soft water is what defined the style as a smooth, but full-flavored pilsner.

The filtering methods mentioned, such as distilling water, can help create a malty beer with a mild, clean bitterness, though a shortcut would be to obtain spring water, which is usually fairly soft but rich enough in mineral nutrients. A bonus of using soft water is that because of the low temporary hardness level, there's little trouble hitting a desired pH with pale base malt.

Brewing salts, such as calcium chloride, can be, but don't necessarily need to be, dissolved before adding them to your kettle.

BREWING SALTS

When you have an idea of your ideal water, look at your water report for what chemicals are too low. If any are already too high, either use filtered water or cut your liquor with distilled water. When dosing brewing salts, ppm is the equivalent of 1 milligram per 1 liter. If you want to adjust the mash pH, add the salt along with the grains; otherwise, the salts can be added to the boil.

BREWING SALTS

Calcium Carbonate	One gram of $CaCO_4$ adds 107 ppm of calcium and 159 ppm of carbonate.	Also referred to as temporary hardness, this typically undesirable chemical raises pH but can balance out the acidity of dark grains.
Calcium Chloride	One gram per gallon of CaCl adds 96 ppm of calcium and 168 ppm of chloride.	Unlike when it's paired with carbonate, calcium increases hardness, lowers pH, and enhances enzymatic mash activity. Chloride enhances mouthfeel in concentrations under 300 ppm; greater amounts can create unpleasant tasting chlorophenols (think plastic bandages).
Calcium Sulfate (Gypsum)	One gram per gallon of $CaSO_4$ adds 62 ppm of calcium and 147 ppm of sulfate.	Calcium increases hardness, lowers pH, and enhances enzymatic mash activity. Sulfate also increases hardness and aids mash conversion while enhancing bitterness. This will amplify bitterness more than calcium chloride or magnesium sulfate.
Magnesium Sulfate (Epsom Salt)	One gram per gallon of $MgSO_4$ adds 37 ppm of magnesium and 145 ppm of sulfate.	Magnesium works like calcium but is essentially only half as effective, while also contributing astringent flavors in high concentrations. Sulfate also increases hardness and aids mash conversion while enhancing bitterness.
Sodium Chloride (Table Salt)	One gram per gallon of NaCl adds 104 ppm of sodium and 160 ppm of chloride.	Sodium enhances mouthfeel when limited to 75 to 150 ppm. Beyond that, it will make beer salty and sour. Chloride also enhances mouthfeel in concentrations under 300 ppm without side effects; greater amounts can create unpleasant-tasting chlorophenols (think plastic bandages).

HOW MUCH WATER DO YOU NEED?

Water chemistry aside, your brew day won't go far if you don't know how much water to use in your mash.

STEP 1

To calculate how much water you need, use a water-to-grain ratio between a 1 quart (0.9 L) per pound of grain to 2 quarts (1.9 L) per pound of grain.

A thicker mash will result in higher-gravity wort, and is useful for big beers that reach the limits of your mash capacity.

A thinner mash has a less-efficient conversion but can pull more sugar from the grains.

STEP 2

Once you calculated your mash's strike water, you will need to work backward from your intended final volume of brew to determine how much to add back in. Add:

The evaporation loss (5 to 10 percent per hour) for your system

The water lost to grain absorption (0.21 gallons per pound [1.8 liters per kg])

Any other losses from your system and the kettle trub (hop matter and other precipitates)

STEP 3

Subtract your strike water from that total, and use the rest as sparge water.

One warning: Measure the gravity of your wort as it drains from the grains. Once it measures only 3 degrees Plato, stop and add any remaining water to the kettle. As the wort becomes especially diluted, it can extract tannins and other undesirable flavors from grain.

THE WATER IN MAJOR BREWING CITIES (IN PPM)

To more accurately recreate or mimic classic beer styles, always consider the chemistry of the original water supply. That said, the iconic cities listed in the table below all brewed a variety of styles of beer that benefited from their water's unique chemical profile, so don't limit yourself to the single style listed.

	Classic Beer Style	Calcium	Magnesium	Sodium	Sulfate	Bicarbonate	Chloride
Antwerp	Belgian Pale Ale	6	11	37	84	76	57
Burton	English Pale Ale	275	40	25	450	260	35
Dortmund	Export Lager	225	40	60	120	180	60
Dublin	Irish Dry Stout	120	5	12	55	125	20
Edinburgh	Scottish Ale	120	25	55	140	225	65
London	English Porter	90	5	15	40	125	20
Milwaukee	Adjunct Lager	96	47	7	26	107	16
Munich	Helles Lager	75	18	2	10	150	2
Pilzen	Czech Pilsner	7	2	2	5	15	5
Vienna	Vienna Lager	200	60	8	125	120	12

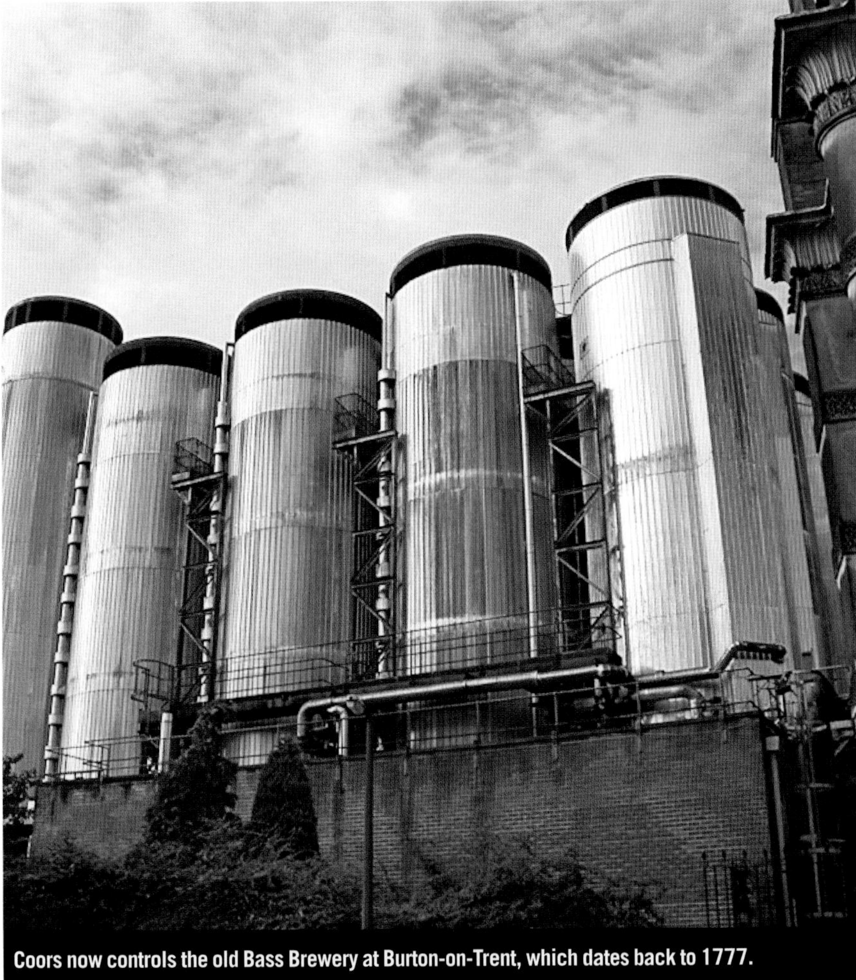

Coors now controls the old Bass Brewery at Burton-on-Trent, which dates back to 1777.

BURTON-ON-TRENT, UK

Few beer lovers would have trouble pointing out the world's famous brewing cities on a globe. That is, until you ask them where Burton is (about thirty miles north of Birmingham, England). While the brewing world is usually run by giants, this relatively small town redefined the pale ale. The many brewers of London, for instance, simply couldn't match the rich, yet drinkable hop profile created and honed by the brewers far outside the city.

Despite the last century's trend of consolidation, Burton still has four craft breweries. With the exception of Burton's largest brewery, Coors Brewers, the UK branch of the U.S.'s Molson Coors, which produces Bass and Carling, the remaining brewers take full advantage of their town water to turn out phenomenal ales as rich as the brewers before them.

Before finding his true home at Stone Brewing, Mitch spent time working at a small brewpub, a large international brewery, and a large winery.

INTERVIEW WITH: MITCH STEELE: HEAD BREWER, STONE BREWING CO., ESCONDIDO, CALIFORNIA, U.S.

THE MAN ENTRUSTED IN BREWING SUCH CRAFT BEER–WORLD STAPLES AS ARROGANT BASTARD ALE AND STONE RUINATION IPA–KNOWS THERE'S MORE TO GREAT BEER THAN HOPS AND BARLEY. EVERY BATCH STARTS NOT IN THE MASH TUN OR KETTLE, BUT IN THE WATER PIPES RUNNING INTO THE BREWERY.

WHAT IS THE WATER SOURCE AT STONE BREWING?

The municipal water. It is moderately hard at 300 ppm hardness and it is loaded with chlorine to knock out microbiological activity. We run all the water through a carbon filter and that strips it of any flavors and chlorine, so it tastes neutral.

It's still hard, but the filter's activated carbon ions absorb chlorine ions and any pipe flavor you might get.

FOR HOMEBREWERS, WOULD NORMAL CARBON FILTRATION MIMIC THIS?

Yes. They can also boil their water for 15 minutes before their mash in and that'll take chlorine out. You have to heat it anyway. Otherwise, chlorine will carry through the whole brewing process and you can taste it in a beer in high levels.

After the carbon filter, we run part of it through a reverse-osmosis filtration system, and that pulls out some mineral content. Only a portion goes through the osmosis filter. So the water comes in at 300 ppm hardness and is leaving at 100 to 120 ppm after it's blended back together.

WITH THE CONTROL OVER FILTRATION, IS THERE ANY WEIGHT TO THE CLAIM THAT CERTAIN BREWERIES HAVE "THE BEST" WATER?

That kind of thinking would go back 150 years or so. Once the industrial revolution came about, chemists began to understand the process and what was happening with Burton water, for example. People started mimicking their brewing salt through additions in the mid-1800s.

LET'S GO BACK TO HARD AND SOFT WATER: HOW WOULD YOU DESCRIBE THESE TYPES OF WATER FOR BREWERS?

The best way to describe hard water is that it has a high mineral content and soft water does not. Minerals in water will affect the brewing process, such as yeast and enzyme performance in mash and yeast performance in fermentation. Hop character is radically different in hard water compared to soft.

Stone
Brewing

In 2010, Stone Brewing produced 115,000 barrels of beer.

FROM A SMALL HOMEBREWING SETUP, DO YOU NEED TO FOCUS MUCH ON WATER, OR JUST BOIL IT AND YOU'LL BE NINE-TENTHS OF THE WAY THERE?

If you have clean neutral-tasting water you'll be fine, but there are things you can do to shape your beer. Boiling removes temporary hardness, which is a technical term for [minerals] that precipitate out. You can add salts to make water harder, or "Burtonize" it with calcium sulfate, gypsum, or calcium chloride. When I homebrewed, I at least threw a teaspoon of gypsum in.

GYPSUM, CALCIUM SULFATE: IT'S A KIND OF SALT?

Exactly, a brewing mineral salt. Most homebrew shops have gypsum, and it's fairly common because most drinking water is soft.

WHY WOULD YOU ADD CALCIUM TO THE WATER?

From a chemistry standpoint, in the mash process, calcium will enhance enzymatic activity of malt enzymes breaking down starches. You get better efficiency and better conversion fairly easily with a little calcium. That turned out to be a big deal with IPAs, because the goal was to make them as dry as possible and not sweet.

The first IPAs were brewed in London, where the water was fairly soft (compared to Burton). But the IPAs out of Burton were clearer with more pronounced hop character. On the brewhouse side, having calcium in your wort is also going to give you slightly better hop utilization.

BURTON-ON-TRENT BECAME FAMOUS FOR ITS HOPPY BEERS, THANKS TO THE WATER. LET'S TALK ABOUT HOW HARD WATER INTERACTS WITH HOPS.

That's the meat of the discussion. At Burton-on-Trent, the water is treated like any other ingredient. They have wells in different parts of the town with different water profiles, and then they mix the water to get the character they want. The brewers realized early on their water was doing something to the beer that made it travel better. It allowed the beer to settle out to a higher level of clarity in a [shorter] amount of time than beer [made] with soft water.

AND THE BITTERNESS OF BURTON'S ALES?

The other thing about pale ales in Burton is they realized they could really hop the beer up and get a really intense bitterness, but it wouldn't be harsh or coarse. It gave [the ales] an enhanced hop flavor from mouthfeel of the water and interaction of calcium ions.

One of the things the brewers at Burton told me is that the water there is so old, and has gone through so many layers of rock, there is no microbiological activity. That's why their beer never spoils. I'm not sure about that, but back in 1800, they mashed longer and could get souring, but that's malt, not water. Boiling should take care of infection. But sometimes the brewers back then would top off their barrels with well water and rinse fermenters. That could lead to spoilage, but I'm still not sure I'm on board [with their theory].

Stone IPA was introduced in 1997 and clocks in at 77 IBUs.

Stone Brewing President and Brewmaster Steve Wagner (left), CEO (and co-author of this mighty tome) Greg Koch (center), and Head Brewer Mitch Steele (right).

The best way to get a water analysis is to call your water supplier and ask for one, or visit their website. Specifically ask for hardness, calcium, and pH. No water company is shy about sharing.

AT STONE BREWING, DO YOU ADD ANY SALTS?

Not regularly. We can filter the water to where we want it as far as hardness. We've done two beers where we've added gypsum, the Stone 14th Anniversary Emperial IPA, and then the [collaboration beer called the Ballast Point/McNair/Stone/Kelsey] San Diego County Session Ale.

It's something I want to explore further, particularly with Stone IPA. The mash pH is a little higher than where I'd like it to be, and if I added a little calcium to bring it down, we'd get a higher efficiency and maybe increase hop utilization. I'm not looking to change the flavor at all, just increase performance a bit.

WHEN WOULD YOU ADD BREWING SALTS?

If you are brewing a hop-forward pale ale and you have soft water, brewing salts will help.

HOW WOULD YOU DO A WATER ANALYSIS?

The best way to do it is to call your water supplier and ask for an analysis, or visit their website. Specifically ask for hardness, calcium, and pH. No water company is shy about sharing. In a standard beer, you want 70 to 100 ppm calcium. For something that is Burton-on-Trent-ish, 300.

SO WHAT'S IN THAT INTERIM RANGE?

Dortmund, Dublin, and London water. In general, most brewing water has a hardness around 100, and that gives you a good range to do lager and ale brewing. You're in the middle of the road. Strict Burton-type water gets that real chalky texture. Burton hardness is around 900, London is around 200. [Stone's water is] on the low end, but I'd argue we make good IPAs.

WHAT'S TOO SOFT FOR BREWING WATER?

In the low 30s ppm for hardness you can risk some hop flavor and have clarifying issues.

COMPARE MUNICH PILSNERS BREWED WITH HARDER WATER AND CZECH PILSNERS WITH SOFT WATER. HOW DOES THE DIFFERENCE IN WATER SHOW UP?

With the Czech pils, the water is so soft they can go to a real high bitterness level without a harsh, bitter feel. A Czech pils is over 40 IBU but doesn't drink like it.

WHAT WOULD HAPPEN IF YOU BREWED A CZECH PILS WITH BURTONIZED WATER?

For a pilsner brewed Burton style, there's 40 IBUs with low-acid hops. And because you'd use boatloads of hops to reach 40, the bitterness would come across as coarse.

HOW DO YOU FIGURE OUT HOW MUCH WATER YOU NEED WHEN BREWING?

You typically use a 3:1 ratio of water to grain (or 1.4 to 1.5 quarts of water per pound [2.9 to 3.1 liters per kg] of grain). That's a starting point.

MOST OF THE WATER USED TO BREW GOES TO WASTE. CAN YOU EXPLAIN OUR WASTEWATER TREATMENT?

Most water used in a brewery is for cleaning. You look at water ratios, and the goal is 4 gallons (15 L) of water per 1 gallon (3.8 L) of beer—and that's on the low side of the industry standard.

A large body of water from our process goes down the drain full of sugar from the mash, yeast, hop particles, and cleaners. We take this brown murky water from the brewing process—it doesn't mix with food or toilets. We take it all down to our wastewaster treatment, run it into a tank, and allow bacteria to consume all the sugar and proteins. Then we separate the water from solids, run it through a reverse-osmosis filter so it comes out clean, clear, and neutral in flavor. It's wonderful water, and we're bringing it into the brewery for cleaning.

BREWING TERM: HOP UTILIZATION

The percentage of bitter alpha acids in hops that are isomerized and absorbed into a beer is the utilization rate. The rate is dependent on the brewing water in addition to boil length and wort density.

The Belgian-owned Brewery Ommegang produces authentic Belgian ales in Cooperstown, New York

BELGIUM, A SLIVER OF HILLS AND CANALS, IS THE WORLD'S MOST UNLIKELY BREWING SUPERPOWER. STACKED BETWEEN GERMANY AND BRITAIN, IT'S A MINISCULE PLOT OF RAINY COUNTRYSIDE. BUT IT'S BEEN A STOMPING GROUND FOR INVADING ARMIES FOR AT LEAST THE LAST MILLENNIUM, SO IT'S A PLACE IN NEED OF A GOOD BEER. BELGIAN BREWERS ARE REVERED FOR THEIR CREATIVITY AND REVERENCE. THEIR BEERS ARE COMPLEX AND CAN ELUDE THE MOST EXPERIENCED BREWERS. THEY'RE NOT ALWAYS EASY TO MAKE, BUT HERE'S HOW TO BEGIN.

CHAPTER 6: BREWING LIKE A BELGIAN

INTRODUCTION TO BELGIAN BREWING

Belgian beer and brewing is easily identified for the fruity and spicy yeast-driven character. That means that while other ingredients contribute, a properly fermented Belgian yeast strain is the essential ingredient and difference between a Belgian pale ale and English pale ale. That said, Belgians also stand out for higher alcohol levels, the use of sugar, and lack of hop character.

In this chapter, you'll learn:

- **Belgian brewing history**
- **Belgian beer ingredients**
- **Brewing with sugar**
- **Belgian yeast**
- **Brewing spices**

BREWERS WITHOUT BOUNDS

As mundane as it sounds, the trajectory of a culture's brewing comes down to tax laws and ordinances. American light lagers are partially a result of Prohibition. The UK's low-strength pub ales were a response to alcohol taxes. And the rigid (though delicious) beer styles of Germany are courtesy of their brewing purity laws. In Belgium, a 1919 law banned liquor from bars and pub areas and helped fuel the trend of stronger ales. Belgium also benefited from the 1790s French Revolution, during which monks were chased into Belgium and later began to set up shop, first in Westmalle.

Add their unusual lack of regulation to their culinary melting pot (thanks to the many invading countries), plus a lack of hop farmers (unlike in the UK or Germany), and you have a perfect storm: beer that is strong and yeast-driven with no rules for proper ingredients. In Belgium, the fifth ingredient in beer is "anything goes." Their brewing is process-driven, aiming to hit a certain flavor profile, instead of being ingredient-driven and forced within certain limits.

Scourmont Abbey, home of Chimay

Brewers at Westmalle follow tradition by using whole-leaf hops instead of pellets.

CHOOSING A MALT

For all the rich, complex notes of a great Belgian, the malt can be surprisingly simple.

Start with good pilsner malt for a base (use the Belgian malting house Dingemans if you want to be authentic).

Some brewers will also add a share of pale malt, then use dark malts sparingly in dark ales.

The Trappists, especially, make little use of specialty malts, largely relying on their dark candi syrups and sugars for color and character beyond the yeast (which does most of the work). But that's not necessarily the only way.

MASHING FOR BELGIAN BEER

If you use a single-step mash, aim for 146°F to 149°F (63°C to 65°C) and then sparge around 165°F (74°C) to continue conversion and maximize attenuation.

For a multistep mash like most Belgian brewers use, keep your protein rest short. In addition to losing head retention from a long protein rest, you'll lose body, which will compensate for the thin, dry feel created by fermenting dry with relatively small amounts of residual sugar.

CHOOSING HOPS

Because there are no hard-and-fast rules to Belgian ingredients, any hops will do, when used correctly. If you want to emulate the famous abbeys and breweries in Belgium, use Noble or Noble-esque hops for bittering and aroma. These flowery and spicy hops, such as Saaz, Hallertauer, and Styrian Goldings, have a clean, not-harsh bitterness thanks to lower cohumulone levels (see chapter 2 for more on cohumulone).

For a similar effect, but with a twist on the Noble character, try Sterling, Liberty, and Mt. Hood hops, which have similarly low levels of cohumulone.

Boulevard Brewery's Brewmaster Steven Pauwels (left) and President John McDonald (right) have crafted some of the best American-made Belgians with the Smokestack Series.

If you want to try brewing a hop-centric ale such as a Belgian IPA, try a mix of Noble hops with other craft beer standbys. Houblon Chouffe, for example, uses Tomahawk for bittering, Saaz for aroma, and then Amarillo to dry-hop.

Urthel's Hop-It and Gouden Carolus Hopsinjoor both use only Noble and European hops, while Stone Cali-Belgique IPA and Flying Dog's Raging Bitch use classic American hops.

ADJUNCT SUGARS

Adding adjunct sugar to a beer may seem repugnant to craft beer lovers or anyone with a distaste for megabrewers and their use of corn and rice adjuncts. However, to brew a true strong Belgian ale, sugar is an absolute necessity. Belgian beer lovers expect a strong beer that won't fill them up. Brewers achieve this mix of strength, complexity, and drinkability by using a highly fermentable sugar for 10 to 20 percent of the malt bill.

Most brewers use dextrose, also called glucose, as a cost-effective ingredient for lightening the beer's body and creating a crisp, dry mouthfeel. Historically, Belgian brewers used sugar derived from beets (what many think of as white sugar comes from cane), but both forms are refined to the point where there is no noticeable difference in taste.

For brewers looking for a sugar with flavor and character, candi sugar is the most traditional Belgian brewing sugar. Think of it like a specialty malt where the sugar is

BREWING TERM: ADJUNCT SUGAR

Brewing adjuncts are typically unmalted grain additions, but adjunct sugar refers to additions of sugar to a beer. Sugar ferments almost completely, unlike malted barley or wheat, which leave residual sugar (with body and flavor) behind. In small proportions, less than 10 percent, sugar boosts alcohol with minimal flavor impact.

cooked as syrup to varying degrees similar to how malt is roasted. These also add color to your beer, and although some syrups or rocks can add wonderful flavors, quality varies by producers.

Candi sugar is made of inverted sugar, which uses the process of heating sucrose with a small amount of acid and converting it into fructose and dextrose. Many brewers also find little advantage to using the clear candi compared to plain table sugar.

USING SUGAR

There are three common points to add your sugar, depending on your goal.

- For a slight caramel flavor, add at the start of the boil for a Maillard reaction.
- For a clean flavor, add at the end of the boil (five to ten minutes remaining) to dissolve and sanitize the sugar.
- To avoid boilovers and scorched brew kettles, dilute the sugar in hot water and add it to the primary fermenter a couple days after pitching the yeast. However, both of these issues can also be avoided by adding the sugar slowly.

CHOOSING BELGIAN YEAST

For all of the inventive ingredients Belgian brewers come up with, the yeast is still king. This is the workhorse and heart within every great Belgian ale. Your job as a brewer is to make that yeast happy and productive. Belgian yeast, however, can be a fickle creature.

Assuming your wort is properly aerated and clean (see chapter 11 for help with that), the yeast production relies on two factors: fermentation temperature, and to a lesser degree fermenter shape.

FERMENTATION TEMPERATURE

Following your yeast lab's temperature guide is a safe start, but professionals often change the temperature over the course of the primary fermentation. By heating or cooling your fermenter, you control the ester and phenol production without cutting short the attenuation.

Trappists and other large breweries like to start fermentation in the neighborhood of 64°F to 68°F (18°C to 20°C) and raise it 10°F to 20°F (6°C to 11°C) over four to eight days. Remember that colder brewing temperatures create cleaner beers and warmer brewing temperatures bring out the fruit and spice.

Guests at the legendary Westvleteren Brewery admire their open fermenters.

FERMENTER SHAPE

Consider the homebrew context: Buying the Westmalle or Chimay yeasts direct from a yeast lab does not guarantee any part of your beer's outcome. Even if you mimic a brewery's temperature process, you can't expect a yeast to act the same in your small plastic bucket or stainless cylindroconical when it's bred to thrive in an open, shallow fermenter with more surface area and less pressure.

A Westmalle brewer adds clear sugar syrup to the kettle.

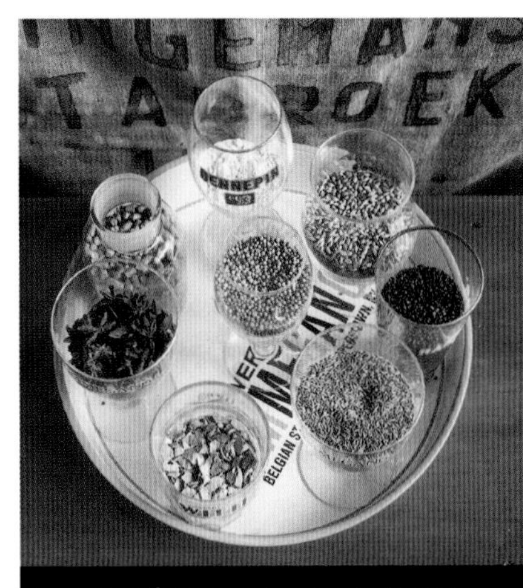

Brewers at Ommegang are no strangers to brewing spices. Clockwise from the top are ginger, barley malt, grains of paradise, cumin, dried orange peel, star anise, hop pellets, and at center, coriander.

FOR THE MOST CONSISTENT RESULTS TRY TWO OPTIONS:

Option 1: Copy the brewery's geometry and temperatures. If your yeast strain hails from a brewery with wide open fermenters, perform your primary fermentation in a loosely covered stainless steel pot. If you can precisely control your fermentation temperature, find the temperature profile for a yeast's brewery to follow.

Option 2: Make the yeast your own. Instead of bending to a yeast strain, experiment with different fermenting temperatures in your existing fermenters. It may not be ideal at first, but a happy medium exists between what a strain is used to and what you can offer.

ADDING SPICE

Purity be damned, we're on the hunt for flavor. Belgians have long used subtle spicing as a way to accent and complement their beers. Unlike a fruit beer or flavored beer, the spices in Belgian beers do not define the flavor—they refine it.

One tenet for spicing beers is that you can always add more spice, but never take it away. So if you are unsure, increase spice gradually and deliberately. Add your spice at the end of the boil to flash sanitize it without boiling off aromatics. (For more on fruit and flavor additives, see chapter 10.)

TIPS FOR ADDING SPICE:

Whole spices should be crushed with a coarse grind. This will allow your beer to clear and filter more quickly. If using a powdered spice after the boil, dilute in a small amount of water to ensure it will mix with your beer.

Coriander: Make sure to crush the seeds before they are added. It can add a mild, spicy fruit and citrus character.

Cardamom: Similar to coriander, but also close to nutmeg. Make sure to remove the seeds from their pods and crush them before they are added.

Orange peel: Sweet orange peel adds an orange liqueur character. Bitter orange peel adds more of an herbal citrus.

Cumin: A peppery spice with a nutty character.

Star anise: Similar to black licorice; can have a cola-like character.

Muscovado (left) is unrefined sugar and has a stronger molasses flavor than standard brown sugar (right).

KNOW YOUR SUGARS

Any sugar can potentially be fermented, though some are easier for yeast to process than others. Find out how different varieties affect your beer.

Candi sugar rocks and syrups: This traditional brewing sugar is derived from sugar beets, but the character comes from the process of heating the sugar. The darker sugar has more of a caramel and rum character, while lighter (though not clear) sugar is fruitier.

Dextrose: Also known as glucose, this is a simple monosaccharide that ferments out clean and crisp.

Invert sugar: A mix of fructose and glucose broken down from sucrose, and the basis for candi sugar. It's largely used by bakers, who consider it sweeter thanks to the fructose.

Sucrose (table sugar): A disaccharide that yeast must break into fructose and glucose before fermenting. While it certainly works, it requires more energy of the yeast and can potentially lead to a slower and less efficient fermentation.

Natural brown sugar: Depending on origin, this comes in a number of forms such as turbinado, demerara, and muscovado. Unlike typical brown sugar that is simply molasses added to white sugar, these unrefined or partially unrefined sugars bring rich caramel and molasses flavors with them.

INTERVIEW WITH:
TOMME ARTHUR: BREWMASTER, THE LOST ABBEY, SAN MARCOS, CALIFORNIA, U.S.

BORN OUT OF THE CRAFT BREWING PIONEER BREWPUB PIZZA PORT, TOMME'S LOST ABBEY IS A BELGIAN OUTPOST IN A CALIFORNIA BEER SCENE DOMINATED BY HOPS. THOUGH AMERICAN IPAS AND BELGIAN DUBBELS MAY SEEM WORLDS APART, WITH TOMME YOU SEE HOW THEIR CREATIVE AND UNBOUND SPIRITS CONTINUE TO PUSH THE LIMITS OF GREAT BEER.

A glass of Tomme's quadruple-style Judgement Day, which uses raisins and dextrose in addition to barley

WHERE DID YOUR INTEREST IN BELGIAN STYLES COME FROM?

I spent a good portion of my early 20s drinking craft beer, but ended up finding Belgian beers later in my drinking evolution. I discovered there was this whole world out there of Belgian beers that were completely different on a flavor level. It was the kind of beer brewing I wanted to be a part of.

SO TALK ABOUT WHAT SPARKED YOUR INTEREST.

The thing about Belgian beers is that so much emphasis was on evolution. All of a sudden, beer wasn't just something that came off a shelf and tasted the same every time. Sometimes you'd get a fresh bottle, or an aged and more vintage bottle, and it's like a favorite book or poem you revisit and find new perspectives.

DO YOU FIND YOURSELF GRAVITATING TOWARD PARTICULAR CATEGORIES IN THE BELGIAN WORLD?

Farmhouse beers. I like the discovery of new things—and they bring that, while also being food-friendly and just great session beers. They have a lot of flavor and there's no true style to them because they're not market-driven beers.

There's a lot of beer with big flavor, even down to 4.5 percent alcohol. That goes back to the historical needs for a provision beer to not get you sick. The beer served a purpose that wasn't just hedonistic pleasure, and in the field you certainly don't want drunk farmers running around.

THE BELGIANS CERTAINLY DO LIKE FOOD-FRIENDLY BEER.

I think the Belgian people, more than most, really focus on the gastronomy. They prize the beer and the food together, and beer can be its own luxury and enjoyment. In the Czech Republic and Germany, it's about the beer hall, and in England it's about the pub.

MOREAU

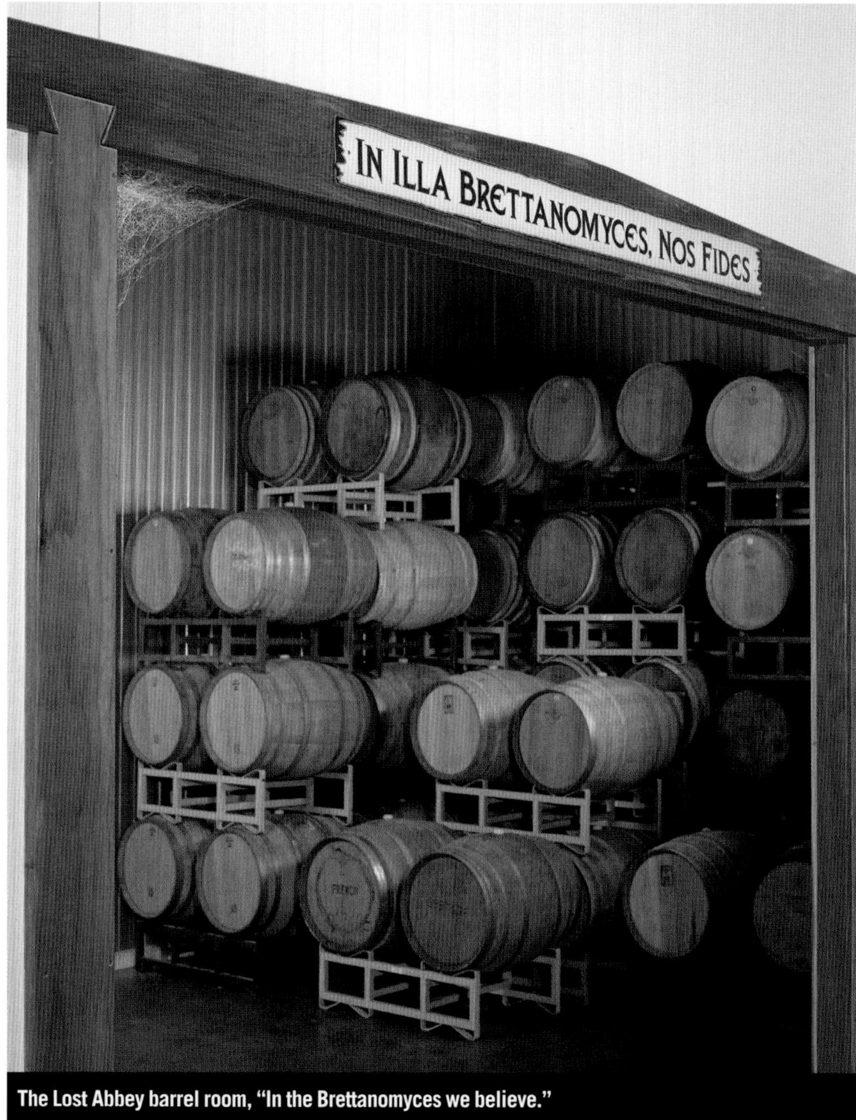

The Lost Abbey barrel room, "In the Brettanomyces we believe."

The process is: A certain amount of yeast with that amount of sugar will give you this kind of funk.

MOVING ON TO BREWING, HOW WOULD YOU STEER DECISIONS WITH SUGAR?

We use 100 percent dextrose, which is just a corn sugar. It serves its purpose in helping us lighten the body and get back to focusing on balance. The biggest choice is to really look at what you want the sugar to do. I don't think most Belgian brewers are looking for the candi syrup to add a flavor so much as he's looking to take out some of the malt sweetness.

DO YOU USE ANY UNUSUAL YEAST STRAINS?

We run five or six different yeasts for all the different brands, and then for a couple of our seasonal beers we add *Brettanomyces* to postfermentation to develop a more predictable profile. The process is: A certain amount of yeast with that amount of sugar will give you this kind of funk. That's the leading theory. We try to ferment down into a standard range, condition off the yeast, then come back and let the secondary conditioning tank be the *Brett*. Then we have a whole slew of things that take place in the barrel room—kind of a Wild, Wild West.

ONE OF THE FAMOUS EXAMPLES WOULD BE ORVAL BOTTLE CONDITIONING WITH *BRETT*.

Two of our seasonal beers, the 10 Commandments, our dark farmhouse beer, gets *Brett* at bottling. Also our Gift of the Magi, which is our holiday release, gets the same sort of treatment. It's a hoppy Bière de Garde style with *Brett*. We've also done some small batches where we add *Brett* at bottling, but we haven't done any 100 percent *Brett*-based fermentations here. Orval and a lot of other brewers have *Brett* as a secondary characteristic, but using it as a primary fermenter is something people only thought possible in the last ten years.

WHAT GOES ON IN YOUR BARREL ROOM?

Typically, 95 percent of the spirit barrels come out sufficiently for blending, while the others pick up an infection, or some weird wood character or leak. With the sour-based beers and microbial refermentation, we're filling a certain amount and then crossing our fingers that 50 percent, if not more, will be usable. Then there are the orphans, the barrels that for whatever reason may not have worked for that batch of beer. We will hold them back for the next release a year later. After eighteen months or two years, we'll taste them one last time and if there's no hope for that one, we'll dump it.

LET'S MOVE ON TO SPICES.

A lot of homebrewers use spices in beers to try to make something more Belgian, even though a lot of the spice character comes from the yeast. On some, you're putting a flavor in that shouldn't be there at that intensity. If you're trying to make a spiced tenderloin at home, you don't want too much rosemary. In brewing you have to look at the yeast first; Belgian yeasts are very spicy in nature, and they have a lot of phenols and other constituents. Too much yeast-driven spice combined with too much spice is going to put you off in left field.

WHAT YEAST STRAINS DO YOU HAVE IN MIND?

The Westmalle yeast is a very spicy yeast. The Hoegaarden witbier yeast is quite spicy. The Chimay yeast, which is called a Trappist yeast, is a lot fruiter and doesn't produce the same amount of phenols as Westmalle. Understanding what the yeast does at different temperatures and pitching rates, and getting to know a yeast really well, singularly using it, will help a brewer understand how much spice will fit that missing piece of the puzzle.

CARBONATING TIP:
After adding bottling sugar (about 1 ounce per gallon [7.5 g per liter]) and capping or kegging your beer, let it sit at room temperature for two weeks before cooling down to drink.

SPEAKING OF FAMOUS YEASTS, DON'T YOU USE THE SAISON DUPONT STRAIN?

Yes, in our Red Barn, Carnivale, and Ten Commandments. You can pick up the Red Barn and tell we're using the Dupont strain. We're getting an enormous amount of yeast character from the fermentation as well as the addition of the spices, but they're very compartmentalized. When they come together after several months, it becomes a much brighter beer. When it's first out, six weeks off of the tanks, it's kind of a mess.

DO YOU BOTTLE CONDITION YOUR BELGIANS?

A secondary refermentation in the bottle is paramount; there's a whole different level of texture and reward. There's no point to go to the length to make all these great flavors in a beer that's not going to have that maturation and evolution.

YOU HAD SOME TROUBLE AT FIRST WITH YOUR BOTTLE CONDITIONING AT LOST ABBEY.

Running a business is very difficult and you have to make a lot of decisions on the fly. We went through a big growth phase and growing pains, where we were hit with needing to get more beer out of the door when we didn't have our warm room. We didn't know we needed one.

We've now allocated the space. So all the beer comes of the packaging line at 55°F (13°C) with a dosage of yeast and sugar. It goes into the warm room at 75°F (24°C) for a week's time. We always package with fresh yeast, rehydrated the day of the bottling. We don't use the primary bottling yeast two or three weeks later, because yeast needs to be healthy and active in order to create a great refermentation.

SO WHAT'S THE YEAST STRAIN THAT YOU ADD?

We picked a basic champagne yeast.

DO YOU BOTTLE FLAT?

There's an atmospheric level of CO_2 from the primary fermentation that we estimate to be a volume and a half of CO_2. We target most of our beers to be 2.8 volumes of CO_2 for bottling, so the packaging sugar is adjusted accordingly.

ARE THERE ANY EQUIPMENT CONSIDERATIONS, SUCH AS FERMENTER TANK SHAPE, THAT AFFECT THE PROCESS?

When you visit breweries around the world, you begin to understand there are a hundred different ways to skin a cat. There's a lot of different tank geometries. In Belgium, there's a lot of open fermentation in square vessels, and atmospherically, yeast behaves differently.

Ale yeast wants to ferment toward the surface. If you spread that out over a larger surface area, you get a much larger flavor impact than in a cylindroconical tank. You get a lot less back pressure in an open environment, and so people who wish to recreate specific beers would be wise to look at the brewery.

ANYTHING MORE YOU WANT TO SHARE?

Trying to brew these at home or commercially without understanding what you're trying to accomplish is very problematic, and there's a lot of flabby Belgian beer out there that isn't well-defined. They're not well put together because they didn't have a clear start or finish point.

Head Brewer Rob Todd mashes in his legendary Allagash White at their Portland, Maine, brewery.

WHEAT, LIKE OUR BELOVED BARLEY, TRACES ITS ROOTS BACK AT LEAST 10,000 YEARS TO EARLY CIVILIZATION AS ONE OF THE FIRST DOMESTICATED GRAINS. WHEAT BEER AS WE KNOW IT LIKELY ORIGINATED WITH GERMANIC TRIBES IN THE MIDDLE AGES, THOUGH IT WAS USED IN BREWING FOR THOUSANDS OF YEARS BEFORE THAT.

AS MUCH AS WE LOVE WHEAT IN OUR BEERS, ITS LACK OF A HUSK TECHNICALLY MAKES IT AN INFERIOR BREWING GRAIN. GRAIN BILLS FOR WHEAT BEER MUST INCLUDE A PORTION OF BARLEY. WHILE 40 TO 60 PERCENT WHEAT IS TYPICAL OF MOST WHEAT BEERS, A PATIENT BREWER COULD GO AS HIGH AS 80 PERCENT.

CHAPTER 7: WHEAT BEER

Wheat malt used for Summit Brewing's Hefe Weizen. The German-style ale's malt bill is 55 percent wheat.

INTRODUCTION TO WHEAT BEER

Wheat beer differentiates from other ales and lagers in that a portion of the normally all-barley grain bill is replaced by a significant amount of malted or unmalted wheat. German brewing law requires that at least half of the malt in a wheat beer recipe be wheat, and certain styles may use different yeast strains or traditionally call for European hops. But any beer with enough wheat to have an effect can be considered a wheat beer.

In this chapter, you'll learn about:

- Types of wheat
- Wheat beer yeast strains
- Mashing and lautering wheat
- Hops for wheat beers
- Brewing Belgian witbier

KNOW YOUR WHEAT

A good homebrew supply store will offer a number of wheat options. There are no bad varieties; the choices depend on the goal of your beer. If you want a hoppy American wheat ale, use red or white wheat. If you're after a true German hefeweizen, go with pale wheat. And if you're brewing a Belgian witbier, use a mix of pale and unmalted wheat. Maltsters use the Lovibond color scale used to measure malt color. Brewers use the roughly equivalent but more accurate SRM scale for beer color.

Variety	Color (Lovibond)	Description	Use
White Wheat	2.5 to 3	A larger, softer American wheat grain. Comparable to red wheat, but with a smoother character.	Base malt for American-style wheat beers.
Red Wheat	2 to 2.5	Has smaller, harder kernels than white wheat. The wheat flavor is also more distinct.	Base malt for American-style wheat beers.
Pale Wheat	1.7 to 2.4	The classic German base wheat malt.	German-style wheat beers.
Cara-Wheat	38 to 49	Like a medium caramel barley, but this trademarked wheat emphasizes sweet character.	Adds body and flavor to any wheat beer.
Chocolate Wheat	300 to 450	Similar to a chocolate barley malt, but with a touch of wheat in the nutty, roasted character.	Specialty grain for dunkelweizens and dark wheat beers.
Unmalted Wheat	1	The unprocessed version of raw wheat. Lends a crisp taste found in Belgian witbier. Unmalted grains have no enzymes.	Belgian witbiers and lambic; adds haze to appearance.
Torrified Wheat	1.5	The popcorn equivalent of raw wheat. Lighter in color and flavor, with better clarity than other wheat grains.	Belgian witbiers.
Flaked Wheat	2	Like instant oats, this wheat is cooked but unmalted for a crisp taste similar to other raw wheats.	Belgian witbiers and lambics; adds haze to appearance.

KNOW YOUR WHEAT BEER YEASTS

Wheat beers are typically ales. And while a handful of breweries use lager yeast, stick to these classic schools of wheat beer yeast before venturing out into less-charted territory

AMERICAN HEFEWEIZEN

First popularized by Widmer Hefeweizen, the American wheat ale yeast is, like a normal American ale yeast, very clean fermenting. It can produce some banana and clove notes, but it largely lets the ingredients speak for themselves. This is a good candidate if you are brewing a fruit infused or hoppy wheat beer.

BELGIAN WIT

Being Belgian, there's no saying what exact flavors Belgian wit yeasts should produce. However, traditional strains tend toward vanilla and spicy phenols without much fruit ester.This is a good choice for Belgian witbiers, but it can be used for any Belgian ale style.

GERMAN

The familiar clove and banana notes of a German hefeweizen are created by the yeast. The standard for the style is known as Weihenstephan 68 (named after the Weihenstephan yeast bank, not the hefeweizen). It is a low-flocculating yeast, meaning it creates a large head of foam while fermenting and then remains in suspension for that cloudy appearance. This is the yeast used in German wheat ales such as hefeweizen, dunkelweizen (dark wheat beer), kristalweizen (clear wheat beer), and weizenbock (strong wheat beer).

Malted wheat is well-modified, only requiring a single-step mash for complete conversion.

A collaboration between Brooklyn Brewery and Schneider, Hopfen Weisse is dry-hopped with Saphir hops.

MASHING AND LAUTERING WHEAT

The first wheat beers may have been entirely wheat, but all modern versions use roughly a 50/50 mix with malted barley. As a grain, wheat is high in glucans and has no husk, making it very sticky. Barley prevents the grain bed from becoming a lump of hot starch and sugar that will clog your lauter tun. The barley husks fluff up the grains to lower the compaction and density.

There are three options for accommodating wheat grains in your mash:

Option 1: You can simply wait around with a slower sparge. Wheat will slow the flow of wort out of a lauter tun, but with patience it will all come.

Option 2: You can add half a pound (225 g) of rice hulls (for a 5-gallon, or 19 L, batch), which effectively adds husks without any flavor.

Option 3: You can use six-row barley instead of two-row. Six-row has more husk to offset the wheat.

With spicier wheat beer styles, such as the hefeweizen, some brewers will use a ferulic acid step in their mash. By holding the mash at 113°F (45°C) for at least ten minutes, the grains will produce a noticeable amount of ferulic acid, which yeast converts to phenol flavors and aroma. German wheat beers often traditionally use a decoction mash (see chapter 1). It's not necessary, but a single decoction mash can help bring out wheat character.

HOPPING WHEAT BEER

Classic European wheat beers only use a touch of hops to reach 10 to 20 IBUs. When brewing at home, that's just an ounce (28 g) of low–alpha acid hops for 5 gallons (19 L). Traditionally, brewers used hops grown close to home, with noble hops from the Hallertau region in German beers and similarly low–alpha acid hops in Belgian witbier.

Only recently have Germans begun experimenting with adding hop flavor and aroma to weiss beer. Both Mahr's Bräu and Weissbierbrauerei Schneider produce hop-forward wheat beers, Mahr's Saphir Weiss and Schneider-Brooklyner Hopfen-Weisse, both with Saphir hops. The variety was developed as a more disease-resistant Noble-type hop, but also brings an earthy tangerine citrus character that blends exceptionally well with the clove and banana of a weissbier.

Some U.S. brewers have embraced hopped-up wheat beers. Munster, Indiana's Three Floyds Gumballhead uses Amarillo hops for a beer that can rival any pale ale or hoppy session beer. And Lagunitas produces A Little Sumpin' Sumpin' Ale, a 7.3 percent wheat ale packed with Cascade, Chinook, Columbus, and Centennial hops for an almost sweet and fruity beer.

There are no hops that are bad for wheat beers, so long as the beer is well-designed. You can even take your favorite IPA and replace half the barley with wheat to make a delicious India wheat ale. The main difference will be that mildly sweet wheat flavor from the grain.

BREWING WITBIER

German weissbier and Belgian witbier both translate to "white beer," but the styles are worlds apart in the eyes of a brewer. Yes, both recipes are largely founded on a mix of malted barley and wheat, but the Belgians diverge from the strict brewing laws Germans adhere to.

ADJUNCTS

Belgians often use unmalted wheat for a portion of the mash to add a more crisp wheat character. It can wholly replace malted wheat, but beware that it has no enzymatic power to convert starches to sugar.

Wheat flour can be added for a softer flavor and decreased clarity (which is appropriate in this style).

Oats are also commonly used for a silky, spiced malt character. Wheat flour and oats shouldn't be used as more than 10 percent of the grain bill.

SPICES

Coriander, orange peel, and sometimes anise are all commonly added spices for a wit. You can read more about them in chapter 6.

Your goal should not be to make a beer with a distinct coriander or anise flavor. That would overpower subtler flavors and result in a less complex beer. Instead, spices should be used in small enough amounts to contribute to the character without defining it.

To be safe, brew two batches and only add spice to one. You can blend the clean batch with the spiced if the spices are too strong.

YEAST

A good Belgian wit yeast is versatile enough to produce entire ranges of Belgian ales, but there's also wide variation in character between strains. Like other Belgian strains, warmer brewing temperatures will produce more fruity esters, while fermenting at the lower end of a strain's recommended temperature range will encourage spice flavors and phenol production.

Hans-Peter has had a decades-long fascination with wheat beer.

INTERVIEW WITH:
HANS-PETER DREXLER: HEAD BREWER, WEISSBIERBRAUEREI G. SCHNEIDER & SOHN, KELHEIM, GERMANY

INDUSTRY LEVIATHANS STICK TO THEIR YELLOW BEERS, BUT THAT SORT OF SPECIALIZATION IS RARE IN THE CRAFT AND SPECIALTY BEER WORLD. HOWEVER, THE WHEAT BEER–PRODUCING SCHNEIDER BREWERY IN BAVARIA HAS NEVER KNOWN ANY OTHER WAY, AND TO THIS DAY IT MAKES SOME OF THE FINEST WHEAT-BASED BEVERAGES ON THE PLANET UNDER THE GUIDANCE OF HANS-PETER.

Brewing is like biological science in combination with engineering. It's very practical. I like that.

HOW LONG HAVE YOU BEEN BREWING WHEAT BEER AT SCHNEIDER?

I started in 1982. That's a long time.

WHAT BROUGHT YOU TO SCHNEIDER?

Going back to the late 1970s, my studies in college were with weizenbier at a research brewery at the university in Weihenstephan. I worked to brew hefeweizen, which at the time was a growing market in Germany. I liked that the style was very different. The lagers were a little bit—how do you say—not so exciting. After that, I went to Greece to brew for a joint venture for one year then went back to Germany. I thought I'd like to brew Bavarian hefeweizens and had an opportunity to start with Schneider.

WHAT INSPIRED YOU TO GO TO BREWING SCHOOL IN THE FIRST PLACE?

I was interested with biological systems as well as practical systems. Brewing is like biological science in combination with engineering. It's very practical. I like that.

I'VE BEEN A FAN OF AVENTINUS FOR MANY, MANY YEARS. ARE THERE ANY NONWHEAT BEERS AT SCHNEIDER?

It's all wheat beer. The portfolio has nine different styles, and in the U.S. market there are five: Original, Aventinus, Eisbock, Edelweiss, and Hopfen-Weisse. In Germany, we have an alcohol-free hefe, a light one, a plain Bavarian hefe, and kristalweiss.

LET'S TALK ABOUT TECHNIQUES OF BREWING WHEAT BEERS. HOW DO YOU ENSURE GOOD LAUTERING?

We use 60 percent wheat malt and 40 percent barley. And we look at raw material to the mash viscosity. And the lauter tun is a little wider than in a normal brewery to reduce the height of the grains. That helps the wort drain faster.

A brewer skims yeast off the top of a fermenter.

A wheat field in Olpe, Germany

IS THERE ANY OTHER SPECIFIC EQUIPMENT TO ASSIST WITH A GOOD LAUTER?

We have a second grain mill: a special mill for wheat malt and one for barley to grind them differently.

WHICH ONE HAS A FINER, SMALLER GRIST?

It's easier to make barley malt finer, because the wheat malt has no husk.

THE TYPICAL PERCENTAGE OF WHEAT MALT IS 60 PERCENT—WHAT'S THE HIGHEST PERCENTAGE YOU'D CONSIDER USING?

We don't do more than 60 percent, but I know in ancient times Bavarian wheats were brewed with 100 percent wheat malt. Now nobody uses 100 percent; it would be terrible to work with.

WHY WOULD THEY USE 100 PERCENT WHEAT?

I don't know—I think they had enough time for lauters.

WHAT HOP VARIETIES DO YOU FEEL WORK BEST WITH WHEAT BEERS?

Interesting. When I started my career, I thought the hops were not important. The wheat beer brewers in Bavaria think you only need a little hops.

After a while, I did some experiments. Now we have the Hopfen-Weisse, together with Garrett Oliver from Brooklyn Brewery. It was a great experience to see what happens if you use a lot of hops.

DO ANY HOP VARIETIES STAND OUT TO YOU?

Saphir hops for the Bavarian pale wheat beer. It brings a very interesting, refreshing citrus note in that fits in a traditional weissbier. And for the Schneider Original and Aventinus, I use Hallertau Tradition and Magnum and they work, but they're not spectacular like Saphir.

MANY CRAFT BREWERS MAKE AMERICAN-STYLE HEFEWEIZENS THAT USE A MORE NEUTRAL YEAST. WHAT'S YOUR OPINION OF THEM?

The American and Bavarian hefe is just different. Even in Bavaria, we have a few different styles. There are the more phenolic styles, more spicy. Then there are more estery styles, which are more fruity like banana. You know, there are also more neutral styles in Bavaria.

IT MIGHT BE HARD TO FATHOM SO MUCH VARIATION IN BAVARIAN WHEAT BEERS.

About 80 percent of Bavarian wheat beer brewers use the same yeast strain, Weihenstephan 68, and I hear from U.S. brewers that many of them use it as well, but it doesn't always act the same way for every brewer. We use a special very old Schneider strain that has always been with the brewery. I don't know where it comes from. It lives in the brewery.

Customers were used to having beer with infection. Thankfully, the market has changed.

YOU USE OPEN FERMENTATION. WHAT STEPS DO YOU USE TO PREVENT INFECTION OR WILD STRAINS?

In the 1990s, we changed the yeast management in the brewery. Before that point, we always had a circulation of yeast harvested from the top of the kettle and taken to the next room. Then we installed a propagation system so that we always have a new strain for every brew. That helps guard against infection.

BUT WHAT ABOUT BEFORE THEN? DID INFECTIONS HAVE TIME TO CHANGE THE CHARACTER?

Yeah, and customers were used to having beer with infection. Thankfully, the market has changed.

DO YOU HAVE RECOMMENDATIONS FOR HEFEWEIZEN YEAST PITCHING RATE AND FERMENTATION TEMPERATURE?

[For homebrewing], I think it's easy to just take a 1-liter propagating yeast start to 100 liters of wort and make sure everything works well. It's enough to start fermentation very quickly and keep the bacteria away. The yeast is very strong at temperatures like 18°C or 20°C (64°F or 68°F).

WHAT DO YOU THINK IS THE FUTURE FOR WHEAT BEERS?

The German focus is different. When I look to brewers from the U.S., I see all these international markets interested in traditional beers. So I see a trend to brew more unpasteurized craft beers.

HOW IS THAT DIFFERENT FROM WHAT'S BEEN HAPPENING IN GERMANY?

In Germany, we have some big players like Franziskaner, Paulaner, and Erdinger. They are, to me, more on the investor side of brewing. Their beers are not very characteristic—they brew beer for everybody. We try to keep the characteristics of a traditional Bavarian hefeweizen and improve on that style. We're a little bit old-fashioned with new, modern techniques.

IS THERE ANYTHING YOU'RE INTERESTED IN BREWING IN THE FUTURE?

We have some ideas; one is to play with the influence of a traditional Belgian. They have very old, very long beer traditions. It could be interesting to use Belgian yeast or Belgian-inspired hops.

YOU'RE ALMOST SAYING SOMETHING VERY SHOCKING. WOULD YOU CONSIDER USING INGREDIENTS LIKE CORIANDER OR ORANGE PEEL?

They're not allowed to be used because of Reinheitsgebot. We're not allowed to use spice in Germany. Only one style, Leipziger Gose, does. They are allowed to use coriander.

WELL NOT TRADITIONALLY, BUT EUROPEAN UNION LAWS MADE IT NO LONGER A LAW.

It's part of the law in Germany; the name is Biergesetz, the beer law. And part of that law is still Reinheitsgebot, under which you're only allowed to use barley, wheat, spelt, rye, hops, water, and yeast for the German market. If you brew for the German market, you have to brew according to Reinheitsgebot.

For example, I make a dry-hop addition in a collaboration beer with Garrett Oliver. Some people here in Germany say it's not according to Reinheitsgebot, but I say it's not forbidden. It's within reason, but it's very restricted in Germany.

WHAT ARE YOUR FAVORITE FOOD PAIRINGS FOR A WHEAT BEER?

It depends on the style. Hopfenweizen is hard to match with Bavarian food, so go with spicy spare ribs, Thai food, things with a lot of spices and fruits. But for typical Bavarian weissbier, like our Original, I'd prefer Bavarian food like schweinebraten or a Bavarian white sausage. Seafood, or pizza and pasta work very, very nicely. And together with Aventinus, blue cheese of course, then dark meat such as beef or venison.

YOU'RE MAKING ME HUNGRY.

Me as well. Talking about beer and food makes me thirsty and hungry.

BREWING TERM: YEAST PROPAGATION

Yeast can reproduce itself. Through propagation, brewers will take a small amount of yeast, feed it, let it divide, and eventually have an ideal amount of yeast to ferment a beer. Brewers often reuse yeast for six batches before propagating a fresh culture.

Cains Brewery began brewing in Liverpool, England, in 1850.

RETURN TO THE ROOTS OF U.S. CRAFT BREWING AND YOU'LL FIND THE ENGLISH ALE. PIONEERS INCLUDING SIERRA NEVADA AND BOULDER BEER QUICKLY DIVERGED AND MADE DISTINCTLY AMERICAN BREWS, BUT THE BRITISH ISLES LAUNCHED BREWS LIKE THE PALE ALE, IPA, BROWN ALE, PORTER, AND STOUT.

Nearly all brewing grains are mechanically malted, but Warminster Maltings's exceptional Maris Otter Pale Ale malt has been floor-malted since 1879.

CHAPTER 8: ENGLISH ALES

INTRODUCTION TO ENGLISH ALE

Brewers producing classic British beer styles use warm, top-fermenting ale yeast that provides subtle flavor to the beers. In general, most English beers are lower in alcohol than American counterparts. And while many styles are hoppy, none match the bitterness of an American IPA. British ales are a lesson in subtlety, and the best examples have a delicious balance of the malts, hops, and yeast notes.

In this chapter, you'll learn about:

- **English malt and hops**
- **English brewing additives**
- **English yeast strains**
- **Diacetyl**

BRITISH BASE MALTS

English maltsters arguably make the finest pale malts in the world. Yes, their crystal and roasted varieties are top-notch, but the base malts are unmatched in flavor. Some malt houses go so far as to continue the age-old tradition of floor-malting barley by hand instead of automation. Even if this were just a marketing gimmick, such malts bring an undeniably superior flavor compared to your standard two-row malt. On a technical note, they are also all highly modified (ready to convert starch to sugar), so a simple single-infusion mash will suffice.

Malt	Color (Lovibond)	Description
Pale Ale Malt	2 to 4	The British equivalent of American two-row malt.
Maris Otter	3 to 4.5	More robust than pale ale malt with nutty and biscuit flavors.
Golden Promise	2.5 to 3	The Scottish counterpart to Maris Otter; has a sweeter character.
Mild Ale Malt	2.7 to 5.3	Another step sweeter than other base malts with more dextrins (unfermentable sugar).

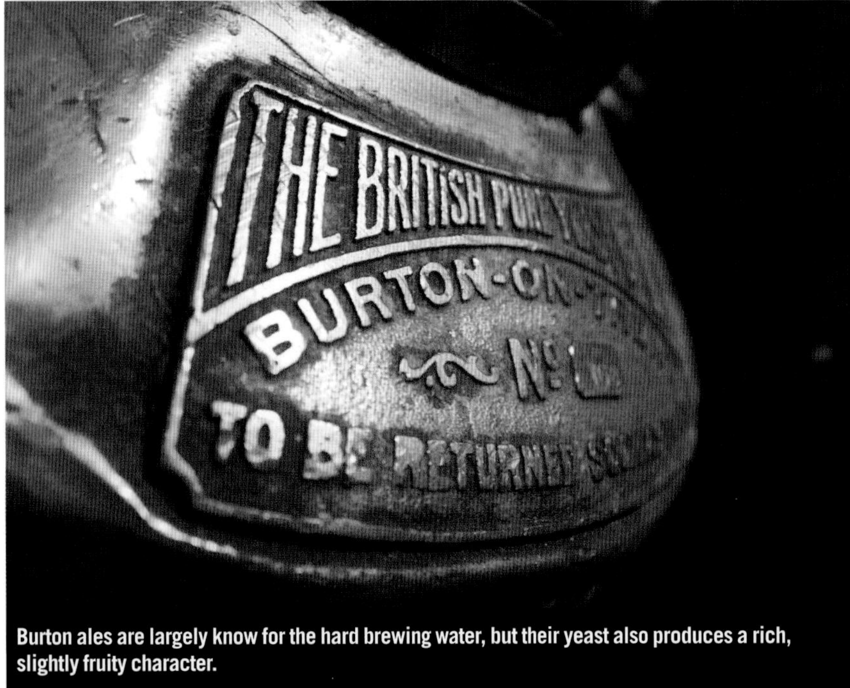

Burton ales are largely know for the hard brewing water, but their yeast also produces a rich, slightly fruity character.

TRADITIONAL ENGLISH ADDITIVES

The Brits aren't usually ones for fruit or spices, but they also don't have the rigid laws of Germany that restricts brewing additives.

ISINGLASS

Derived from the swim bladders of sturgeon (yes, the fish), isinglass is a traditional fining agent that, when mixed with beer or wine, acts as a filter and improves clarity. English brewers would add isinglass to their cask as a final filter. The isinglass finings attract yeast and other particles floating in your beer, and then pull them to the bottom of your tank. Use 1.5 to 2 ounces (43 to 57 g) for a 5-gallon (19 L) batch. Chill the beer as cold as possible, then transfer onto the finings in a secondary fermenter.

FLAKED MAIZE

This form of processed corn is mostly used to lighten pilsner-style lagers, but British brewers used it a century ago to dilute the nitrogen from their barley. This improved clarity while working with the lower-quality barley of the time. Like any sugar adjunct, it can also lighten the body and mouthfeel of a beer. You can use flaked maize for up to 10 percent of your malt bill.

GRUIT

Hops didn't become a mainstay of beer until the Middle Ages, and the British Isles were actually one of the last areas to adopt the pungent flower. Up until about the seventeenth century, brewers used a bitter mix of spices called gruit that consisted of herbs, some of which are questionably safe at best, including yarrow, bog myrtle, wild rosemary, and wormwood. A Scottish variation called Froach, which used heather, remained popular until the eighteenth century. For a safe and interesting unhopped ale, try using 2 to 4 ounces (57 to 113 g) of dried heather tips in a 5-gallon (19 L) batch.

HOPS

Just as American hops can be roughly lumped together for their citrus character, most English hops have a distinctive spicy aroma with a milder fruity, citrus component. These hops have a softer bitterness with lower cohumulone levels (see chapter 2 on bittering hops). Golding, Fuggle, and Challenger are all popular varieties for flavor and aroma. Challenger is a touch stronger in character, also having more alpha acids, but these are the essential hops necessary to make a traditional English ale.

While British ales aren't known for big hop character like American pale ale, British brewers certainly love their hops—just in a more restrained manner. The hoppier styles, which include the bitters (ordinary, special, and extra special), all benefit from dry-hopping. Just be aware that British yeast strains are known to cover or absorb some hop character and bitterness.

YEAST

English beer is brewed with ale yeast. Though most American styles descended from English originals, the American yeast is much cleaner fermenting in terms of flavor, while British yeast can be assertive with fruity, sometimes candylike, notes. The strains don't tend to dominate a beer like a hearty or wild Belgian strain would, but it creates complementary flavors like a mild weizen yeast might.

British yeast strains are no different from any other in that their output is a product of the environment you give it. Starving a yeast slightly of oxygen or fermenting it in the high end of its temperature range will increase the fruity ester output, while a colder fermentation yields a cleaner beer.

DIACETYL

Diacetyl adds a slick mouthfeel and flavors that can range from butterscotch to movie theater popcorn butter, or even rancid meat. The "Big D" can take over any beer, but English strains are often predisposed to its production. It's stylistically appropriate in English bitters and brown ales, but can appear in any beer.

Infections can produce diacetyl, so in a clean brewing environment, the chemical is still a natural product of fermentation. Yeast, thankfully, will gobble up diacetyl if given enough time and warmth. That means a cold-fermented beer might need a "diacetyl rest" of sitting at 60°F (16°C) for two days. In the case of an ale, give the new beer two extra days before you'd normally transfer to a conditioning tank or secondary.

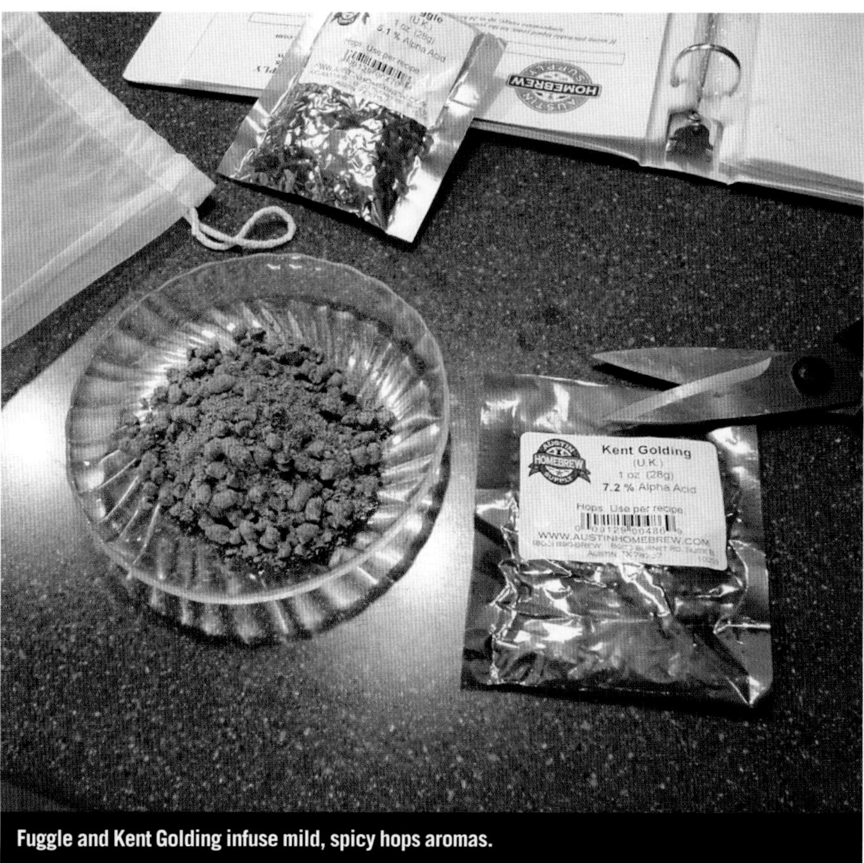

Fuggle and Kent Golding infuse mild, spicy hops aromas.

British strains range from dry with only a light fruit character from northern brewers, to sweet and malty around London. This allows for a great deal of freedom when brewing along their stylistic lines.

TEST FOR DIACETYL

Take a small sample of beer and heat to 140°F (60°C) for an hour. If no popcorn butter or butterscotch flavor comes out, your beer is ready to move on.

Alan Pugsley and his Shipyard Brewing in Portland, Maine, brought Ringwood English ales to the United States.

RINGWOOD BREWING

In the late 1970s, back when American homebrewing was only being legalized, a brewer named Peter Austin did his part to revive Britain's beer scene by opening the Ringwood Brewery. After a few years, he was joined by aspiring brewer Alan Pugsley, and the two made full-flavored ales that were a mix of malt and fruit ester that caught the attention of Americans seeking inspiration for their own breweries. Soon, Pugsley and Austin began exporting their brewhouse across the pond to brewers who wanted to capture the same distinctive character, leading to the opening of Magic Hat, D.L. Geary, Middle Ages, Gritty McDuff's, and along the way, Pugsley's own Shipyard Brewing.

Though the new Ringwood-style brewers are concentrated in New England, Peter's original brewery has undoubtedly had the largest single effect on British-style brewing in the U.S. The beers are distinctive and, if they follow all the traditional steps, use an open fermenter with only about four days before being racked off the yeast. The yeast is infamous for its diacetyl production, which in small amounts lends complexity to the beer; an extra two days in the fermenter keeps the buttery molecule in check.

FULLER'S
LONDON PRIDE

John Keeling joined Fuller's in 1981 and became the brewing director eighteen years later

INTERVIEW WITH: JOHN KEELING: BREWING DIRECTOR, FULLER, SMITH & TURNER, LONDON, ENGLAND

AS THE BRITISH BEER CULTURE FUMBLES WITH THE NOTION OF MODERN CRAFT BEER, THANKS TO CASK FANATICS AND FIZZY PALE LAGERS, JOHN HAS HARDLY BLINKED. INSTEAD OF ISOLATING THE LANDMARK LONDON BREWERY IN THE FACE OF IMPORTED LAGERS, HE'S DRIVEN FORWARD WITH NEW BEERS AND INGREDIENTS ON A CONSTANT DRIVE FOR A MORE FLAVORFUL PINT.

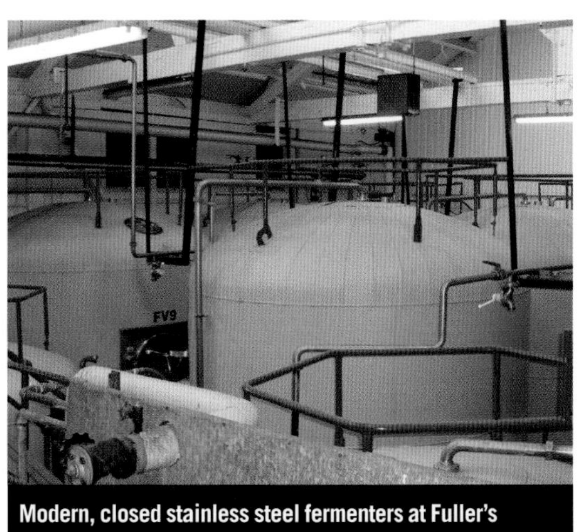

Modern, closed stainless steel fermenters at Fuller's

HOW WOULD YOU DESCRIBE THE CHARACTER OF ENGLISH ALE YEAST?

The yeast flavors that come through are esters, fruity. I think it depends on fermentation conditions and the system you use. At Fuller's, we use cylindroconical vessels, but up to about 1983, we used open squares.

WHAT DO YOU THINK ABOUT THE CHANGE BETWEEN OPEN SQUARES AND THE CYLINDROCONICALS?

In 1982, we needed new fermenting vessels, so we had a choice. We could find new squares or look at modern vessels. We actually experimented with the two types of systems side-by-side. We found from time to time, open squares produced a beer that couldn't be beaten. But most of the time, the cyclindroconical produced better beer. On average, a better flavor and ability to settle in a cask. We said, let's make the beer as consistent as we can at a high standard. We're not going to quite hit the high notes from the open square, but nor will we hit the bottom notes we get often.

DID THE PUBLIC NOTICE?

Oh yes, we got phone calls from people asking, "What have you done to my beer? It tastes better." Also Fuller's had not won brewing prizes for years, and all of a sudden we started winning again with the new beer. It was a strong affirmation we made the right decision.

BACK TO THE FULLER'S YEAST. COMPARED TO OTHER TYPICAL ENGLISH YEAST, COULD YOU DESCRIBE THE CHARACTER?

A strong fruity character comes through that's a combination of hops and the yeast. As our beers tend to get stronger, you notice this orange character like a marmalade or pithiness, and that's our yeast.

WHAT DO YOU THINK ARE THE BEST FERMENTATION TEMPS FOR ENGLISH ALES?

Every yeast does ferment a bit differently. And one of the most important things in brewing is the relationship between a brewer and his or her yeast. You get to understand it, it gets to understand you as well, and you can play tunes together. We pitch in at 17°C (63°F), and allow it to naturally warm to 20°C (68°F). When a quarter of the gravity remains, we chill it to 6°C (43°F).

TELL ME MORE ABOUT THE RELATIONSHIP WITH YEAST.

The difference between making cornflakes and beer explains it. That's like the difference between riding a bike and horse. If you're riding a bike, you want to turn right, you turn the handlebars and you'll go right. Just like making cornflakes; it's the same every day. Whereas when you're making a beer, it's like riding a horse. If you want to turn right, you turn the reins and only if the horse agrees will it go right. If it agrees with you and trusts you, it will turn with you. That's the same relationship you have with your yeast.

A LOT OF PEOPLE THINK OF BRITISH BEER AS BALANCE.

Some folks misinterpret what balanced means; they think you're in the middle of the road. Balance to me is making a balance of the complexity of flavors you generate, not being neutral.

WHAT MAKES A GOOD SESSION BEER? HOW DO YOU ACHIEVE A FLAVORFUL, LOWER-ALCOHOL BEER?

In England, beer is always drunk in pubs rather than at home. So you drink it standing up and in the company of others. You want a drink that is sociable and promotes that chitchat over a long period of time. There's no point in something that makes you really drunk and incoherent.

SO ON ONE HAND, THAT'S WHAT PEOPLE HAVE WANTED.

Yes, and I think cask lends itself to that drinkable, low-gravity because it allows a lot of flavors to be produced. I think hops are a key to it. With dry-hopping, you can generate a lot of flavor without adding alcohol. When I was a young brewer, I went to Bass in Burton to see how they make beer. One of their old brewers told me the beer with the greatest drinkability is a beer with the yeast removed late in the day. If you're making a keg beer, filter it, and drink it six weeks later; it's not like a beer where the yeast has just dropped out.

STILL, ENGLAND HAS HAD ITS OWN TROUBLE WITH DECLINING CASK SALES.

For a long time in the brewing world, flavor wasn't that important. It was the profit margin and making the beer cheaper. Now with the explosion in the last twenty years, flavor has come back to its rightful position. I think flavor is now king, and the bigger breweries need to wake up to the fact that accountants decide how they make their beer. There are two types of brewers: those judged by the taste of the beer they produce and those who are judged by the cost of the beer they produce. If you're making beer on cost, you're being judged by accountants.

The Fuller's brewery is London's only remaining brewery.

The Fuller's Vintage Ale is released every year with slight recipe variations such as switching the Fuggle hops to Northdown and Challenger.

One of the most important things in brewing is the relationship between a brewer and his or her yeast. You get to understand it, it gets to understand you as well, and you can play tunes together.

YOU MENTIONED A DIFFERENCE BETWEEN KEGS AND CASKS.

With keg beer, you will get drinkability, and bottled beers are far better made than when I was studying at Bass. The difference between cask, keg, and bottle is mostly the gas content, CO_2. It can have a big effect on how you perceive flavor.

CAN YOU GIVE ME AN EXAMPLE?

Some bigger beers need effervescence to bring out flavor. One of our beers we made recently, a brewer's reserve, is just not the same beer when you taste it flat. You need the bottle-conditioned fizziness and it lifts the flavor. Then I think lower-gravity beer for drinking is better with lower carbonation, like in a cask beer.

WHAT DO YOU THINK ABOUT THE UK BEER CULTURE'S RESISTANCE TO FLAVORFUL, INTERESTING KEG BEER?

People get into mind-sets. For example, Northerners prefer a big creamy head, but that's psychology. And so some people assume all beer without head has something wrong. Likewise, certain people assume there's no good keg beer because they've never had a good pint. If you tried it twenty years ago and it was overpasteurized and lacking flavor, that's no comparison to keg beer now. We have to be thankful to American brewers for starting to push past those old pasteurized beers.

DO YOU BREW DIFFERENTLY KNOWING WHICH PACKAGE IT'S DESTINED FOR?

We make our beer stronger for bottle and keg because they have to last longer. We do pasteurize a lot but also bottle condition some. Our bottle-conditioned beers tend to be stronger and will last up to six years. But we also make bottle and keg stronger because processing is a bit traumatic with filters, pasteurization, and bottling. In the end, I just want as much or more flavor. But you cannot make a bottle taste exactly like a cask.

SO WHAT'S NEXT FOR FULLER'S?

We're about to start making beers from the past and try to match them as best we can. It's interesting to look through the old brewing books. We were using American brewing hops in 1902 to make pale ale, though I think it's simply because they were cheaper. You also see the family trees for beers. If you follow that pale ale's history, it becomes Special Pale Ale. Turn a few more pages and it's London Pride.

BUT WHAT'S IN THE FUTURE FOR YOU?

One of the things I'm determined to do is get our brewers exposed to the world of brewing at a younger age than me. I do think younger brewers need to get a heads-up and see different beer cultures, and there's no finer way than to get around the world and do it.

Five to six different barrels will be blended for a batch of Cantillon Gueuze.

SOUR BEERS ARE ANYTHING BUT SPOILED. THESE EXPLOSIVELY RICH ALES USE A LONG, BUT VERY INTENTIONAL, PROCESS OF INOCULATING WORT WITH NATURAL YEAST AND BACTERIA TO CREATE BEERS SIMILAR TO THOSE BREWED MILLENNIA AGO. MANY HOMEBREWERS ARE TAKING UP THE CHALLENGE OF CULTURING AND CONDITIONING WILD YEAST BEERS, BUT THE HEART OF SOUR BEER LIES IN THE LAMBIC ALES OF BELGIUM.

CHAPTER 9: LAMBIC BREWING

Creating a true lambic is as much about process as patience and faith. If you're brewing a lambic-style ale correctly, the beer will be in charge and your job is just to encourage it along as best you can.

In this chapter, you'll learn about:

Traditional sour Belgian lambics

Brewing lambics

Lambic ingredients

Wild and sour yeast strains

Fruit lambics

INTRODUCTION TO LAMBICS AND SOUR BEER

Most brewers ferment their ales and lagers in clean, sterile environments to guard against infection. Lambic and sour brewers intentionally allow wild yeasts in, to either ferment by themselves or along with normal brewing yeast strains. Wild yeast can come live in the fermenters, drop into beer from surrounding air, or be added like another strain, with a specimen from a yeast lab. Because of their wild, undomesticated nature, lambic and sour beers are very difficult to control and can take years to mature.

CHOOSING YOUR INGREDIENTS

To brew a lambic, the malt bill is a simple mix of 35 percent unmalted wheat and 65 percent pilsner malt. Adding a small portion, 5 to 10 percent of the malt bill, of maltodextrin will help mimic a traditional lambic mash.

The hops are trickier, as traditional two- and three-year-old hops can be difficult to buy. However, that's how the bitterness is kept below 10 IBU. Hops are added largely for their antiseptic properties to protect against unwanted bacteria (these do exist in lambic brewing).

Hopping rates run a little under 1 pound (455 g) per barrel (31 gallons, or 117 L), which leaves you with about 2 ounces (57 g) for a 5-gallon (19 L) batch. And if aged hops are unavailable, use the lowest–alpha acid hops available, such as French Strisselspalt.

TURBID MASH AND BOIL

The traditional lambic mash was born out of a 200-year-old tax (since repealed) on mash tun size. To convert as much starch as possible, brewers packed their mash tuns full of grains with minimal water. They then pulled out wort and heated it while adding near-boiling water to reach the next mash step.

This sounds bizarre and inefficient, but it makes a perfect low-gravity mash for lambic brewing. The extra unconverted dextrins and starches fuel *Brettanomyces* while starving less-desirable bacteria that act early in spontaneous fermentation.

The schedule here, developed by Wyeast Laboratories, is a good compromise between the complicated traditions of nineteenth-century Belgium and modern homebrewing.

LAMBIC MASHING SCHEDULE

- Dough-in at 113°F (45°C) and rest for 15 minutes.
- Add 195°F (91°C) water to the mash to raise the temperature to 126°F (52°C) and rest for 30 minutes.
- Add 195°F (91°C) water to the mash to raise the temperature to 149°F (65°C) and rest for 30 minutes.
- Add 195°F (91°C) water to the mash to raise the temperature to 162°F (72°C) and rest for 30 minutes.
- Heat mash to 172°F (78°C) and rest for 15 minutes before sparging.

Cantillon's Classic Gueuze has used the same recipe since 1900.

FERMENTING BACTERIA AND YEASTS

Sour Cultures	Time Active	Character
Enteric bacteria	1 week	Sulfur, rotting notes that fade with aging. Plays a minor role in flavor but supports later yeast growth.
Kloeckera apiculata	1 week	Almost a hop-like fruit character. Typically plays a minor role in flavor but supports later yeast growth.
Lactic acid bacteria	4 months	Sour and tart flavors. Some strains produce buttery diacetyl. *Lactobacillus* is more prevalent in Flanders sour red and brown ales, while the milder *Pediococcus* produces the lactic acid in lambics.
Brettanomyces yeasts	8 months	Classic barnyard funk. An oxidative yeast, but overaeration and low pH (sub-3.4) prevent growth. Available in three different strains, all of which happily ferment unconverted starch.

At Norway's HaandBryggeriet, brewers use fresh oak barrels as well as former wine and spirits barrels for their sour ales.

Naturally, the boil is no easier. Because of their inefficient mash, brewers would boil for at least three hours in order to evaporate a little more than 20 percent of the wort. That means starting with 6.5 gallons (25 L) of wort to boil down to 5 gallons (19 L).

INOCULATION AND FERMENTATION

A common misstep homebrewers make is cooling their lambic wort too quickly. This can be difficult to manage, since you may have to insulate your pot or carboy to slow the process, but wort needs to sit, exposed to the world, for eight to twelve hours before racking to primary fermentation at 64°F to 68°F (18°C to 20°C). Commercial brewers consider an ambient temperature around freezing ideal, but a homebrewer's smaller batch would chill too quickly in these conditions.

Once wild yeast has set in, the fermentation is still exceedingly slow and may not begin in earnest for more than a month or two. Well over one hundred types of yeast and bacteria will be present in the beer, but about four of them do most of the work. (See table at left.) They can be added with blended culture from a yeast lab, but will likely also be floating through the air around your fermenter. Of course, natural, open-air inoculation is considerably less predictable than a yeast blend.

Typically, lambics are brewed in the cooler months and sit in oak barrels for primary fermentation for nine to twelve months. About halfway through the process, the beer becomes "sick" as *Pediococcus* takes hold, with thin lines of slime appearing throughout the beer. This step lasts about three or four months, shortly after which the ale is deemed ready to be a jong, or young, lambic.

Brewers at Odell Brewing in Colorado transfer their *Brettanomyces*-conditioned Saboteur ale into American oak barrels to mature.

BRETTANOMYCES STRAINS

B. bruxellensis	This milder *Brett* is famously used to condition Orval, but still holds a sweaty, horseblanket-type character.
B. claussenii	A relatively low-impact strain used to sour Irish stouts like Guinness, with a mild fruity character.
B. lambicus	The *Brett* strain commonly used in lambics. It's the strongest and most distinctive strain, with barnyard spice and sour-cherrylike flavors.

BUYING LAMBIC YEAST CULTURES

No one will sneer or think less of you for using a sour yeast culture in place of your local microbiota. Wyeast and White Labs both have individual sour strains and lambic blends for primary inoculation or secondary conditioning. These contain the necessary *Brettanomyces*, *Lactobacillus*, and *Pediococcus* along with an ale yeast. They differ in their proportions and strains, but with the right base beer and nurturing, will produce wild beer with high attenuation.

Souring a cleanly fermented beer is an option favored by many brewers who produce phenomenal wild ale, but don't assume a packet of yeast will do all the work. Remember that *Brettanomyces* feed off unfermentable sugars and that barrel aging also imparts a strong character to sour beers through the wood itself and the slight oxygen it allows in the beer.

BLENDING AND BOTTLING

While it's not required of sour beers, brewers will usually blend barrels of beer to produce a single batch. Blending, as with cider apples, increases complexity while balancing strong, acidic, and smooth characteristics. Master blenders start with a beer in mind, then mix barrels and batches to reach that end.

If you're making a gueuze, which consists of one-, two-, and three-year-old lambics, the basic goal is to blend a rich, powerful beer with a blander vintage to make it palatable so the great flavors can be enjoyed. Sour beer brewers, however, will routinely dump beers that are too acidic to blend or are infected with *Acetobacter*, which turns the beer to vinegar.

Brett-inoculated beers finish dry, 1.010 or lower. In the case of a gueuze, the young beer provides relatively fresh yeast and enough sugar to carbonate over the course of a year. Otherwise, a traditional brewer might leave an older unblended lambic still. Add any priming sugar with caution and at lower levels than usual, as *Brettanomyces* is a slow, but aggressive yeast.

BREWING FRUIT LAMBICS

No more than 1 percent of the fruit beers labeled "lambic" are honest-to-God lambics. If it's sweet and clean, it's no more a lambic than your bland commercial lager is a pilsner. True fruit lambics marry the tart, funky flavors of a gueuze or straight lambic with a rich, fresh-fruit character.

Start by using 1 to 2.5 pounds of fruit per gallon (119 to 300 g per liter), depending on the desired strength of impact and the fruit's character.

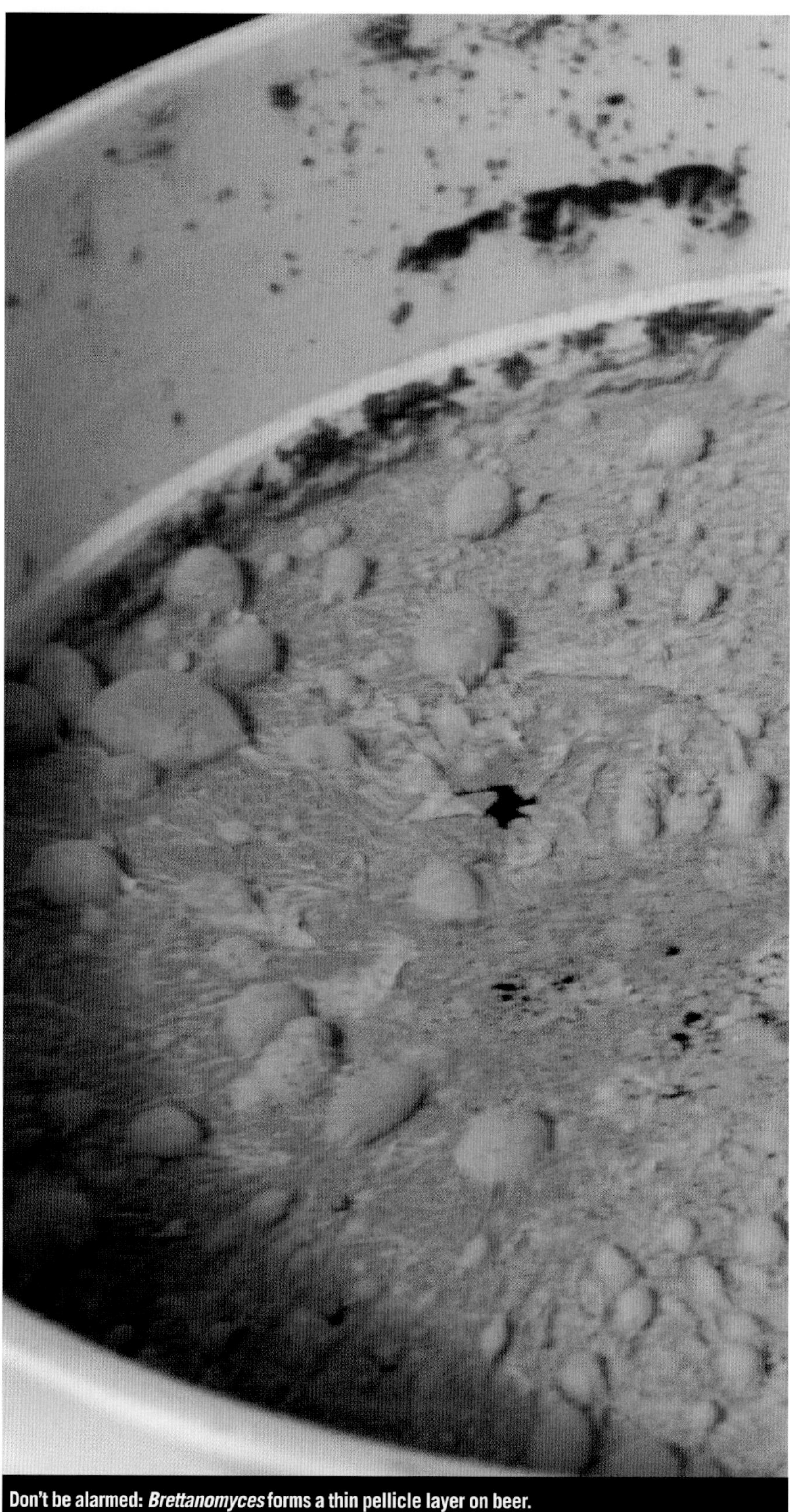

Don't be alarmed: *Brettanomyces* forms a thin pellicle layer on beer.

LAMBIC GLOSSARY

Krieks: cherries
Framboises/Frambozen: raspberries
Peches: peaches
Cassis: black currants

Krieks from Cantillon and 3 Fonteinen use whole, crushed cherries complete with pits.

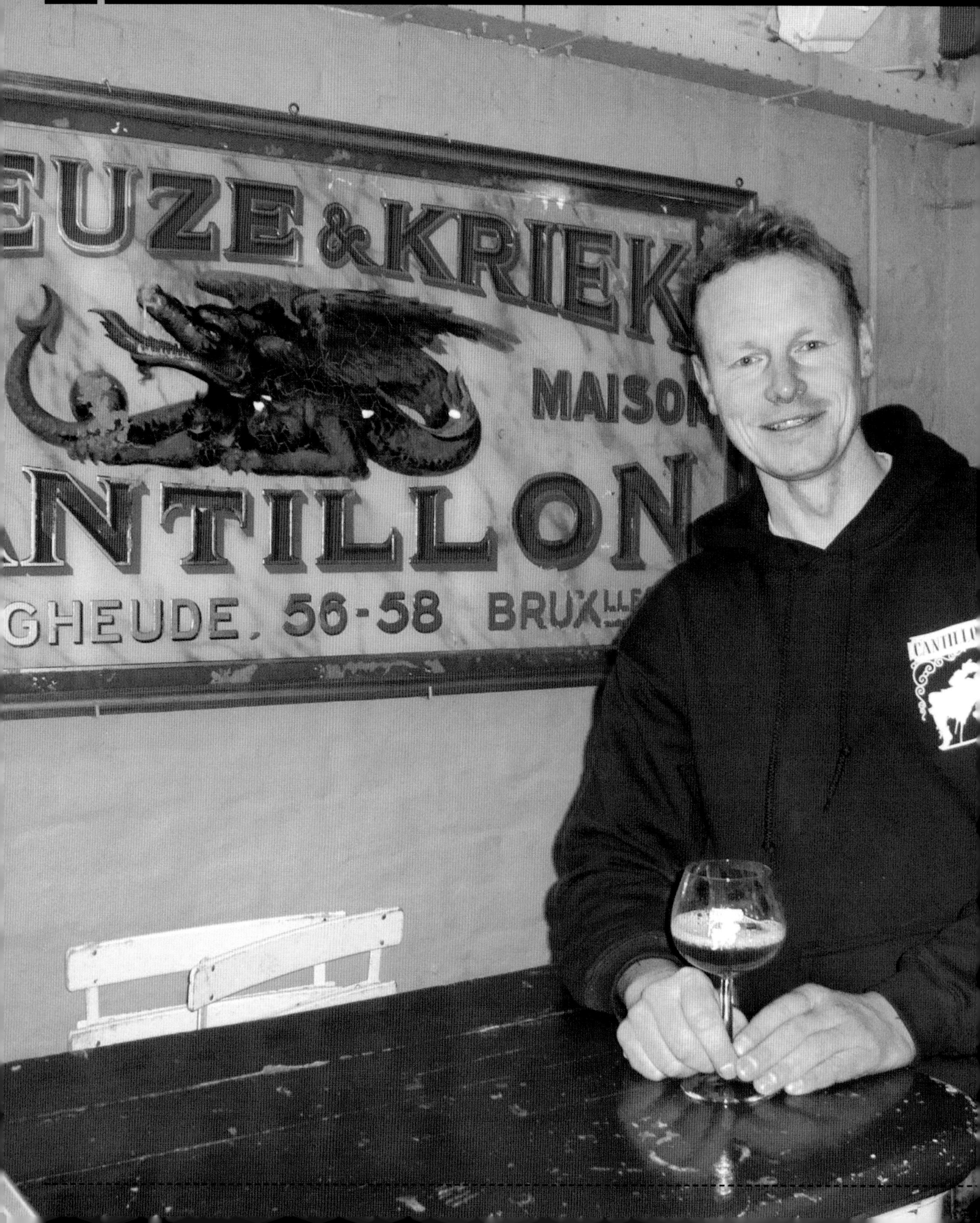
EUZE & KRIEK
MAISON
ANTILLON
GHEUDE, 56-58 BRUX

Jean Van Roy is a fourth-generation brewer at Cantillon in Brussels, Belgium.

INTERVIEW WITH: JEAN VAN ROY: BREWMASTER, BRASSERIE CANTILLON, BRUSSELS, BELGIUM

THERE EXIST OLDER BREWERIES, BUT NONE CAN MATCH THE TRADITION OF CANTILLON. JEAN VAN ROY LEADS THE OPERATION, BREWING HIS GREAT-GRANDFATHER'S LAMBICS FROM 1900.

HELP US UNDERSTAND BELGIAN BEER CULTURE. WHY CAN'T YOU EASILY FIND CANTILLON BEERS IN BRUSSELS?

Belgians are not great beer connoisseurs in general, but they think they know everything about it. I think it's simply because the big Belgian breweries control everything.

BUT THERE ARE OTHER BEERS LABELED "LAMBIC" THAT ARE READILY AVAILABLE.

The majority of beer called gueuze, lambic, kriek, and so on are fake. For the common Belgian customer, a gueze, kriek, or framboise is a sweet beer. And it's why Cantillon is not found everywhere.

HAVE YOU EVER CONSIDERED BREWING OUTSIDE THE LAMBIC STYLE?

Not really, because first of all, I'm not a brewer. I learned everything at the brewery from my father and grandfather, who were also not brewers. We learned everything from our ancestors. It would be difficult for me, not because of the work, but because of the philosophy, to brew another beer than lambic. I love my product. For me, lambic may not be the best beer in the world for flavors, aromas. It's not the top beer, but because the product is alive, it is its own life. No, it's lambic or nothing.

THAT'S INTERESTING TO HEAR YOU DESCRIBE YOURSELF AS "NOT A BREWER."

I didn't study to be a brewer. Even a lambic brewer is not a master brewer. Because a master has to control the product, he has to dominate the beer. A lambic brewer works with his product. I'm a guide for my beer.

The shallow attic coolships cool wort overnight while exposed to the Brussels air.

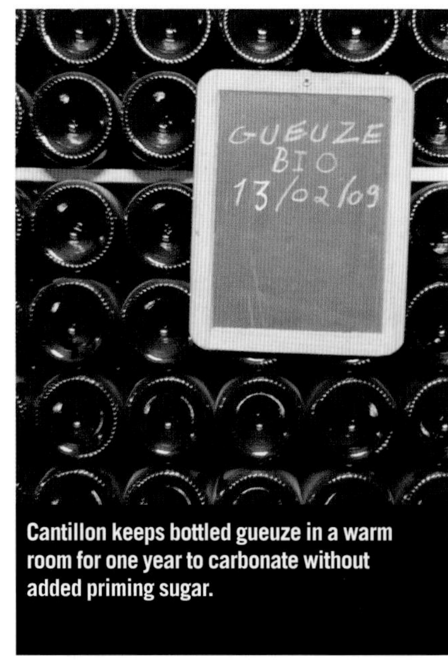

Cantillon keeps bottled gueuze in a warm room for one year to carbonate without added priming sugar.

IN SOME WAYS, DON'T YOU THINK BEING A GUIDE IS MORE CHALLENGING THAN DOMINATING YOUR BEER?

We begin to play a role in the beer conception when we blend a beer. The blending is very important, but before the blending, we have to feel our product, we have to understand the product. The beer needs this love to grow. I'm sure of it. I think that lambic is alive and it's a bit crazy, but the beer feels it. The most important thing we can do for the beer is when the beer is just brewed, to give it passion.

WOULD YOU GUIDE US THROUGH YOUR PROCESS AND HOW IT DIFFERS FROM NORMAL BREWING?

The most important difference is the cooling. We don't use industrial refrigeration; that's why we brew in the winter. The best temperature for us is around 0°C (32°F), because when the wort is coming on the coolship, it is coming on at 85°C or 90°C (185°F or 194°F) and the day after we have to fill the barrels with the wort at 18°C to 20°C (65°F to 68°F). In the winter you have a classic yeast activation, but less bacteria than in the summer.

The wort stays one night in contact with the air. At night, we have natural inoculation, the most important of them are the *Brettanomyces lambicus* and *Brettanomyces bruxellensis*. The day after, we fill the wooden barrels, but we don't close them, and we await the first fermentation. It can start after two to three days, or if the wort is cold, we can wait weeks or months.

WHAT IS THE PURPOSE OF THE LONGER BOIL?

First of all, it's because we have to evaporate a lot of water to extract maximum sugar from the grains. So at the Cantillon brewery, we bump the boiling around 9,500 liters (2,509 gallons) and we evaporate a minimum 2,000 liters (528 gallons).

Lambic brewers also use copper kettles, which can impart some flavor. You can try to get the same effect by boiling in a copper stockpot instead of in stainless or aluminum.

A brewing engineer [once] said to me that boiling in copper develops special things between water and ionization. I spoke some years ago with a French distiller, and they are working with copper as well. They don't know why exactly distillation in stainless steel doesn't give the same result. They think ionization plays a role.

COULD YOU MAKE LAMBIC BEER WITH A STAINLESS KETTLE?

I think so, but probably not the same one. Some people—even in the U.S.—are producing beer from spontaneous fermentation [in stainless]. There's more, though. I think each building plays a role. Cantillon is a typical lambic because we've produced that beer at the brewery since 1900. If tomorrow I built myself another brewery at my home eight kilometers (5 miles) from the brewery, and produced a beer from spontaneous fermentation, the result will be different.

WHAT DO YOU THINK ABOUT PROTECTING THE WORD "LAMBIC" AS A REGIONAL DESIGNATION?

No, it's too late. We are not strong enough. The majority of the beers called lambic are not real lambic. And to receive such a certification, we have to be strong. And that's impossible. You have one brewery and three blenders who produce 100 percent in traditional lambic. The brewery is Cantillon.

At Cantillon, we (my father and mother) fought in the 80s to protect the name lambic. That's why we founded the Brussels Gueuze Museum as well. If tomorrow some people are ready to fight to protect lambic, we will do it with them.

ARE THERE FRUITS YOU WOULD NOT CONSIDER USING?

There are no limits for lambics—you can use what you want. Each year, I make a small experiment. I've done it with rhubarb, elderflower, and a special grape variety. It's not just to see the results, but also to learn about my beer. The lambic with elderflower was a great discovery.

Even a lambic brewer is not a master brewer. Because a master has to control the product, he has to dominate the beer. A lambic brewer works with his product. I'm a guide for my beer.

WHEN DID YOU DECIDE YOU WANTED TO CONTINUE THE TRADITION AT CANTILLON?

I never decided. I watched my parents; they did everything for the brewery, for beer, for the process. I was born in the brewery.

DOES THE POPULARITY OF YOUR BEER OUTSIDE BELGIUM SURPRISE YOU?

Yes, and it's always a surprise; I can't explain it. It's always emotional for me because I'm proud of my product when I see that. I think a lot of my ancestors, especially my great-grandfather.

YOUR GREAT-GRANDFATHER COULDN'T HAVE IMAGINED THIS.

No, impossible. The only people who drank lambic forty years ago were people from Brussels. Belgian beers and European beers have to take care because those countries like the U.S., Canada, and Italy will begin to produce better beers than the original ones.

THAT'S QUITE A STATEMENT.

That's true. For me, the last great white beer I tasted was not Belgian but American or Italian.

WHAT ARE YOUR THOUGHTS ON AMERICAN SOUR BEER?

It's getting better and better. At the beginning, the beers were not balanced enough, but now I find more and more quality. I think the U.S. will produce great sour beer in the future.

IS THIS GOOD FOR YOUR BUSINESS AND THE LAMBIC CULTURE?

I think so, because the problem with lambic is you don't find enough of this beer on the market. When people drink it for the first time, they are surprised. And if they don't receive the right information, the reaction will be, "Oooh, that's sour—that's bad." Here I'm speaking for me and am alone in thinking that the sour beer production is a good thing for lambic. I think all the other lambic producers are afraid.

TIP: LAMBIC-STYLE BOIL

Traditional lambic brewers boil their wort for four to six hours. Aside from condensing the wort, it also helps extract more bitterness from hops and counteract the high protein levels brought in by unmalted wheat. Over the course of a long boil, proteins coagulate and drop out of suspension. For a similar effect, boil your wort for at least two hours.

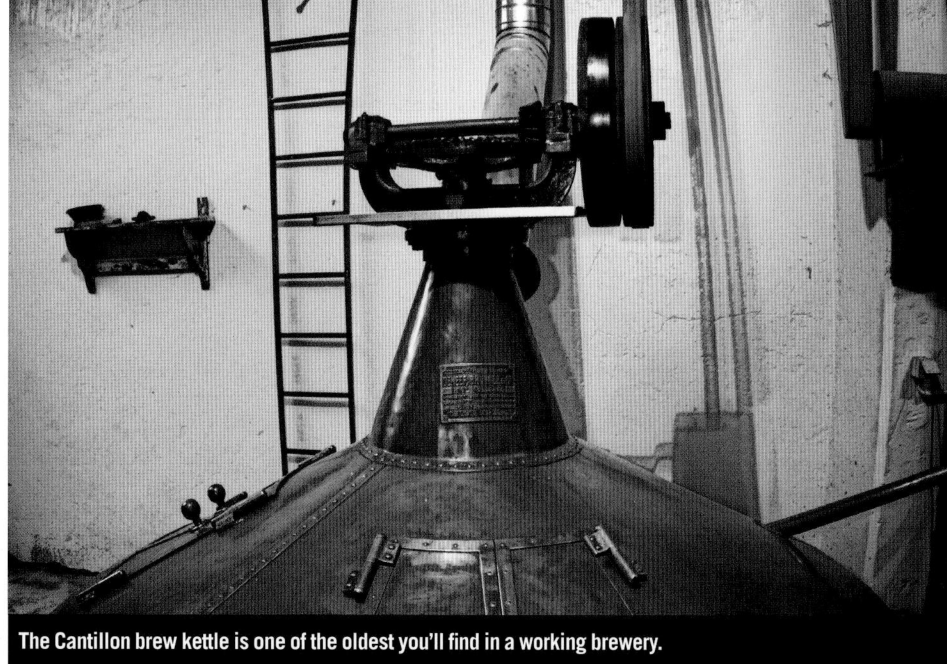

The Cantillon brew kettle is one of the oldest you'll find in a working brewery.

Your next batch of beer could be waiting at the grocery store.

TRUE HANDCRAFTED FRUIT BEERS ARE A THING OF BEAUTY AND A PINT TO BEHOLD. FORGET THE SICKLY SWEET JUNK PANDERING TO THE ALCOPOP CROWD. WE'RE TALKING ABOUT THE REAL DEAL—BEERS DESIGNED AROUND ARTISAN FOODS AND FRUIT. THINK OF THE BELGIAN KRIEK OR AN IMPERIAL COFFEE PORTER. THESE AREN'T BREWED BY ACCIDENT; INFUSING AN OUTSIDE INGREDIENT IS A MATTER OF TIMING, SANITATION, AND PORTION CONTROL.

CHAPTER 10: BREWING WITH FRUIT AND MORE

INTRODUCTION TO FRUIT BEER

Not to be confused with soda-like alcopops, fruit beer is always beer at heart. A fruit or flavoring may complement the backing malts and hops, or can even take center stage, but the majority of fermentable sugars should come from malted grains.

In this chapter, you'll learn about:

- **Preparing fruit**
- **When and how to add fruit**
- **Ideal fruits for beer**
- **Other flavorings**

PREPARING FRUIT FOR BREWING

Preparing fruit for brewing is simple. Select fresh fruit from the grocery, or better, the local farmers' market, and begin by washing and freezing the fruit. As the water in the fruit expands while freezing, it breaks the skin, which will help the juice blend with your beer.

SANITIZING FRUIT

Fresh and frozen fruit will both need to be sanitized unless you are adding it after your boil. Heat the fruit in a small amount of water to 170°F (77°C) for 10 minutes. Another option is to soak the fruit in a spirit. Soaking your fruit in vodka for 15 minutes will make your fruit ready to ferment and leave you with a lightly fruit-infused vodka you can either add to the beer or save for your bar.

At Denver's Wynkoop Brewing, a brewer adds roasted pumpkin to the mash. Homebrewers should use smaller chunks to compensate for a smaller system.

ADDING FRUIT TO THE BREW

There are three common points in the brewing process at which you can add fruit: at the end of the boil, during primary fermentation, and to the conditioning tank.

End of the boil: Adding fruit postboil, especially unsanitized fruit, will clean it without heating off too much of its character. Note that boiling fruit releases pectin and creates a hazy appearance in the finished beer.

Primary fermenter: When adding to the primary fermenter, it's best to wait a couple days before adding the fruit. This lets the yeast adapt to fermenting barley sugars first, ensuring fruit doesn't compromise the base beer.

Secondary/conditioning tank: Adding to the secondary or conditioning tank allows you to age the beer longer on fruit while the alcohol provides a bit more insurance against spoilage. For most batches, one or two weeks will add a good level of flavor and still allow time to add more fruit if desired. If possible, use a fermenter with an open top when you add the fruit (old stainless milk jugs are perfect). Squeezing fruit in and out of a glass carboy is a royal pain.

DOSING FRUIT

New fruit brewers often ask "how much should I add?" but there's no easy answer. Your dosing should be determined through a combination of the flavor intensity of the fruit, the amount of fruit character you desire, and character of the beer's malt and hops. Use the lower end of recommendations for lighter beers or for lighter fruit character, and the high end for big flavors or for matching a big beer.

RASPBERRIES AND BLACKBERRIES

These beer-friendly fruits can be added in quantities anywhere between 4 ounces to a pound per gallon (30 to 120 g per liter).

CHERRIES AND MANGOS

These both have milder flavors. To have an effect on the final brew, you will need to add as much as 2 pounds per gallon (240 g per liter).

BLUEBERRIES AND STRAWBERRIES

These require similarly high dosing along with a lighter base beer: Add as much as 2 pounds per gallon (240 g per liter). When brewing with lighter-tasting fruits, it's best to work with lower hopping rates.

CITRUS

Citrus fruits make a delicious complement to American hops. When brewing with them, all you want of the fruit is the peel and zest to use as a spice. Sour oranges, such as Seville, work well, as do tangerines and grapefruit. The zest or peel of one orange added at the end of a boil will add a basic citrus character to your brew.

FORMS OF FRUIT

If you're not brewing with whole fruit, you will need to adjust your dosing. Fruit purées do not contain seeds, making them about 10 percent more potent (10 ounces, or 280 g, of purée is 11 ounces, or 310 g, of fruit). Juice is even more potent, though the final flavor depends heavily on the quality of juice (look for farm-fresh instead of sweetened and pasteurized). A juice concentrate needs anywhere from 2 to 6 ounces per gallon (15 to 45 g per liter) to impart flavor. Read the concentrate label for its fruit equivalent to plan a more accurate addition.

A blackberry ale waits to be brewed by homebrewer Matt Mets. Left to right: Specialty grains, extra light dry malt extract, flaked barley, yeast packet (back), pale liquid malt extract, raspberries (back), blackberries (middle), fruit flavoring, and Fuggles hops.

FRUIT FLAVORING

You've probably noticed those little plastic bottles of natural fruit flavor in your homebrew store. They're perfectly capable of making a good beer. Adding a 4-ounce (120 ml) bottle of apricot to a 5-gallon (19 L) batch of wheat beer at bottling produces a real crowd-pleaser with minimal effort, but don't expect to impress any beer snobs. The drawback with flavorings is that often the character is very simple and can have a sweet, candylike taste. There's nothing morally wrong with using these (although co-author Greg thinks there is), but use the real thing if you want a deeper, more complex character in your brew. Also, check that the flavoring is either intended for beer or doesn't include preservatives that will inhibit carbonation.

BEYOND FRUIT

Fruit is an enticing and easy example of blending beer with outside flavors, but it's not the only one. Most culinary elements that have a manageable fat content (yes, chocolate works), and can be sterilized, added, or infused into beer in some way. Here are a few successful ideas:

PUMPKIN AND SQUASH

Cube and roast any form of squash until the meat starts to brown. Add at least a pound per gallon (120 g per liter) to the mash tun with the grains for a mild flavor. Be aware that the squash adds a small amount of sugar.

New fruit brewers often ask "how much should I add?" but there's no easy answer. Your dosing should be determined through a combination of the flavor intensity of the fruit, the amount of fruit character you desire, and character of the beer's malt and hops.

Use coarsely ground coffee beans as you would for a French press coffeemaker.

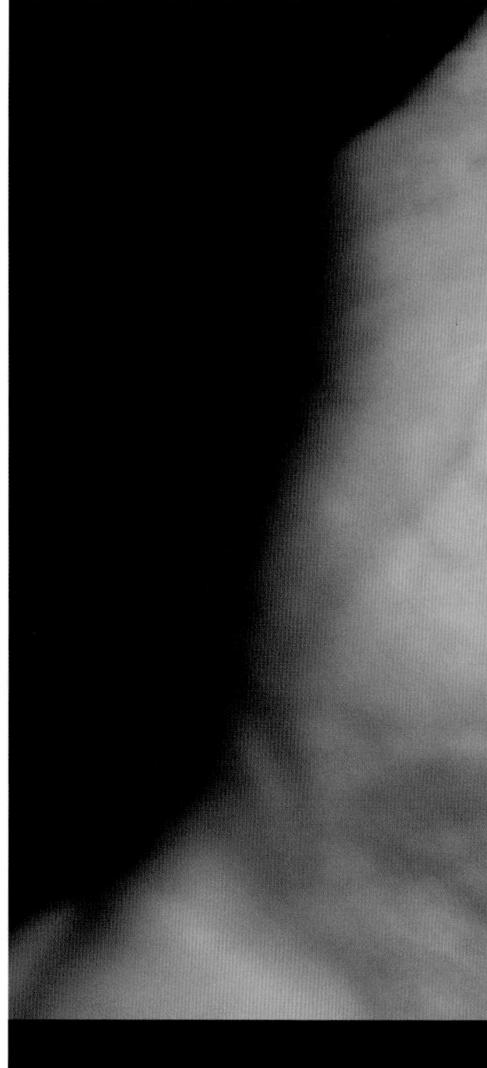

COFFEE

There are two preferred methods for coffee infusions among brewers. First is the cold extraction, in which you soak your beans (coarsely ground) in water overnight and then add the resulting coffee to your condition tank. The second is to "dry-hop" by adding the beans straight to the tank. The latter is simpler, but the extraction method allows you to slowly dose the coffee and control its effect.

CHOCOLATE

First off, forget the chocolate syrup. You can add an ounce per gallon (8 g per liter) of dark, semisweet, or baker's chocolate at the end of your boil for a slight chocolate flavor, but 2 to 3 ounces per gallon (15 to 23 g per liter) will be more forward in the beer's character. Avoid transferring any fats and cocoa butter from the chocolate (they will separate during the boil) from the brew kettle to your fermenter; they can inhibit yeast and eventual carbonation.

For a more earthy cocoa flavor, add cacao nibs to your secondary fermenter in the same amount you would add whole chocolate. Cocoa powder will create a similar character, but it only needs a quarter-ounce per gallon (2 g per liter) for a basic impact. The powder also has the lowest oil content if you're worried about fats derailing your brew. A good bet is to add 2 to 3 ounces (55 to 85 g) to your 5-gallon (19 L batch) at the end of your boil.

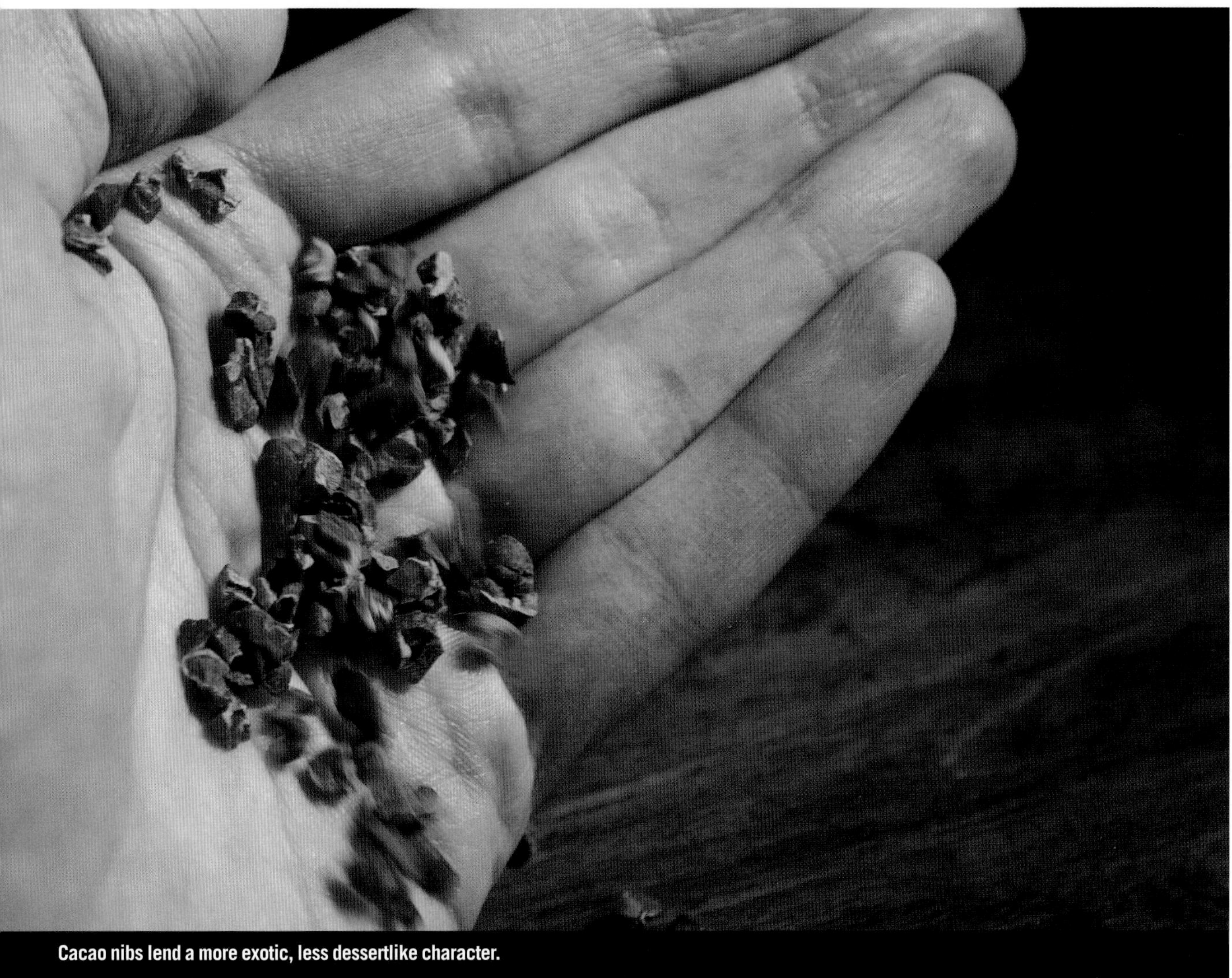

Cacao nibs lend a more exotic, less dessertlike character.

PEPPERS

Adding heat is a deliciously dangerous endeavor. Capsaicin, the heat component in peppers, can easily overpower a beer and render a batch useless beyond using as a cooking aide. Adding peppers to the end of your boil will add more heat than anything. Making a secondary addition will bring out more pepper flavor and aroma. Use either roasted or freshly chopped peppers, depending on your desired flavor.

A simple addition is one seeded habanero (or equally high-test pepper), or a dozen midrange peppers, such as serranos. Remember to taste-test often as the heat infusion increases over time.

VANILLA BEANS

Adding just one bean to a 5-gallon (19 L) batch can add a wonderful flavor, though it's wise to start by adding a half bean or less. Split the bean lengthwise, then scrape out the insides, chop the bean pod, and add everything to your secondary.

Sam has brewed more than a dozen different fruit or flavored beers with ingredients such as cacao and arctic cloudberries.

INTERVIEW WITH: SAM CALAGIONE: FOUNDER, DOGFISH HEAD CRAFT BREWERY, REHOBOTH BEACH, DELAWARE, U.S.

Fort, Sam's 18 percent ABV raspberry beer, is fermented with 20 pounds (9 kg) of fruit per barrel.

WHEN DID YOU FIRST DEVIATE FROM TRADITIONAL BEER STYLES?

My first batch I ever brewed was a fruit beer. Back in 1993, it was a pale ale made with sour cherries. I had this recipe from the homebrew store, a malt extract kit with a little bag of probably very old and useless hop pellets. On my way home, I stopped at the grocery store and bought a bunch of sour cherries.

WHERE'D THAT SPARK COME FROM?

I always had a bit of a contrarian bent. I figured if I wanted to start homebrewing, I'd want to try and do things that hadn't been done before. I was so naïve to the whole brewing movement. I didn't know of beers like kriek and stuff, so I was reinventing the wheel.

But right from the gate, the whole inspiration for getting into brewing was the opportunity for creative expression. So for my first beer, I wanted to flex my creative muscles.

LET'S COVER SOME TECHNICAL ASPECTS. HOW DOES THE TIMING OF WHEN YOU ADD THE FRUIT AFFECT THE FINAL PRODUCT?

Different fruits work in different ways. We like to add things late in the boil, generally. For homebrewing, you can always flash sterilize things by adding them to boiling water and then puréeing and adding them to a carboy. If it's already puréed and sterile, we'll add it during primary fermentation on the cold side. If we're talking raw fruit, we invariably add it on the hot side unless we're doing a sour.

SO WHAT DO YOU DO FOR A SOUR FRUIT BEER?

If you want a beer with the wild buggers in it, wild fruit will have that, and we'll add them during fermentation. Frankly, the more rotten the better. For Festina Lente, we purposely went to a local peach orchard and said, "Give us your slimiest, grossest, fly-infested peaches." That's what we wanted. I know that makes it sound enticing.

ENGINE

A flight of beers at the Dogfish Head brewpub includes ales brewed with coffee, green raisins, brown sugar, and licorice root.

The Dogfish Head Craft Brewery in Milton, Delaware, was converted from a cannery to meet growing demand.

If you want a beer with the wild buggers in it, wild fruit will have that, and we'll add them during fermentation. Frankly, the more rotten the better.

TALK ABOUT THE DIFFERENCE BETWEEN USING FRESH FRUIT, PURÉE, AND FRUIT FLAVORING.

We haven't played around with fruit flavoring, other than our vanilla extract liquid that we use with some beers. Usually, we have vanilla beans and cut them open and accentuate that with vanilla extract. That's the only extract we use. Otherwise, we only use puréed real fruit that's been aseptically prepared or fresh fruit.

I'm not a fan of extracts or artificial flavors. I'm sure there are brewers making competent beers, but we kind of philosophically have a problem with that.

LET'S TALK ABOUT OTHER KINDS OF FOODS. WHAT'S THE PROCESS YOU GO ABOUT DECIDING WHEN TO ADD THEM?

We start with our little Sabco, a glorified homebrew system on steroids, for 12- to 14-gallon (45 to 53 L) experimental batches. We don't do focus groups. We vet ideas in that Sabco by doing a test and then saying, [expletive], that worked, or oops, that sucked. We rarely do two batches on the Sabco. We know enough about brewing with exotic ingredients that we have confidence about tweaking recipes around an idea.

PLEASE GIVE ME AN EXAMPLE.

If it's a tart fruit, like sour cherries or orange skin and rinds, we know they're going to add more aroma. If it's a really sweet fruit, like raspberries and blueberries, we know it's going to add more flavor or taste. There weren't any books on that; it was just trial and error of starting as a brewery that only brewed 12 gallons (45 L) at a time, so we brewed two or three batches a day.

ANY GENERAL RULES OF THUMB? PLEASE SHARE SOME OF YOUR EXPERIENCE.

Basically it's all over the map; there's no substitute for personal expression and subjectivity and volume. Too much peppercorn for one person isn't enough for another. We had that experience with peppercorns in 1996—some people wanted to vomit because of what we loved.

SO WAS THAT THE CASE OF THE WEEK OR MONTH FOR THE EMPLOYEES THEN?

No, but there was Au Currant with currants and people called it "Aw Come On," because they were so sick of getting it, even for free.

But some general guidelines are: We like to add spices earlier than we add fruit. We have spices in the mash tun and kettle, and most of our fruit goes in the whirlpool. For homebrewers, this is at the end of your boil when you turn off your heat source and are simmering. It's hot enough to flash pasteurize it.

But we are adding most of our whole spices, whether its allspice and cinnamon for Punkin Ale or chicory and licorice root for Chicory Stout, early in the boil. In the case of our grapes, we find red and white grapes work well after fermentation has started. Honey we found works better at end of the boil. Honey should still be in the kettle.

WHAT'S YOUR MOST SPECTACULAR FAILURE?

My most spectacular failure was 1997 through 2000. [Laughs.] We kept brewing beers like Immort Ale and Chicory Stout and expected people to want them and lost money at our production brewery. We needed our restaurant to keep us from going bankrupt. So besides entire chunks of decades, our five-barrel brewpub pilot system lets us fail publicly in a marginal way while we swing for the fences with things we've never done before.

WHAT ABOUT INGREDIENTS YOU THOUGHT WERE A SPECTACULAR IDEA?

The ingredient was lavender buds in 1996. We brewed a beer with lavender and peppercorns called High Alpha Wheat and it was a wheat beer with high-alpha hops and lavender, so it was a perfect storm of stupidity from known brewing history right out of the gates. It probably tasted more like perfume than beer. I suffered through most of that 12-gallon (45 L) batch by myself at the bar.

HOW DO YOU DETERMINE THE VARIETY OF THE HONEY THAT YOU USE?

We make honey-based teas, such as a mild English breakfast tea—that's what led us to orange blossom honey and thyme honey, which are probably the ones we use the most. And then we use this unprocessed, really raw Ethiopian honey for Bitches Brew. Homebrewers can make three super-hot teas, to release the aromatics, and try three different honeys of the same volume and figure what they like. Have a giant tea party.

ARE THERE ANY FRUITS, VEGETABLES, OR HERBS ON YOUR RADAR?

I hear you can make a good beer with parsley, sage, rosemary, and thyme. Is that too self-serving for [the collaboration beer Dogfish Head/Stone/Victory] Saison du BUFF? This palm fruit, or dom is what it's called in Egypt, is a really pungent, molassesy fruit that's dried. I pulled it out of a market in Cairo and smuggled it back in a camera bag. We're going to brew about 22 pounds (10 kg) in a 5-gallon (19 L) batch.

ANY RECOMMENDATIONS FOR BALANCING FRUIT WITH THE HOPS AND BARLEY?

I'd just say there are some styles that work well in the context of hop-forward beers. We've had no luck with raisins or cherries working in hoppy beers. We've had great luck with apricots. Certain raspberries and acidic blueberries can work well. Our Aprihop came from us playing around with hop varieties that the growers said had notes of apricots.

Lots of different hop varieties [are] described as grapefruit notes or pineapple notes. Why not take one of those significant notes in the hops and amplify the fruit it's referencing? The hops you see describing a flavor of fruit—that's a natural jumping-off point.

There's no substitute for personal expression and subjectivity and volume. Too much peppercorn for one person isn't enough for another.

IS THIS TO SUGGEST WHEN YOU'RE FEELING CREATIVE, WE SHOULD KEEP AWAY HOPS THAT HAVE CAT URINE?

Oddly enough, no—they go so well together. We made a beer with saliva, so all I'm going to say is "urine-vited" to try our newest beer. But pineapple is one fruit that I think has not been played around with enough.

I WANTED TO ASK ABOUT THAT BECAUSE OF PINEAPPLE'S HIGH ACID CONTENT.

The acid content scares people, but blueberries have a high acid content and a lot of brewers have successfully brewed with that. We're friendly with the guys at 21st Amendment who make a watermelon-wheat. Watermelon doesn't have a lot of acid, but brewers stayed away from it for a long time because you needed so much volume to make an impact on the flavor. But they did a great job.

AND HOW COME YOU WEREN'T ON THE LEADING EDGE OF THE BACON BEER FRONT?

Yeah, that one did get away from us. Garrett Oliver made a really fun bacon beer, with just a tiny bit a few years ago and brought it to GABF [Great American Beer Festival]. No, I don't think we'll be doing a bacon beer, but we're psyched other breweries are out there flying their pork flag.

BACON ASIDE, WHAT ADVICE DO YOU HAVE FOR HOMEBREWERS?

Carboys are cheap. Split batches into different carboys and add fruits and spices at different points. The awesome thing about that is you have two or three different versions of your beer with the same wort and you're creating a conversation with your friends when they come over. That's a great way to figure out what your tastes are geared to.

BREWING TIP: FRUIT AND HOPS

Sam dry-hops his fruit-IPA hybrid Aprihop with Amarillo hops. This creates a beer that balances fruit sweetness with bitter and combines the floral, citrus hop notes with the juicy apricot fruit.

When first brewed in 2003, the 21 percent alcohol, 120 IBU 120 Minute IPA from Dogfish Head redefined the bounds of IPAs. (Please excuse the plastic cup.)

THE PATH TO STRONG BEER IS PAVED, PAINTED, AND PATROLLED BY BREWING YEAST. SURE, THERE ARE OTHER CONSTRAINTS. YOU MIGHT NEED A LARGER MASH TUN, OR A THICKER GRIST TO ACCOMMODATE THE TUN YOU HAVE. YOU MIGHT KEEP YOUR KETTLE ON THE HEAT LONGER TO BOIL OFF MORE WATER. AND YOU CAN SUPPLEMENT MALT WITH EASILY FERMENTABLE SUGAR TO LIGHTEN THE BODY.

CHAPTER 11: BREWING BIG BEER

You can do all these things or none of them; the biggest factor in a high-alcohol brew is picking the right yeast strain and keeping it happy. In reverence for the magical little *Saccharomyces*, brewers will talk about having a relationship with their yeast, or even caring for it like a child.

INTRODUCTION TO BIG BEER

Making big beer and doing it well is less about ingredients and more about brewing process. By pushing beer to its limits, you lose the wiggle room and shortcuts that make normal beers relatively easy to brew. And at the heart of big, extreme beer you have a focus on yeast, the engine behind brewing. To make good beer, you need happy yeast, but for high-alcohol brews you want euphoric yeast. Even if strong or extreme beer doesn't appeal to you, all the methods relating to it can be applied to any beer for improved results.

In this chapter, you'll learn about:

- **How much yeast to use**
- **Making a yeast starter**
- **Brewing with champagne yeast**
- **High-strength strains**

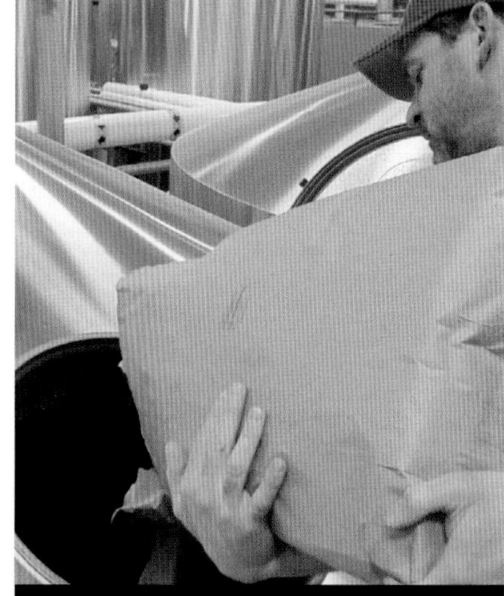

Pizza Port Carlsbad's Jeff Bagby adds sugar to a collaboration strong scotch ale at Stone Brewing Co. The yeast pitch rate for this 9 percent beer was targeted to be 20 million cells per milliliter of wort.

Poured here at the Borefts Bier Festival, the 26 percent alcohol Black Damnation V was created using eisbock techniques at Belgian brewery De Struise.

There is no perfect pitching rate, but big beers need more yeast.

PITCHING RATE FOR YEAST

There is no perfect pitching rate, but big beers need more yeast. Generally speaking, a beer needs 0.75 to 1.5 million yeast cells per milliliter of wort for every degree Plato (0.004 specific gravity). One million cells is a good starting point for your average homebrew. That means if you brew a 5-gallon (19 L) batch of pale ale with a starting gravity of 14 Plato (1.056), you need 266 billion yeast cells (1,000,000 x 19,000 x 14).

Homebrewer yeast packs and vials contain a little more than 100 billion yeast cells. This is adequate for most beers below a starting gravity of 1.068 (17 Plato); however, a higher pitching rate provides a more complete fermentation to prevent unwanted residual sugars, and faster fermentation, which helps prevent infection.

Phenol-driven beers, like German wheat beers or Belgian ales, are the exception to the "more yeast is better" mentality. These styles actually benefit from slight underpitching to accentuate the phenols. A 100 billion–cell pack can actually be ideal. Overpitching can completely eliminate the flavor profile.

Stronger lagers need more yeast than average. In general, lagers require twice the normal amount of yeast necessary to overcome the colder pitching temperature, which slows the yeast. Some homebrewers will pitch their lagers warm, in the 60°F (16°C) range, but this can lead to unwanted fruit esters.

MAKING A STARTER

Starters are essentially small batches of beer that are brewed for the sole purpose of propagating yeast to increase your pitching rate. Pitching your packet or vial into a healthy environment will typically double your yeast count.

The basic tried-and-true recipe is:

100 g light malt extract (LME)

1 L water

2 g (½ tsp) yeast nutrient

Hops will do nothing for yeast health, so they never enter the equation. Otherwise, this is a roughly 1.040 gravity wort, which is an ideal condition for yeast. Any higher gravity would begin to add undue stress on your yeast, but lower would be inefficient.

Boil the mixture for 15 to 20 minutes, then cool to room temperature and pour into a sanitary vessel covered with tinfoil. Shake the cooled wort to aerate and pitch your yeast. Ferment for 24 to 36 hours and either pitch into your full batch of beer, or refrigerate (for up to a week) until your wort is ready.

The basic 1-liter starter will increase your cell count by 50 percent, and a 2-liter starter of the same relative strength will about double the count. However, regular agitation of the starter will about double your yeast cell count in a 1-liter starter and nearly triple the count in a 2-liter.

That agitation can come from a stir plate that spins a small metal pill in the bottom of the starter with magnets, or by simply shaking the starter every hour. By disturbing the starter, you introduce more fuel (oxygen) for the yeast while removing CO_2, which inhibits growth.

A homemade stir plate demonstrates its whirlpool effect.

A small yeast starter is ready to inoculate the wort. Often homebrewers will also make overnight starters in growlers.

CHAMPAGNE FERMENTATION

Champagne yeast is so voracious in its fermentation that it can convert sugars most yeast can't make a dent in. While most beer yeast strains peter out above 10 percent ABV, common champagne strains have an alcohol tolerance of about 17 percent. Because of this virility, nearly all of the strongest beers in the world use a second fermentation with champagne yeast to ferment out remaining sugar and boost alcohol content.

Despite its strength, champagne yeast still needs a healthy environment and should be added while the beer is still fermenting strongly. Add the champagne yeast when a beer has reached half to two-thirds of its alcohol. To find this, check your wort gravity every twenty-four hours after pitching to observe when it is two-thirds of the way from your starting to your estimated final gravity.

AGING AND CONDITIONING

Not all beer styles require the same period of aging, despite their strength. A 9 percent double IPA or Belgian tripel could be ready to bottle within three weeks of brewing, while a 9 percent stout could take months to mellow out. Or it could be ready in four weeks.

There are only two real points of consensus among brewers (and a few would probably still disagree). First is that at more than 10 percent alcohol, a beer needs more serious aging, in the realm of three months. Second, cellar temperature, 50°F to 55°F (10°C to 13°C), is the ideal environment to let beer mature. This colder temperature improves yeast flocculation (dropping out of suspension), but is still warm enough to let the yeast do its magic of absorbing off-flavors and lending complexity to existing characters.

CHOOSING HEALTHY YEAST

Purely pitching hundreds of billions of yeast cells is a good start, but like any living thing, yeast needs to be properly fed. Basic minerals such as copper, calcium, iron, and nitrogen are all required, and malted barley is an excellent source of these. If you're brewing high-gravity beer or a hybrid with honey, fruit, or juice taking up a large portion of the recipe, ½ teaspoon of yeast nutrient per 5 gallons (0.1 g per liter) of wort will ensure happy yeast.

Once the nutrients are available to yeast, it just needs oxygen to get working on the sugar. The stronger the wort, of course, the more oxygen necessary. Wort needs 8 to 15 parts-per-million (ppm) of oxygen to properly support the yeast. Eight ppm is about the maximum saturation reached from the air around us, and shaking your carboy of wort for 45 seconds will reach that.

HIGH-TEST YEAST STRAINS

Thanks to yeast banks like White Labs and Wyeast, alcohol-tolerant yeast is available to suit nearly every style of beer. The British Isles alone have Irish, Scottish, and English strains capable of 12 percent brews, and each with its own twist. There are at least as many Belgian strains and more than enough clean American versions. There are a few strains, however, that stand out for brewers looking to push the limits of high-gravity beer. Remember that the alcohol tolerance levels where yeast stops producing are not absolute; they depend on yeast health and conditions.

White Labs/Wyeast Name	Alcohol Tolerance (% ABV)	White Labs/Wyeast	Character
Trappist/High-Gravity Trappist Ale	12 to 15	Both	Balanced mix of Belgian esters and phenols with a generous temperature range and high attenuation.
Belgian Golden Ale/Belgian Strong Ale	12 to 15	Both	Favors ester production but also maintains malt character despite excellent (high) attenuation.
California/American	11 to 15	Both	A powerful, clean-fermenting strain favored for malty and hoppy brews alike.
Irish Ale	11 to 12	Both	Creates a slight fruitiness and crisp beer with low amounts of diacetyl.
Super High Gravity Ale Yeast	25	White Labs only	Requires a lot of attention (see whitelabs.com for details) but can produce very strong malty beers with some fruit esters.
Zurich Lager	15	White Labs only	This lager yeast ferments clean with minimal sulfur and diacetyl.
Champagne Yeast/Pasteur Champagne	17	Both	This superdry wine (and cider) yeast can take on Belgian characteristics when used in extreme beers. It's best used in combination with beer yeast, for more complete fermentation.

For big beers, pure oxygen is necessary for higher saturation levels. The basic technique is to fill the open space in the top of a fermenter with oxygen from a tank before shaking. This will provide close to the 15 ppm of oxygen for yeast.

You can also copy professional brewers and use a stainless steel (easy to clean) diffuser stone hooked up to an oxygen tank. A stone with 0.5 micron pores can reach 15 ppm in 60 seconds.

Additionally, it's worth risking oxidation to aerate beer midfermentation if yeast is prematurely slowing down. If your fermentation appears to be lagging (the airlock will be bubbling less) before the beer is about two-thirds of the way fermented, re-aerate with a diffuser stone or by shaking the carboy with the airlock removed to reintroduce oxygen.

White Labs California Ale yeast has a 15 percent alcohol tolerance before it stops fermenting.

REDHOOK
ESB
BREW DOG
www.brewdog.com
www.brewdog.com

James Watt (right) with his friend and BrewDog brewer and cofounder, Martin Dickie (left).

INTERVIEW WITH: JAMES WATT: COFOUNDER, BREWDOG, FRASERBURGH, SCOTLAND

JAMES WATT AND HIS BREWDOG COFOUNDER, MARTIN DICKIE, WERE COMPLETELY DISILLUSIONED WITH BEERS IN THE UK. MARTIN SAYS, "THERE WAS NOTHING BETWEEN GENERIC MASS-MARKET MONOLITHIC INDUSTRIAL BEERS AND THE LITTLE GUYS HERE MAKING BEERS THAT WERE QUITE SLEEPY, QUITE STUFFY, OLD-FASHIONED, AND CONSTRAINED BY TRADITION."

Watching the American craft beer movement and "guys just following their muse," BrewDog launched a brewery that handcrafted beers across flavor spectrums, styles, ingredients, and ABV—including the world's strongest beer.

SO THIS IS WHAT KICK-STARTED BREWDOG?

We started making U.S.-influenced beers on the weekend in our garage. And when we started our business in 2007, our biggest goal was to make other people as passionate about good beers as we are. More stylistic diversity, pushing the envelope, being bolder—that's what we set out to do.

HAVE YOU BEEN SURPRISED BY SOME OF THE NEGATIVE REACTION TO YOUR HIGH-ALCOHOL BEERS?

We've enticed negative reactions and been quite good at acting surprised when it happens. The controversy over high-strength beer has given us a platform to communicate ideas about beer. We want to open a debate of what beer is, how you can enjoy it, and just show people there is an alternative to the beers out there.

IS THAT PART OF WHAT DREW YOU TO THE CHALLENGE OF MAKING THE WORLD'S STRONGEST BEER?

We knew we were going to get a lot of publicity for this, but we wanted to use it to challenge people's perception of what beer is. We also pushed the envelope to take our favorite beer styles and see how far we can take them, see what that would do to the flavor.

In the UK, "beer" is something where you go out, drink eight pints of something that's cold and fizzy. You fall over, have a kebab, wake up with a sore head, and tick Saturday night off your to-do list. We wanted to introduce people to a completely new approach to beer: beer that's made with passion and enthusiasm, no junk in it, [and which] people can drink for the flavor and experience, not just the effect.

"DON'T TRY THIS AT HOME" DEPARTMENT: CHEST FREEZER

Normally a chest freezer is modified with a temperature regulator to accommodate lager brewing, but with a freezer's normal -20°F (-28°C) setting, it can be used for ice distillation. After placing a conditioning beer in the freezer, every week or so, drain off the liquid from the ice into a new vessel. Repeat until the beverage is fortified to your satisfaction. Of course, distillation (even amateur) without a license is illegal in the United States and many other countries.

BrewDog makes beer ranging from 1.1 percent to 55 percent alcohol.

YOUR STRONGEST ALES USE A FREEZE-DISTILLATION PROCESS, BUT THERE'S CONTROVERSY OVER WHETHER THEY'RE STILL BEER AFTER THEY ARE DISTILLED.

I think it's beer. I think the term freeze-distillation confuses people. In normal distillation, you use extreme heat to purify. We use extreme cold. We're concentrating the flavors, aroma, and mouthfeel, and turning up the volume by taking the water out. That's where the big distinction is.

HAVE YOU COME UP WITH A BETTER TERM THAN FREEZE-DISTILLATION?

We should have thought of something more eloquent before we launched. Now we call it "penguin-temperatures brewing."

WILL YOU KEEP UP THE FIGHT FOR THE STRONGEST BEER?

I think we're all out. We just wanted to make three high-strength beers. First was our stout—we brought that up to 32 percent—that was Tactical Nuclear Penguin. And after that, we wanted to make a quadruple IPA and hopped the hell out of it at every single stage. We actually ice-hopped the beer. [Sink The Bismark] is 41 percent but has a huge hoppy nose, cinnamon, toffee-biscuit malt sweetness, and you still get an avalanche of hops. It sort of hammers your tongue.

WOULD YOU BE WILLING TO SHARE YOUR TECHNIQUES?

Yeah! We welcome other people to take up the challenge and push it further than we've done or refine the technique. That's what craft beer is all about. What amazed me when I went to the U.S. was how open everyone was. It's improved our beer massively. Brewers in the UK are so closed, guys hardly even tell you what size bottle they use. If anyone wants to chat about our beers or where to find penguin suits, we'd be happy to talk.

LET'S DIVE INTO JUST THAT.

The inspiration came from the German eisbock technique, which is used to take a beer from 8 percent to 12, 13, or even 14. The key thing is water has a higher freezing temperature than alcohol. So if you can chill your beer low enough, what freezes first isn't going to be the alcohol.

WHAT KIND OF VESSEL DID YOU USE?

Most people use their cylindroconical tanks and then get glycol that can go to -10°C (14°F). You pump this around your tank; that's what we tried to do initially. We got the beer down to -7°C (19°F), but the freezing locked up the valves and inlets and outlets of the tank. We calculated that to get to 32 percent, we'd have to reach -20°C (-4°F).

Tactical Nuclear Penguin, at 32 percent ABV, was BrewDog's first of three record-breaking beers.

SO YOU WERE STALLED.

Later, I was on a fishing boat and thinking about how to do it. Instead of freezing the tank, what about putting the beer in a container and taking it somewhere cold? We're in a fishing town, so the original idea was to take it to a blast freezer where they freeze fish. So we got a 500-liter container and filled it with beer we'd aged for eighteen months. Then the problem was that because the blast freezer smelled quite strongly of fish, it might taint the beer. We reluctantly left it in there for twelve hours and it didn't freeze a single bit. We thought if we have to leave it for ages, we definitely don't want to leave it in there and get a mackerel-infused imperial stout. A few days later I was eating ice cream from a local factory and I thought we could persuade them to give us some space.

COULD YOU BE CERTAIN THEY WEREN'T MAKING A MACKEREL SORBET?

It was worth the risk. After three days it was -3°C (27°F), despite the ambient temperature being -20°C (-4°F). After ten days, it got down to -7°C (19°F). Every five days, we'd transfer and leave a little ice behind. Tactical Nuclear Penguin took six weeks, and when we got it tested, it was 28 percent. It amazed us how much beer we lost. We tested the water as well and it'd have 3 or 4 percent alcohol in it. You'll start out with 1,000 liters (264 gallons) and end up with less than a couple hundred bottles.

HOW FAR WERE YOU ABLE TO PUSH THE ABV BEFORE YOU STARTED THE PENGUIN-TEMPERATURE PROCESS?

For the End of History, we pushed it to 20 percent ABV with a champagne yeast from the start. It can operate at higher alcohol levels and is able to convert proteins and sugars ale yeast can't.

SO WHY NOT PITCH AFTER AN INITIAL ALE FERMENTATION?

When you're pitching yeast at 11 percent, it's not happy and it's tough to make headway. If we start with the champagne yeast, it's not just feeding on starch and it gets a good head of steam up, so when it hits 12 percent, it's already working quite well. Even then, the champagne yeast, at 15 percent, is going to start to die off.

Every four hours, we'd take a tiny bit of sugar and put it into the fermenting wort, and it was just enough to keep the yeast alive and keep the fermentation going. It was a bit like having a baby. Every four hours, day or night, it got some care and attention. Gave the tank a big hug and kiss, crossed our fingers, and hoped that it kept fermenting. We were able to get the base beer just over 20 percent.

DID YOU GET THE FLAVOR YOU WANTED? CHAMPAGNE YEAST HAS A REPUTATION FOR NOT BRINGING ANY CHARACTER.

We found when you push a champagne yeast as we did, the flavor characteristic was very reminiscent of classic Belgian yeast flavor characteristics. That's why with the End of History, the flavors you develop in a Belgian blond ale would be really beneficial once we got up to 55 percent. We thought this kind of vanilla, banana, clove, ester mix would help soften and balance the massive amount of alcohol.

FINALLY, FOR THE END OF HISTORY, WHAT INSPIRED YOU TO PACKAGE THE BOTTLES INSIDE TAXIDERMIED STOATS AND SQUIRRELS?

With the 55 percent beer we made, because it was the last one, we wanted to do something that was quite epic with the packaging. And it infused three things we're very passionate about: craft beer, art, and taxidermy.

For the End of History, BrewDog decided to try something new for its packaging.

Firestone Walker Brewing conditions a portion of every pale ale batch in oak with their patented Firestone Union oak barrel brewing system.

IN THE STAINLESS, SANITARY WORLD OF BREWING, WOOD-AGED BEER STANDS OUT AS A PLACE WHERE SCIENCE MUST GIVE WAY TO THE ART OF BREWING. BARREL- AND WOOD-AGED BEER STANDS AS ONE OF THE BEACONS OF EXTREME BREWING BY PUSHING THE BOUNDARIES AND FLAVOR OF BEER. BARRELS ARE A DEVIL TO CONTROL, AND BREWERS ARE OFTEN AT THEIR MERCY, WHICH CAN BRING AN AMAZINGLY COMPLEX NEW CHARACTER TO OLD RECIPES, OR DESTINE A BATCH FOR A DRAIN-POUR. IRONICALLY, BARREL CONDITIONING IS A THROWBACK TO THE DAYS BEFORE COPPER AND STAINLESS BREWING VESSELS.

CHAPTER 12: BARREL AGING

The two main options for barrels (and thus wood additives) are American and French oak. Both impart vanilla, but American oak has a more aggressive character with lower tannins. Technically, American oak can come from anywhere within the United States, which does not guarantee a consistent flavor, so check with your cooperage (barrel maker) for the origin. The white oak from Oregon, for example, is a different species that holds more in common with European oaks.

French oak, the more traditional barrel wood for wine, imparts a subtler, spicy character with high tannin levels. The wood has a tighter grain, meaning it releases flavor more slowly and there's less oxygenation. French oak proponents claim the slower extraction produces a more complex character. New French barrels typically run double the price of American oak, but Hungarian oak has a history as being the less-expensive substitute.

In this chapter, you'll learn about:

- **Types of wood used**
- **Effects of temperature and barrel size**
- **Methods for adding wood**
- **Preparing a barrel**
- **Dosing spirits**

French cooper Alain Nunes handcrafts three barrels a day for the Château Margaux wine estate.

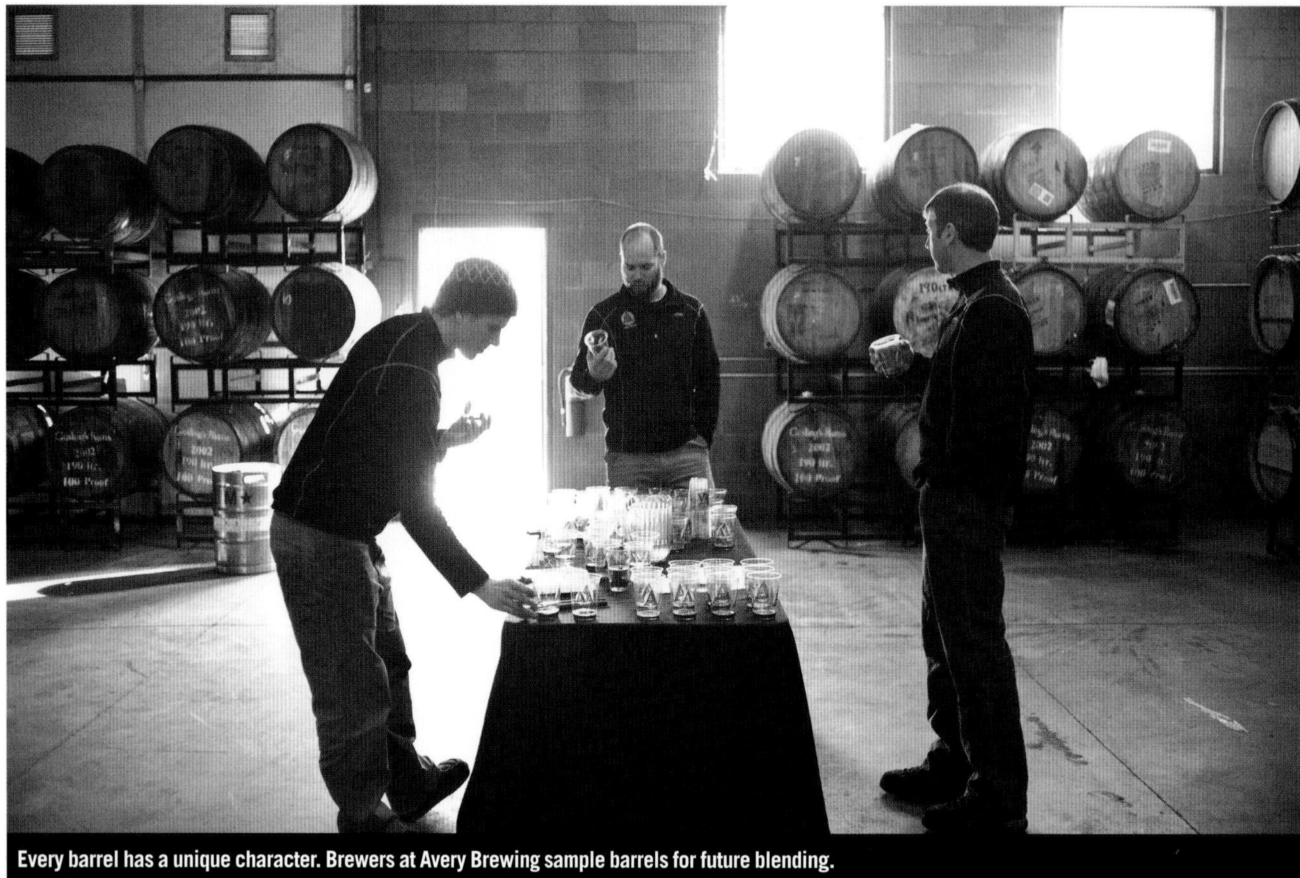

Every barrel has a unique character. Brewers at Avery Brewing sample barrels for future blending.

TOASTED WOOD

Just like specialty grains, wood is dried and toasted to varying degrees to achieve particular flavor profiles. Most brewers use a medium or medium-plus toasted oak; however, bourbon barrels are also charred to create a charcoal layer over the toasted oak. Naturally, toast levels vary by cooperage, but some basic profiles hold:

- Lighter toasts are more subtle with fresh fruit flavors.
- Medium toasts project more vanilla and spice.
- Heavy toasts show more caramelized and roasted notes and need the shortest maturation time.

WOOD AND TEMPERATURE

Just like yeast, wood also responds to temperature changes. A rise will draw your brew into the wood, while a drop in temperature pushes it back out. A mildly unstable temperature may not actually be a bad thing if you're looking to speed your infusion process.

SIZE MATTERS

It's easy to talk about barrels and wood in terms of weight or capacity, but surface area determines the rate of flavor extraction. The smaller the barrel, the greater the ratio of surface area to liquid.

Although a professional brewer might leave his ale in a 60-gallon (227 L) barrel for six months, a homebrew-scale 5-gallon (19 L) barrel can work its magic in a mere two weeks. The same theory works for other forms of oak. Oak powder works quicker than thin-cut chips, which then are still faster than cubes and spirals.

BEYOND THE BARREL

Wood additives are largely produced to help vintners supplement a barrel's character when they become neutral and lose their flavor. In the hands of inventive brewers, they can infuse wonderful character into any beer style and fairly accurately recreate a bourbon barrel at a fraction of the cost and headache. However, additives cannot perfectly mimic the barrel-aging process—the porous structure of wood allows for slight oxidation. Like most flavor additions to beer, oak and other wood additives should be added to the conditioning tank as beer ages.

OAK ESSENCE

Available in liquid or powder, this is the fastest way to add oak character, but it is considered the least consistent. Dosage runs from 1 to 4 ounces per 5 gallons (1.5 to 6 g per liter). The liquid is instant, and the powder needs no more than a week. Expect a lightly toasted oak character, and be careful to filter out the powder; otherwise, your beer will have a distinct sawdust taste.

OAK CHIPS

These roughly cut wood chips release their flavor in as little as a week. They're generally regarded as a more aggressive method and character, but have proved to be a great addition to hoppy beers. They are also the easiest way to simulate a bourbon barrel. Here's how:

- Soak the chips (or any of the other solid options) in your favorite bourbon overnight.
- Drain or include the liquid depending on the desired intensity.
- Add the chips to the beer for just one to four weeks. You can always just add sanitized (steamed for 15 minutes) chips and bourbon separately.

Typically, 2 ounces (55 g) of chips will make a noticeable impact after a week in a 5-gallon (19 L) batch.

SPIRALS

Produced by the experts at The Barrel Mill, these American and French oak spirals minimize mess and claim to do eight months of maturation in six weeks. Although professionals use 4-foot (1.2 m) segments in their tanks, one or two 8-inch (20 cm) spirals will do for most 5-gallon (19 L) batches.

BEANS AND CUBES

Beans and cubes are designed to release flavor at the same rate as traditional barrels, and the producers claim the slower extraction creates a smoother, more complex character. They need at least two months of aging (six months is ideal), but they can also mature and be reused for up to a year of total contact time. Use 2 to 3 ounces per 5 gallons (1.5 to 4.5 g per liter).

ADDING SPIRITS

Numerous laws (which vary by locale) prevent commercial brewers from adding straight liquor to beer, even if it's just flavoring. Homebrewers, however, are safe from these regulations.

One cup (235 ml) of spirits for 5 gallons (19 L) generally provides balanced flavors. Adding 1.5 ounces per gallon (11 g per liter) will bring a noticeable aroma, flavor, and lighter mouthfeel.

PREPARE YOUR BARREL

If you dive in and either buy a small wine barrel or organize a group brewing session to fill a larger bourbon barrel, prep your barrel to make sure your beer doesn't go to waste.

INSPECT FOR INFECTION

Your first step is to check for infection. Stick your nose in the bunghole and take a big whiff. If there are any signs of acetic acid (smells like vinegar), nothing good can come from the barrel. If the barrel is used, pour out and collect any remaining liquid. It'll give you a taste of what you can expect from the aging. New barrels should have a sweet oak smell.

HOT WATER SWELL AND CLEANING

The repeated rinses from swelling a new barrel (sealing the cracks) should be all the cleaning needed. If you have a used barrel, wash out any deposits with hot water. To swell, fill the barrel one-tenth full with hot water. Put the bung in place and slosh the barrel to coat the inside with water. Let it stand for 30 minutes on its head, then repeat on the other side. Drain and refill all the way to test for any seepage.

In the hands of inventive brewers, wood additives can infuse wonderful character into any beer style and fairly accurately recreate a bourbon barrel at a fraction of the cost and headache.

Eight-inch (20 cm) oak infusion spirals offer an ideal compromise for homebrewers seeking an authentic barrel character without committing to an actual (and expensive) barrel. Most 5-gallon (19 L) batches require only one or two spirals.

SCOTT'S OBSESSION WITH OAK BARRELS PREDATES HIS LOVE OF BREWING, WHICH SAYS A LOT CONSIDERING HE WAS HOOKED ON HOMEBREWING AT AGE SEVENTEEN. NOW AT THE HELM OF HIS OWN BREWERY, HE PRODUCES ABOUT A DOZEN DIFFERENT BARREL-AGED BEERS YEARLY.

Scott Vaccaro stands with the apple brandy barrels used for his Golden Delicious American tripel and Smoke from the Oak porter.

INTERVIEW WITH: SCOTT VACCARO: FOUNDER, CAPTAIN LAWRENCE BREWING CO., PLEASANTVILLE, NEW YORK, U.S.

HOW LONG HAVE YOU BEEN IN BUSINESS?

We moved in August of 2005 and were brewing by December.

THAT'S A QUICK TURNAROUND. I COULD HAVE TAKEN A LESSON FROM YOU.

It was the most stressful four months of my life. I think I aged about five years.

YOU WERE AN AVID HOMEBREWER FIRST.

I was seventeen years old and went over to my buddy's house after school to hang out, like any other day. I walked in the kitchen and my friend's dad was standing over the stove, stirring a big pot. I asked what he was doing and he said, "Making beer."

At that point in my life, beer was pretty taboo. I wasn't close to being legal to drink, though I dabbled in my fair share of Schaefer longnecks. I asked him if he'd show me how to make beer. I couldn't believe you could do that at home. My parents were happy to let me do it at home as long as I kept it under control and didn't go try to intoxicate the neighborhood kids. I immediately bought Charlie Papazian's book, *The New Complete Joy of Home Brewing*, and that was the start of my brewing career.

YOU TOOK A DIVERSION FROM BREWING IN COLLEGE.

I ended up following my father's footsteps of going to Villanova to be an accountant. I continued to homebrew but didn't know I could make a career of it. While reading Zymurgy my freshman year, I came across UC-Davis, did a little research, and realized I could get my bachelor's in fermentation science. I immediately called home and said, "Listen, accounting is great and all, but I'm going to fail out of this school if you keep me here. I was born to brew."

WHAT STARTED YOUR INTEREST IN BARREL AGING?

This is going to sound strange, but I always had a fascination with oak barrels. At first, it had nothing to do with beer. I remember being much younger, fourteen, and trying to come up with different blends of iced tea I could stick in an oak barrel.

When I started homebrewing, I was constantly trying to formulate in my head how many batches I'd have to brew to fill up an oak barrel that was 50 or 60 gallons (190 or 227 L), but it didn't make any sense. I'd have to kill myself brewing for a week straight and wouldn't be able to drink it all.

We happened to open Captain Lawrence on the same street as a winery, and not having anyone to tell me what not to spend my money on, I procured some 60-gallon (227 L) red wine barrels to fill up with smoked porter. I just kept buying barrels. We're a pretty cramped location, but I have sixty or seventy.

WHEN YOU BEGIN A BARREL-AGED BEER, DO YOU HAVE A SPECIFIC RESULT IN MIND, OR IS THERE AN INTERPLAY WITH ALLOWING IT TO EXPRESS ITSELF?

It goes both ways. We've been doing it for five years pretty consistently and we're still working those kinks out. A few of the beers we use particular barrels, like apple brandy barrels for Golden Delicious, when we have a specific goal in mind. And then we have some of sour beers where we're taking wine barrels, and sure we'd love to get a little bit of the oak flavor, vanilla, some of the wine, but we just say, "Okay, let's see what happens."

CAN YOU ACHIEVE MASTERY OVER THE BARRELS?

If you consistently use the barrels in the same way, you can control some of the flavors, but there are always wild card barrels out there. Right now, we don't have temperature control over our barrels, and in New York we get huge swings where it can be 105°F (41°C) in the brewery and I'll freak out. Then, in the winter it gets into the 50s and 60s.

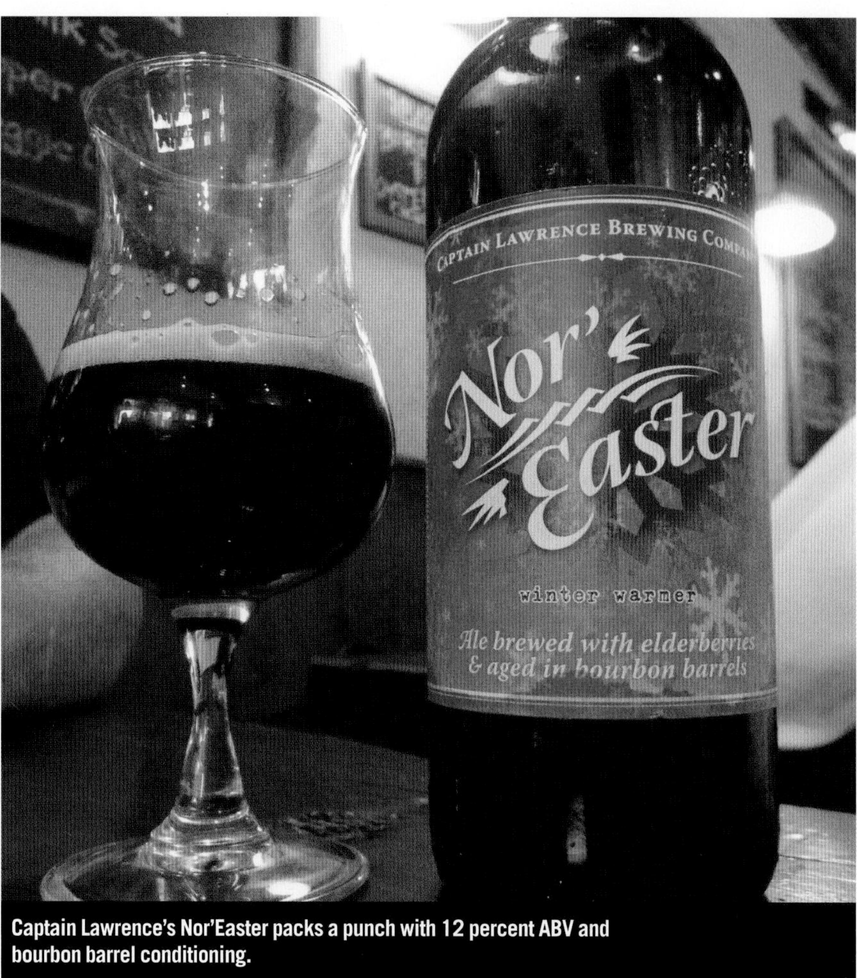

Captain Lawrence's Nor'Easter packs a punch with 12 percent ABV and bourbon barrel conditioning.

WHEN YOU HAVE BARREL-AGED BEER THAT TURNS OUT NOT-SO-GOOD, IS THERE A WAY TO SAVE IT, BLEND IT OUT?

We've dumped a lot of beer. If you're going for a sour beer and it's a little too acidic, you can use small portions and blend it into something that's a little softer, and it adds depth of flavor. I always tell homebrewers: Listen, if you're going to do a barrel beer, brew ten gallons, put five in a barrel and five straight up that you can blend in later if you need. You can also see the difference and have more room to play.

SO WHAT ARE YOU UP TO NEXT WITH BARREL AGING?

We're releasing a new formulation of the Smoke from the Oak series. We haven't had huge success with expressing the true flavors of those barrels without getting some off-flavors. We've upped the alcohol content from our regular smoked porter to give it a little more stability at 9.5 to 10 percent.

WHEN IT COMES TO AGING AND THE BARRELS, IS THERE A RULE OF THUMB TO HOW LONG IT WILL TAKE?

With the whiskey and rum and the apple brandy, we've had varying degrees of success with extracting the flavor over time. We've found in our brewery, if you let them sit for more than eight months, they get hot—they just soak way too much. [With] the wine barrels, if you don't want microbial activity, keep it cool and age it a lot longer. So it depends on the spirit and the degree at which you'd like to extract the flavor.

I always tell homebrewers: Listen, if you're going to do a barrel beer, brew ten gallons, put five in a barrel and five straight up that you can blend in later if you need.

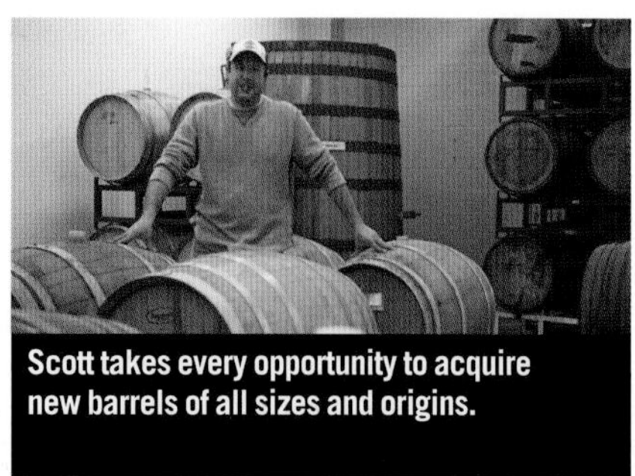

Scott takes every opportunity to acquire new barrels of all sizes and origins.

The first time we did our Golden Delicious, we aged [it] a year, and it was extremely hot. The second time, we did three months, and that was soft. Now we've settled on six months. The rum barrels, on the other hand, come with some serious flavor to them and for those, three months is perfect.

HOW DO YOU CHOOSE THE STYLE OF BEER TO MATCH THE WOOD AND PREVIOUS CONTENTS?

We look for complementary flavors and then also try straight experimentation. Using apple brandy barrels, I thought, was a no-brainer. We use them for our Golden Delicious, which is dry-hopped with Amarillo. [We call it] a Belgian-style American tripel because it expresses these really fruity tropical flavors, and then from the apple brandy barrels, it gets that kind of apple spice and vanilla flavor out of that barrel. For bourbon and rum, we thought strong dark beer, something more traditional would be perfect. I always say, for a homebrewer as a rule of thumb, strong and dark ages well in brown spirit barrels.

We tend to use our wine barrels primarily for sour beers because to get the flavor of wine into a smoked porter or brown ale, the flavors are very subtle. You'll get a nice vanilla and some interesting character, [but] to me the flavors don't justify the time.

LET'S TALK ABOUT WHAT INSPIRES YOU. WHAT'S ON YOUR RADAR?

At the beginning of it all, the inspiration came from Michael Jackson's books. He did such a beautiful job of describing these beers and making me want to drink them. Reading about Cantillon and Boon made me realize there's this whole other world of beers. After reading about these beers while not being able to drink them, when I finally got a chance to try them was a whole 'nother revelation. Now I need to go try to make them or something in style or inspired by.

IT TAKES ME BACK TO THE FIRST TIME I VISITED CANTILLON IN '95, I WAS CLUED IN FROM MICHAEL JACKSON'S BEER HUNTER SHOW.

Yeah, it's amazing. I went over and spent an afternoon drinking there. It was my last stop after six weeks. I stayed in hostels and had a sheet sewn up like a sleeping bag and carried three cases of Cantillon lambic back with me and that was my carry-on.

WHAT DO YOU THINK ABOUT THE UBER-ENTHUSIAST CROWD AND THEIR FASCINATION WITH ANYTHING BARREL AGED?

I just see it as a function of people looking for where they are going to get the next intense flavor. Maybe first it was superhoppy and next it's going to be sour, and they go for barrel aged. I just look at it as the search for the next [intense] flavor.

Captain Lawrence uses Cruzan barrels for its Smoke from the Oak Rum Barrel ale.

BREWING TERMS: HOT AND SOFT ALCOHOL

Used in reference to spirits, and sometimes strong beer, hot refers to a strong, burning alcohol taste and feel. Soft means that a spirit has a mild character. In terms of barrel aging, a beer that's hot has too much character from a spirit, while a soft flavor might be too subtle.

ORGANIC BEER HAS FINALLY ARRIVED, AND NOT JUST BECAUSE IT'S FINALLY GETTING THE SHELF SPACE IT DESERVES. WHILE BEFORE BEER LOVERS COULD WRITE OFF A MARGINAL BATCH OF BEER WITH "WELL, IT IS ORGANIC," THE EXCUSES ARE GONE AND BOTH PROFESSIONAL AND HOMEBREWERS ARE MAKING AWARD-WINNING BEERS WHERE ORGANIC INGREDIENTS ARE THE REASON FOR THE BREW'S SUCCESS, NOT THE EXCUSE FOR ITS LACK THEREOF.

CHAPTER 13: ORGANIC BREWING

Organic brewer Matthew Speckenbach removes spent grains from the lauter tun at Hopworks Urban Brewery.

AN INTRODUCTION TO ORGANIC BEER

Organic beer is defined by using organic ingredients. In the professional world, there are two types of organic beer. There's beer brewed with organic malts but nonorganic hops. For many organic-certification agencies, this qualifies as organic. Then there's beer brewed with both organic hops and organic malts. Great brewers will go a step further and look to reduce waste in their brewing process and adopt environmentally friendly cleaning and sanitizing products.

In this chapter, you'll learn about:

- **What organic beer is**
- **Organic barley**
- **Organic hops**
- **Growing organic hops**

WHAT MAKES IT ORGANIC?

Of beer's four basic ingredients (water, yeast, hops, and barley), only the barley must be certified-organic to call it organic. Legislation may eventually require hops, but if you're a true believer in organic beer, you'll use organic hops anyways. Yeast is a microorganism that only requires a clean environment and sugar to survive and grow. And so long as you brew with clean, filtered water (and why on Earth wouldn't you?), you're safely in the organic camp.

Hops and barley farmers use different organic standards, but you can expect that the products will be grown without chemical fertilizers, pesticides, fungicides, or additives that might find their way into your beer. This approach also ensures a more careful, nurturing approach to cultivating your ingredients. Essentially, you are getting a higher-quality product that's better for the soil, limits pollution, keeps drinking water clean, and supports sustainable farming practices. Who knew beer could do so much good?

HOPS

The fragrant green flowers that give pale ales their zing and balance the sweetness of barleywines have been slow to arrive in organic options. The two-year cycle required to produce a full harvest makes growers reluctant to invest in new plants. To further complicate hop farming, the USDA and National Organic Standards Board decided in 2008 that beers labeled "organic" need not actually use organic hops. Silly as it seems, many organic brewers supported the exception because of the limited supply of organic hops. Of course, without the requirement, many "organic" brewers avoid organic hops for the cheaper and more readily available options anyways.

The fragrant green flowers that give pale ales their zing and balance the sweetness of barleywines have been slow to arrive in organic options.

The United States' organic hop market is a relatively new player in the global market. And although German and Belgian growers are slowly developing and planting new organic varieties, oddly enough, the oldest and most stable source of organic hops has come from New Zealand. The island nation's isolation and temperate climate provide near-perfect growing conditions that never see the likes of downy mildew, verticillium wilt, or other hop diseases. New Zealand growers battle their one pest—the two-spotted mite—through natural predators and use a combination of mussel shells, steam, and grazing sheep to control weeds.

New Zealand growers offer a full range of options, from aroma hops (Motueka, Riwaka) to bittering hops (Green Bullet, Pacific Gem, Pacific Jade) and wonderful dual-purpose hops (Nelson Sauvin). U.S. growers tend toward high–alpha acid bittering hops that are more disease resistant, but are slowly adding more aroma and dual-purpose varieties such as Cascade and Centennial.

BARLEY

Although organic hop farmers tend to be a small and passionate group, the barley farmers are largely growing their crops for the profit margins. The maltsters, such as Briess, Great Western, or Weyermann, who buy grains and malt them for brewing, are the folks you can thank for making dozens of options available today.

In the early days of organic brewing, your options were essentially one base malt and a couple darker specialty grains. Now you can pick from a variety of base malts, even a traditional English pale malt (Warminster), and have the freedom of a full spectrum of specialty grains, from wheat to chocolate and crystal malts, to brew whatever you please.

Organic maltsters produce conventional malts in much greater quantities, but like brewers making organic and conventional beer, their systems are purged of nonorganic ingredients and cleaners when switching over. As they sell both types of malt, they're reluctant to disparage their non-organic products, but many brewers agree that even organic base malt has more flavor.

True organic brewing is more than the sum of its ingredients. It's the dedication to low-impact methods, Earth-friendly farmings, and hands-on love and care for the ingredients. Every pint you raise is a celebration of the soil and purity of ingredients.

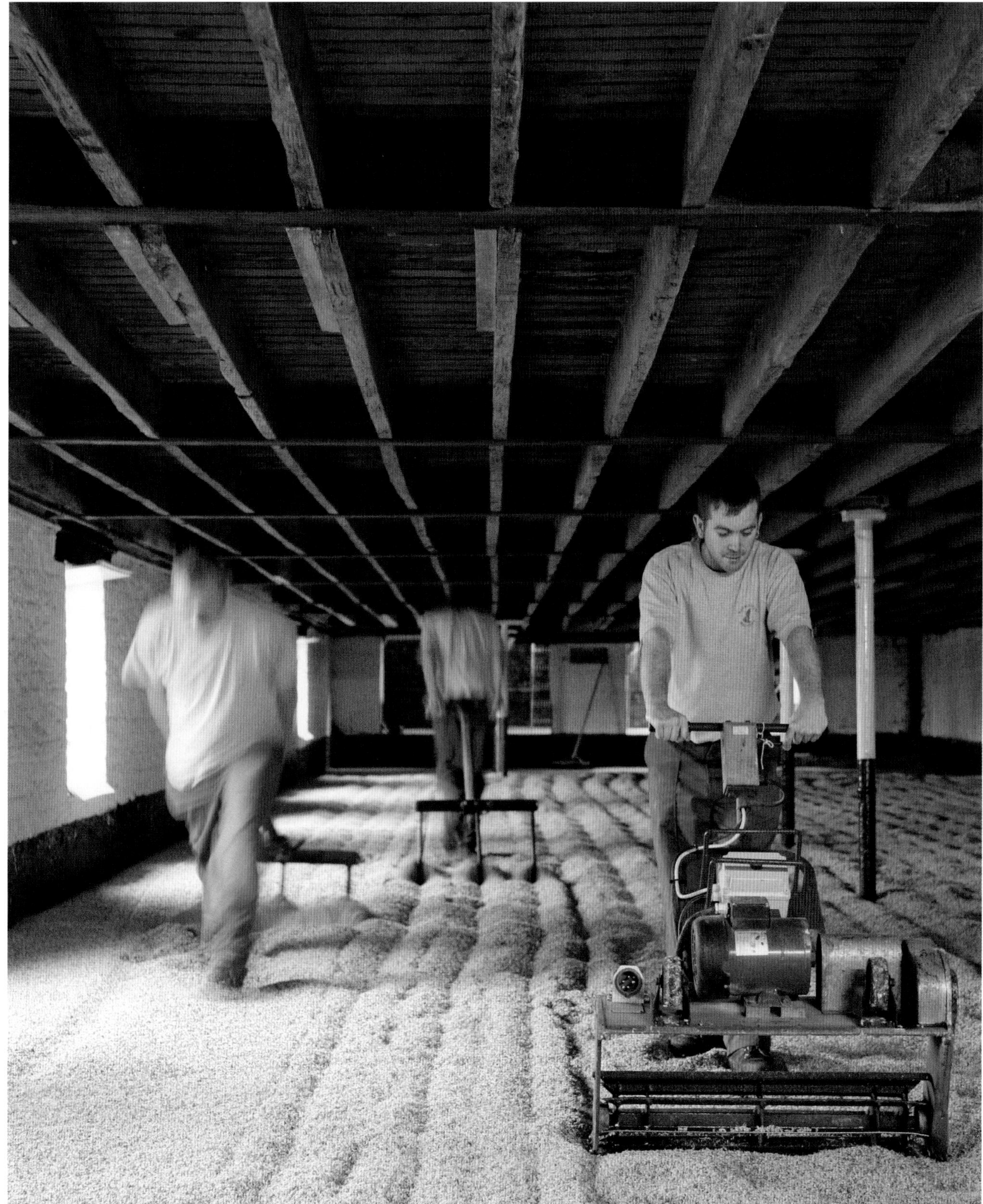

Warminster Malting produces exception grains with the same man-powered barley malting process they've used since 1879.

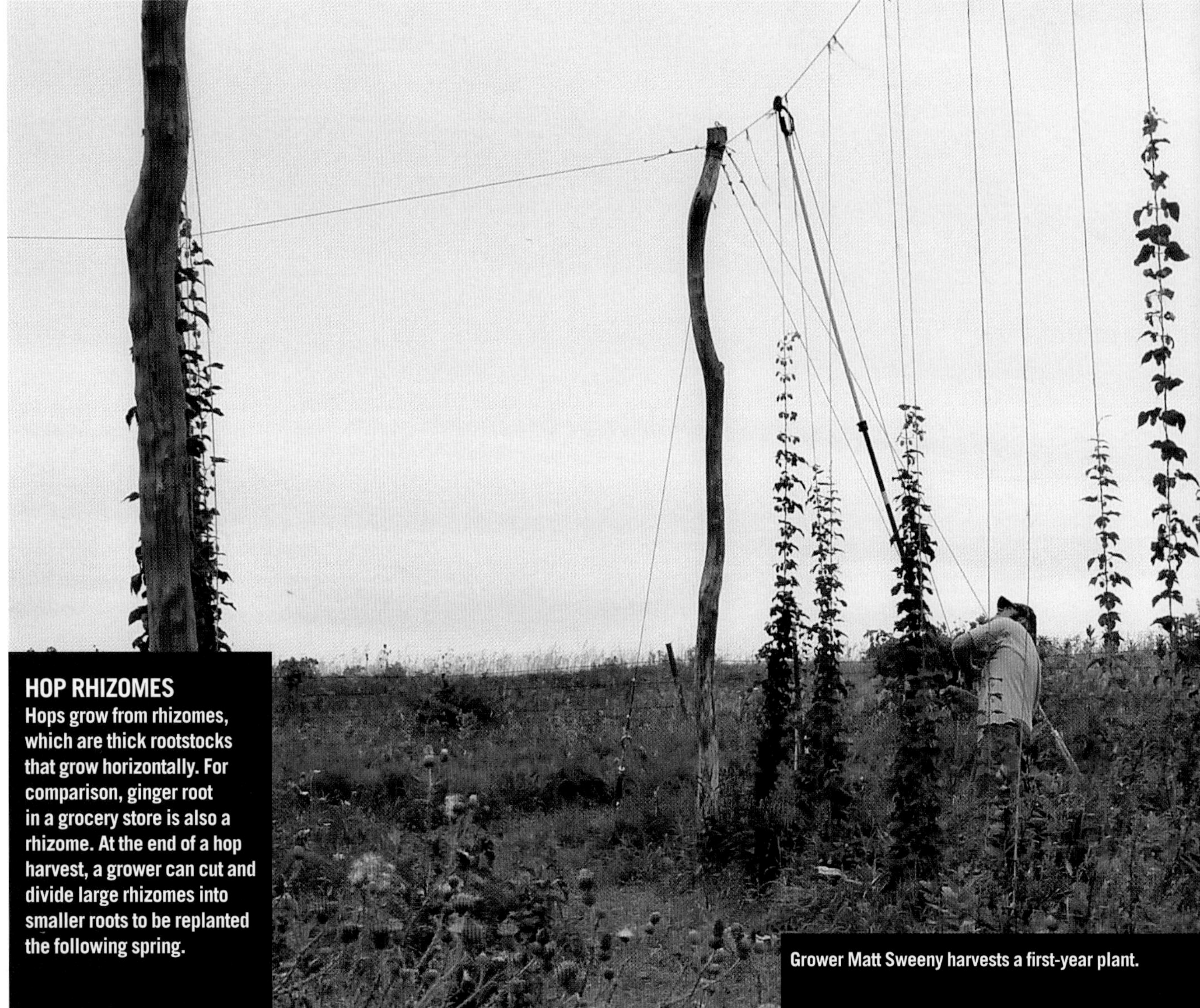

HOP RHIZOMES
Hops grow from rhizomes, which are thick rootstocks that grow horizontally. For comparison, ginger root in a grocery store is also a rhizome. At the end of a hop harvest, a grower can cut and divide large rhizomes into smaller roots to be replanted the following spring.

Grower Matt Sweeny harvests a first-year plant.

GROW YOUR OWN

Growing backyard hops is a great way to add a personal touch to beers, but they're also an attractive trellising plant and bring a rich aroma around harvest time. Hops grow on bines, a vine-like plant that corkscrews up around trellises and wires. Many homebrew stores take preorders for rhizomes, the underground stem and base of the hops plant, over the winter, and they arrive in April for planting.

HOPS SELECTION

Hops are a hearty plant that can flourish in any moderate climate. Historically, hops have been farmed all across the northern half of the United States, the Hallertau region of Germany, and Southeast England. For hotter areas, pick Chinook, Golding, or Liberty. If you have a shorter, colder season, try Fuggle, Hallertau, or Saaz. Hops are bred for aroma, bittering, or a combination of both. Planting hops with both qualities in mind allows you to brew most styles entirely from your own crop, though a mix of resilient hops proves more fruitful.

PLANTING

Rhizomes are planted horizontally with the buds pointing up and thin roots down under an inch (2.5 cm) of loose soil and covered with mulch to trap moisture and provide nutrients. After the last threat of frost, plant the rhizomes at least 4 feet (1.2 m) apart and clear the ground of weeds. Hop plants can grow more than 20 feet (6 m) in a season if given a tall-enough trellis, direct sunlight, and plenty of water.

BEST DISEASE-RESISTANT HOPS

Variety	Usage	Downy Mildew	Powdery Mildew	Verticillium Wilt
Brewers Gold	Bittering	S	MR	MR
Bullion	Bittering	S	MR	R
Cascade	Aroma	MR	MR	MR
Chinook	Bittering	MS	MR	R
Crystal	Aroma	R	S	R
Hallertau Magnum	Bittering	S	R	MR
Hallertau Tradition	Aroma	MR	R	MR
Liberty	Aroma	MR	MR	U
Perle	Aroma	S	R	MR

U = unknown, S = susceptible, R = resistant,
MS = moderately susceptible, MR = most resistant

"Field Guide for Integrated Pest Management in Hops." Oregon State University et al. 2010

Freshly picked hops drying on screens

PRUNING

Once the hop plants reach 1 to 2 feet (30.5 to 61 cm) in length, look to remove weaker bines. Train two or three bines onto each trellis wire, and remove new growth that appears over the summer. Once they grow taller, trim the lower 2 to 3 feet (61 to 91 cm) of the bines to aid growth and pest resistance.

HARVEST

Hops are picked in August and September (in the Northern Hemisphere). Look for the flowers to fade to pale green and the yellow lupulin sacks around the base of petals to darken to mustard yellow—that's when they're ready. The flowers will also become drier and feel papery. Check hops from the tops and bot-toms of bines and then remove the bine, leaving the lower 3 feet (91 cm). Pick the hops off the bine by hand and place them into a small or breathable container before drying.

DRYING

Hops deteriorate quickly and should begin drying for storage the same day they're harvested. The flowers need dry heat (less than 140°F, or 60°C) and air circulation. Lay them out on screens (clean window screens work fine) in a dark, well-ventilated room and mix daily to allow the whole flower to dry. The hops are ready for storage once the center stem of the flower becomes brittle. Pack the hops in freezer bags or any airtight container and store them in a freezer.

INTERVIEW WITH:
TED VIVATSON: PRESIDENT, EEL RIVER BREWING COMPANY, FORTUNA, CALIFORNIA, U.S.

NESTLED ON THE BANKS OF ITS NAMESAKE EEL RIVER, TED'S BREWERY IS A BEACON FOR GREEN BREWING. SLOWLY EXPANDING THROUGHOUT AN OLD PACIFIC LUMBER MILL IN SCOTIA, CALIFORNIA, EEL RIVER BREWING IS THRIVING IN A SPACE FORMERLY OCCUPIED BY WHAT TED DESCRIBES AS THE ANTICHRIST TO THE ENVIRONMENTAL MOVEMENT. THE BIOMASS-POWERED BREWERY IS A FIRST IN THE BEER WORLD, JUST AS EEL RIVER WAS ALSO THE FIRST CERTIFIED-ORGANIC BREWERY. SINCE GOING ORGANIC, TED AND HIS CREW HAVE CREATED ALES THAT RIVAL (AND BEAT) THE BEST IN THE WORLD, TAKING MEDALS AT COMPETITIONS, INCLUDING THE WORLD BEER CUP AND GREAT AMERICAN BEER FESTIVAL.

HOW'D YOU GET YOUR START IN ORGANIC BREWING?

It was actually consumer driven. An older customer from the hills came in. I hate to say "old hippie," but it's what best describes him. He asked, "You make a naked beer? Make me a beer just like my granddad drank. I don't want all the crap in it: any fungicides, herbicides, synthetic fertilizer, or sewer sludge. I don't want none of that crap."

That really made me start thinking. At the time, it was really provocative and crazy. We were still a new craft brewery and pretty much had the training wheels on, but I'm thinking, "Wow, this is cool. Who's going to have the ingredients?"

SO IT'S 1997 WHEN YOU STARTED GOING ORGANIC. WHAT INGREDIENTS WERE AVAILABLE?

I worked with Roger Briess. He was cutting edge as an American maltster, but at the time there were very limited ingredients, especially specialty malts.

HOW DID YOU APPROACH YOUR FIRST ORGANIC BEER?

Our biggest problem was perception and what I call the "organic carrot syndrome." I always remember going into a co-op for produce. They had conventional carrots that were absolutely beautiful for 25 cents a pound. And next to them were organic carrots for 90 cents and they looked like someone grew them through a box of rocks.

It always struck me that people thought if they were going to buy something organic, they were going to have to settle. I thought that was total BS. Organic products should be better and comparable in price.

So I decided we had to make an award-winning beer that's accepted by my peers and that just happens to be certified-organic. The only ingredients we really had at that time were for an amber ale with a base malt and two specialty malts. We brought hops from New Zealand [Hallertauer] and started serving it in the pub.

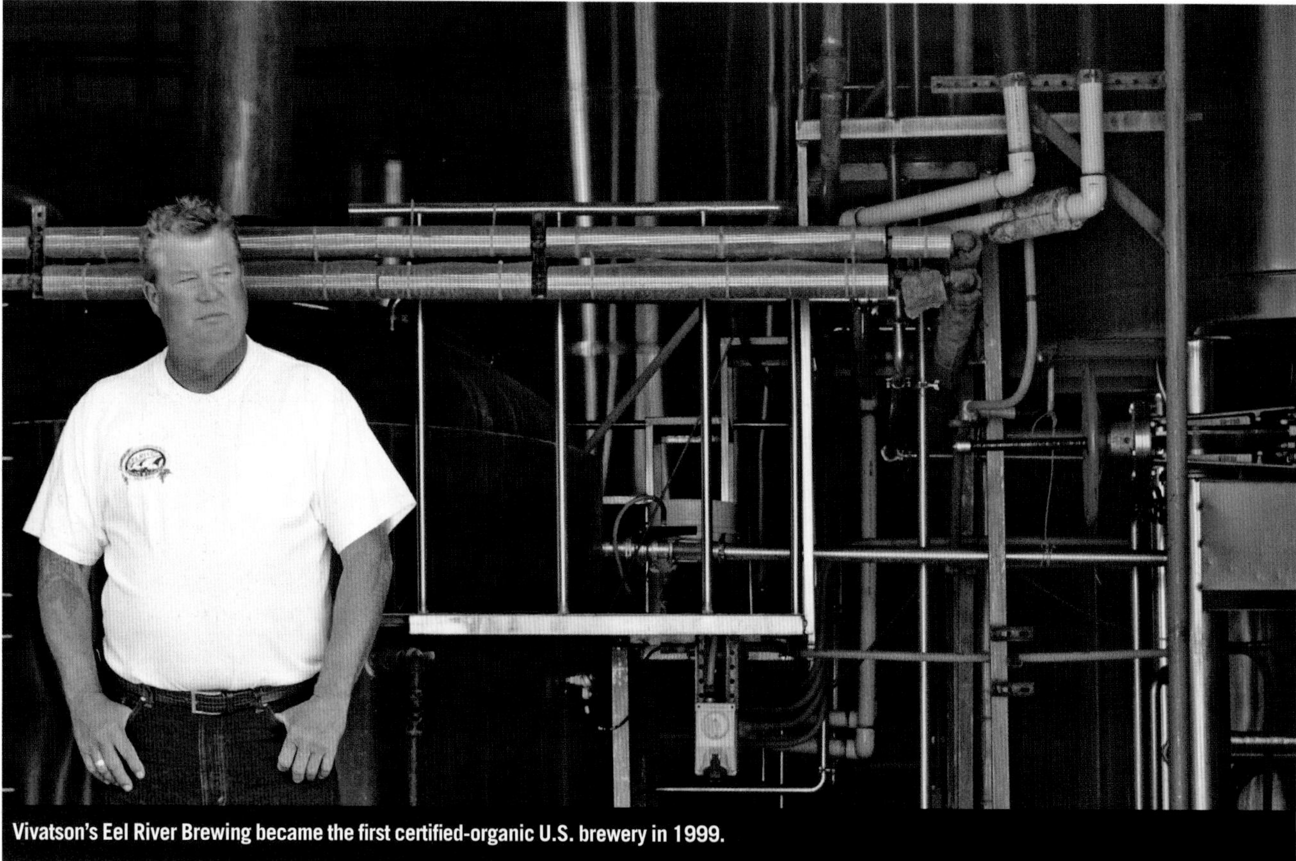

Vivatson's Eel River Brewing became the first certified-organic U.S. brewery in 1999.

Sometimes I find the organic mantra holds us back, and sometimes it helps. I tell young brewers, you have to make an exceptional beer and then people will buy it, whether it's organic or not.

AND IT WAS A HIT. WHAT WAS YOUR NEXT MOVE?

We tried making a porter, and that was difficult. Our porter before was the Ravensbrau, which was an outstanding brown porter that people still talk about. We had to transition to a darker robust because of the ingredients available, but now our porter is rated one of the top twenty-five in the world by DRAFT Magazine.

Then we went to our IPA, and that was the hardest. We figured we couldn't make a good West Coast IPA like Bear Republic or Russian River, so we went with an English IPA, which turned out phenomenal.

YOU STARTED WITH NEW ZEALAND ORGANIC HOPS. NOW THAT THERE ARE DOMESTIC HOP GROWERS, ARE YOU USING THEM?

We traditionally use NZ Cascade, Motueka, Rakau, Hallertauer, Pacific Jade, and Pacific Gem, but we just got a contract with Roy Farms in Oregon. I remember years ago when I asked Yakima Chief to grow some organic hops for us and they just laughed. Now it's economically feasible.

HAVE ANY FAVORITE ORGANIC HOPS YOU'D RECOMMEND?

Try some of the New Zealand heritage hops like Motueka and Riwaka. They've been raising hops for decades and they're getting back into the growing for the love of beer. You're going to get grapefruit and citrus, all those sorts of things. They're very fun.

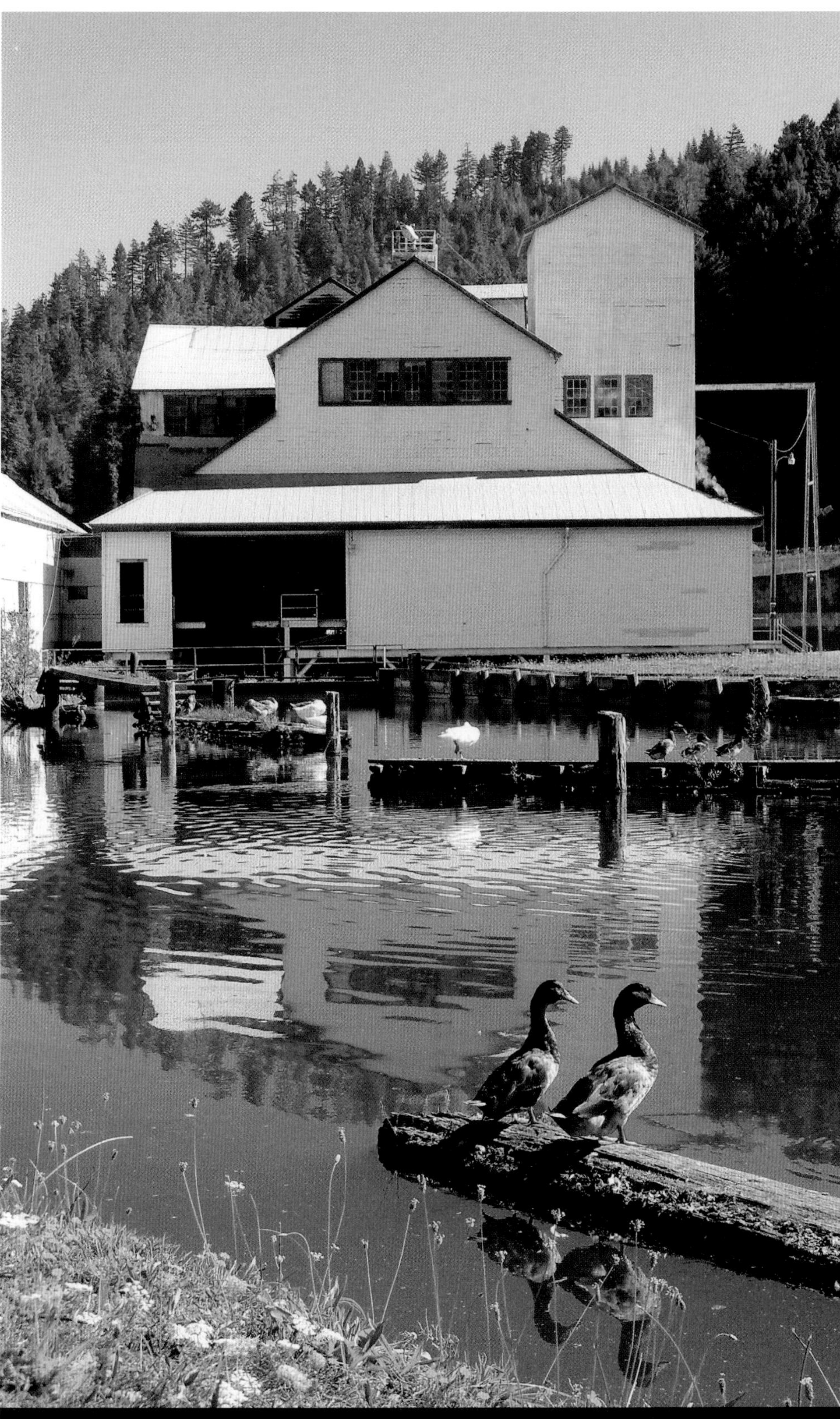

The biomass-fueled Eel River Brewing Company

ENGLISH IPAS VS. AMERICAN AND WEST COAST IPAS

An English IPA is the original, traditional version of the IPA, an acronym for India Pale Ale. It got its name from being, simply, a pale ale originally brewed to be higher in alcohol and with extra hops (as a preservative) to survive the trip from England to India in the nineteenth century. Stylistically, English IPAs have an earthy, floral, and fruity hop character with biscuitlike malts. American IPAs have more hop flavor and bitterness with less malt character. The use of American hops brings sharper citrus fruit and pine notes. The West Coast IPA is a hoppier, more bitter substyle of the American IPA.

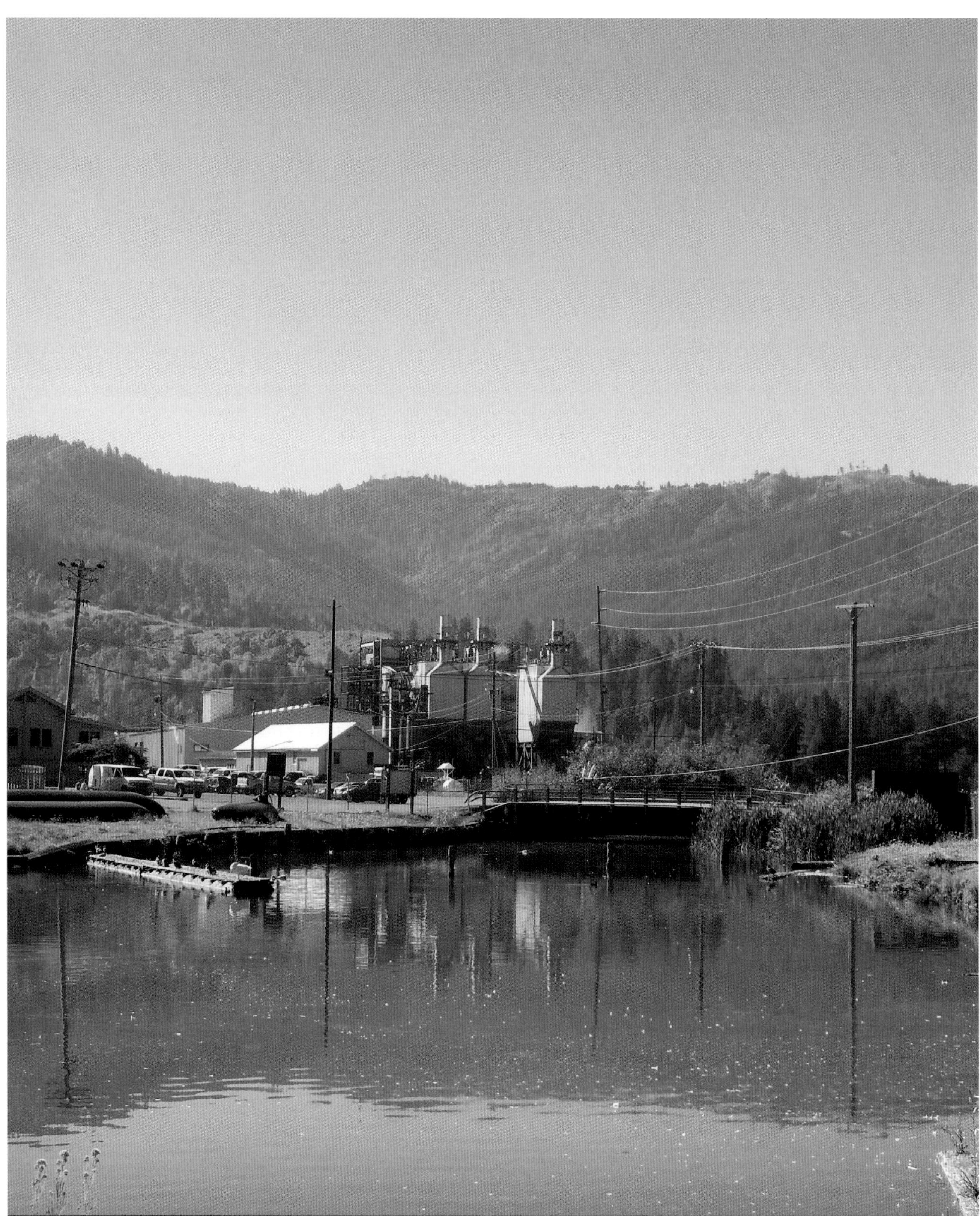

The brewery resides in a former lumber mill on the Eel River.

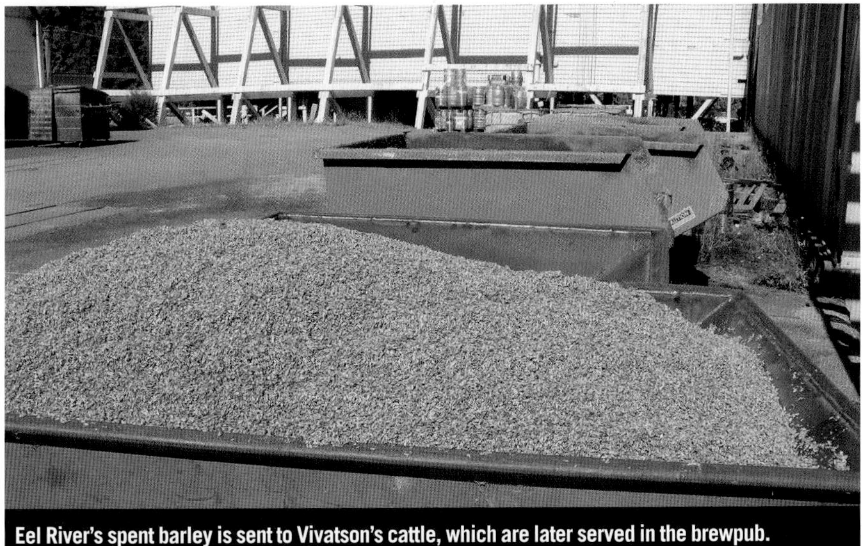

Eel River's spent barley is sent to Vivatson's cattle, which are later served in the brewpub.

DOES USING ORGANIC INGREDIENTS MAKE A BEER TASTE BETTER?

Yes, it's a proven fact that organic foods taste better. But it also offers peace of mind, and what's that worth?

CAN WE ASSUME YOU FEED YOUR SPENT GRAINS TO LOCAL CATTLE?

We actually raise our own cattle for the Fortuna pub. It's pretty cool. I raise them at my place, and we get natural beef. It's not certified-organic, but there are no shots or any of that. I take them at six- or seven-weight (600 or 700 pounds) to Redwood Meats, an organic facility in Eureka, for finishing.

WERE THERE DIFFICULTIES BREWING BOTH ORGANIC AND CONVENTIONAL BEER AT FIRST?

We had to do one batch at a time and purge our system—the grain mill, auger system, everything. A lot of chemicals had to be switched over. We couldn't use an iodine cleaner anymore; we use biodegradable cleaners like peracetic acid. It was rather tedious, but when we built our new facility we were all-organic.

SO CAN YOU CALL YOUR BEER 100 PERCENT ORGANIC?

Beer is impossible to make 100 percent organic because CO_2 and oxygen are not certified. They're considered brewery processing aides. So, I don't agree with that, but God doesn't certify CO_2 and oxygen. We're never going to be 100 percent certified-organic, but we do the best we can and stick to what we believe in.

NOW WHAT'S YOUR TAKE ON THE USDA EXCEPTION ALLOWING CERTIFIED-ORGANIC BEER TO USE CONVENTIONAL HOPS?

This is a huge sticking point with me. I brew purely organic, but I don't speak out against unpure organic brewers. I believe in the organic industry. It's in its infancy, and because a lot of people would like to see us not around, I support the exception.

A few years back, major breweries bought out all the organic hops and it would have just about put everyone out of business if they required 100 percent organic hops. Until the industry is really strong and the growers are there, I believe it needs to be that way. It's in everyone's best interest because you don't want to give the powers to the big ones. I don't trust them.

SO THEN WHAT'S YOUR TAKE ON ANHEUSER-BUSCH'S ORGANIC BEERS?

If they're going to make an organic beer, more power to them. It's going to make American hop growing economically viable and expose more people to organic products, so to me it's a win-win.

My only problem is they don't own up to it. If it's Budweiser, why didn't they come out with Budweiser Organic Amber Ale instead of Wild Hop or Stone Mill, where you have to put on your reading glasses to find out who really made it? Be proud of what you brew.

SO WHAT'S THE OUTLOOK FOR EEL RIVER?

Right now, we brew around 10,000 barrels. We're comfortable with our growth. For the last couple of years, we have had about 50 percent growth. We've got people who say "Dammit, I want organic!" And we've got people who just want great beer. We cater to both. We've got to stay innovative and fresh. As new ingredients come out, we've got to push the envelope.

A member of New Belgium Brewery's tasting panel compares batches of the same beer.

GOOD BEER DRINKERS USUALLY HAVE TWO DEFINING MOMENTS IN THEIR JOURNEY THROUGH THE BEER WORLD. THERE'S THEIR FIRST BEER, USUALLY A CHEAP, YELLOW, FIZZY, AND OCCASIONALLY WARM LAGER, MAYBE FROM THEIR UNCLE OR A CUP OF CHEAP KEG BEER AT A PARTY. CHANCES ARE IT WASN'T A PLEASANT EXPERIENCE, BUT IT SETS THE STANDARD FOR BEER TO COME, AND IF THE EVENT WAS ENJOYABLE ENOUGH, THEY MAY TRY THAT BEER AGAIN.

CHAPTER 14: TASTING AND EVALUATING YOUR BEER

A double flight of beers from Howe Sound Brewing in Squamish, British Columbia, Canada.

INTRODUCTION TO EVALUATING BEER

Then somewhere down the road, often years later, comes the good beer. Beer that not only tastes great, but is so wonderful you actually want to taste it, not chug it, for a change. Forget searching for cheap beers with no aftertaste—you want all the flavor you can get. Drinking beer for its character, not its alcohol content and availability, is what craft beer, homebrewing, and beer appreciation is all about.

Whether you want to fine-tune your homebrew or your tongue, learning to taste and evaluate beer will lead you to better beverages all around.

Everyone has an opinion on beer, but thoughtful evaluation requires more than a thumbs up or down. Judging a beer requires that you taste and enjoy a beer for what it is, regardless of personal preference. Most IPAs rate higher than light lagers, but a true taster also has to consider which is a better representation of their style. More important, judging beer identifies imperfection and room for improvement so that a brewer can learn their mistakes and make better beer.

In this chapter, you'll learn about:

- **Perfecting the beer pour**
- **Judging appearance, aroma, taste, and mouthfeel**
- **Diagnosing off-flavors**

A Belgian server finishes with an extra tall pour to create a proper head.

To taste better, you need to buy fresh beer. So exercise caution buying a beer that:

- **Has exposure to sunlight from the shelf. UV rays create the skunky beer phenomena.**
- **Is leaking. Always check the tops of corked bottles. If the cork is partially pushed out or there's residue around the edge, back away.**
- **Has grown dusty. Not all beer is dated, but all beer can collect dust.**
- **Is on clearance sale or deep discount. This may indicate the beer has been hanging around too long.**
- **Is out of season. Pumpkin beer isn't meant for March, and summer beers are typically stale by mid-fall.**

THE PROPER POUR

Before you can really taste or even admire a beer, you need to give it a proper pour. There are unending variations of what should be a simple task. There's the classic no-foam pour where you let beer sneak down the side until your glass is filled. You can squeeze a few more ounces into your cup, but this mutes the aroma. There's the showier pour straight to the bottom. This does a fine job of releasing aroma but leaves a huge head between you and the liquid you're dying to sip.

Instead, hold your glass at a 45-degree angle and pour the beer onto the middle of the wall. About halfway through the pour, turn the glass upright and pour the rest straight down to create a 1- to 2-inch (2.5 to 5 cm) head. For more effervescent beers, wait longer to turn the glass; for low-carbonation, pour straight down earlier. It's a bit of an art, but it's a skill you won't mind practicing.

APPEARANCE

You can't judge a beer by its label and packaging, but a quick inspection can tell you what flavor is in store. Dusty bottles on the store shelves, for instance, may indicate a beer is well past its prime. For homebrewed beer, hold your bottle up to light to look for a ring around the inside of the neck—this indicates an infection. Infections often lead to overcarbonation, so open any ringed bottles over a sink.

Color: A beer's color only gives a small indication of flavor. Two identical-looking red ales could have completely different characters: An all-Munich malt beer will have a sweet caramel and bready taste, while adding just a few ounces of black patent barley to pilsner malt during brewing will create the same appearance with none of the flavor.

Still, every beer style has an appropriate range of color defined by its SRM (Standard Reference Method). This scale runs from 0 to about 70 with light lagers registering a 2, imperial stouts pulling 50 to 70, and an amber ale in the neighborhood of 20. Good homebrewing software will calculate your SRM along with original gravity so you can check against your style's guidelines.

Clarity: Hazy beer is appropriate and preferred for some styles, such as German and Belgian wheat beers (hefeweizens and witbiers). In brewing competition, some haze is acceptable for India Pale Ales due to chill haze. Clear, clean beer typically results from good sanitation, and using a bit of Irish moss at the end of a boil draws out tannins and proteins. Properly maturing your beer in the secondary fermenter also creates clear beer; as a beer ages, yeast and other particles fall out of suspension.

AROMA

The only thing that could be simpler than drinking is sniffing, right? There's a lot you can learn by smelling your beer. Aroma is the gateway to flavor.

Beer is a complex but delicate drink, and the pour releases volatile notes that disappear within minutes, if not seconds. The second you set your beer down, dive in nose first. Take several short sniffs and focus on both the upfront character and then the background.

If you stop to take notes or ponder the beer, an occasional swirl of the glass will help raise the head and release a new burst of aroma. You can also let the aroma build by placing a coaster or your hand over the glass during and after the swirl.

TASTE

It should go without saying that you can't properly taste beer out of a bottle or can. But for anyone who needs reminding, there are two problems with trying to taste this way:

■ First, you can't smell the beer. The majority of our perceived taste comes from aroma, and you might notice food tastes more dull when you have a snuffed-up nose.

■ Second, the small opening on cans and bottles forces you to pour faster, accelerating the beer onto your tongue and releasing more carbonation, which in turn clouds the flavor.

To properly taste beer:

■ **Step 1:** With your beer poured, the color examined, and the aroma suitably sniffed, take a sip and swirl it around your mouth to coat your tongue.

■ **Step 2:** Swallow, and then exhale through your nose to bring the flavor back.

■ **Step 3:** For all the various flavors and notes, pick them out one at a time and examine whether you like them, and then whether they're appropriate for the intended style.

In formal homebrew tasting, there are rarely wrong answers, just ill-informed ones. A written description from judging and style guidelines can only help so much to understand how a style should taste. You need to try commercial examples to understand how similar beers stack up. To be a better taster, yes, you need to drink more beer, albeit thoughtfully. Take notes and keep tasting logs; this is likely to be the most enjoyable research and study you can find. Through sampling the standards and quintessential beers of a style, you begin to develop a library of potential flavors.

Know your limits: Beyond learning the notes and characteristics of a beer, you also need to know your limits. Everyone's palate reacts differently to certain chemicals and a good judge understands their strengths and weaknesses. Again, hone this by drinking more beer, and also discussing it with friends to hear what they can taste and you can't.

MOUTHFEEL

The feel of a beer is the final sense to evaluate and can be the most ambiguous. Light American lagers (such as Bud or Miller Lite) feel light and refreshing because they can have about the same weight and density as water (We suggest drinking water instead). Bigger beers, with more unfermented sugar (such as Aventinus Weizenbock or Old Rasputin Imperial Stout) are literally thicker with a high density.

Carbonation also forms our perception of mouthfeel. Some people falsely assume Guinness Draught is a big and alcoholic beer because it feels thick on their tongue. It's actually no stronger than a light beer. The difference comes from its nitrogen carbonation, which has smaller bubbles and makes it feel heavier, but also smoother.

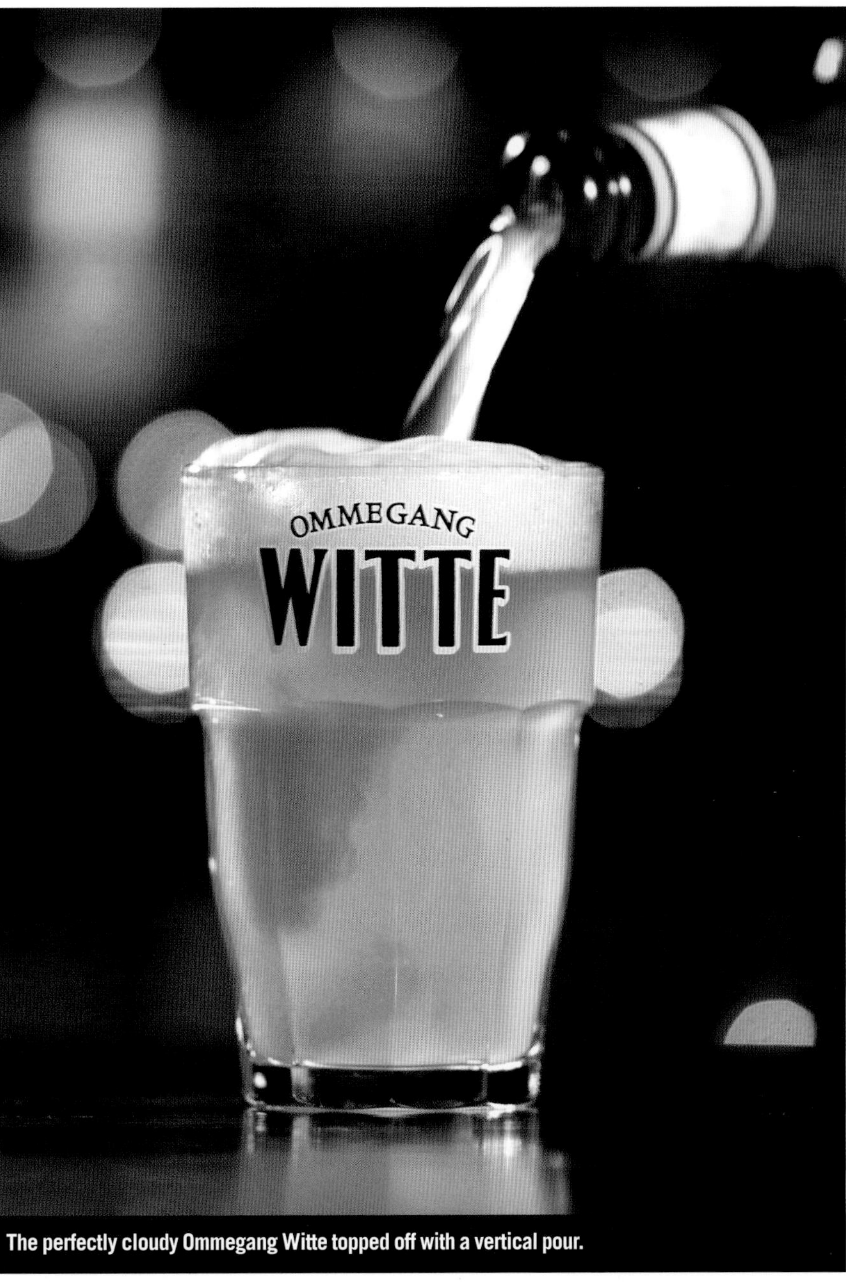

The perfectly cloudy Ommegang Witte topped off with a vertical pour.

TROUBLESHOOTING OFF FLAVORS

When good beer goes bad, there's a group of usual suspects to round up.

You taste	Diagnosis
Sour, puckering mouthfeel; tastes and feels like a dirty lemon or grapefruit; beer may have a film on top.	You have a wild yeast infection most likely due to unsanitary equipment or conditions. Keep your brewery clean and your beer sealed from the world.
Plastic bandages, cough medicine, plastic, chlorine, or assorted medical supplies.	You're most likely tasting chlorophenol, a chemical created through the bonding of chlorine from your brewing water or cleaner with normally tasty phenols created by your yeast. It may also be wild yeast contamination. Either way, check your water and sanitizer.
Alcohol, as in bottom-shelf spirits or cleaning solvent.	If your beer is stronger than about 7 percent, continue aging. Otherwise, these fusel alcohols come from fermenting too warm and/or with poor aeration.
Wet cardboard in dark beer and paper in lighter beers, or if you're lucky, sherry.	Oxidation. Oxygen is one of beer's mortal enemies, and exposure during conditioning and bottling will make your beer taste like the sports section.
Astringent, dry, chalky bitterness like grape skins.	It could be an infection, but it is likely tannins from the malt. Mashing grains too hot, sparging for too long, or grinding them too fine will unleash this unpleasant aftertaste.
Butterscotch or movie theater popcorn butter.	Diacetyl. This fermentation by-product is appropriate and desirable in some English ales, but otherwise it indicates the beer was taken from primary fermentation too soon or wasn't adequately aerated.
Boiled or canned vegetables, commonly corn.	DMS, or dimethyl sulfide, can be an infection, but often results from a poorly vented brew kettle. Keep your equipment clean and pot uncovered to let the DMS boil off.
Fruit punch, berry flavors when there should be none.	While perfectly normal in Belgian ales, it's a mark of too-hot fermentation in cleaner beer styles like a pale ale or pilsner.
Fresh, green apples.	Acetaldehyde. This is another sign of young beer. Adequate primary and secondary fermentation will clean this flaw out.
Apple cider.	Blame your sugars. You either have old, stale malt extract, or you added too much sugar.

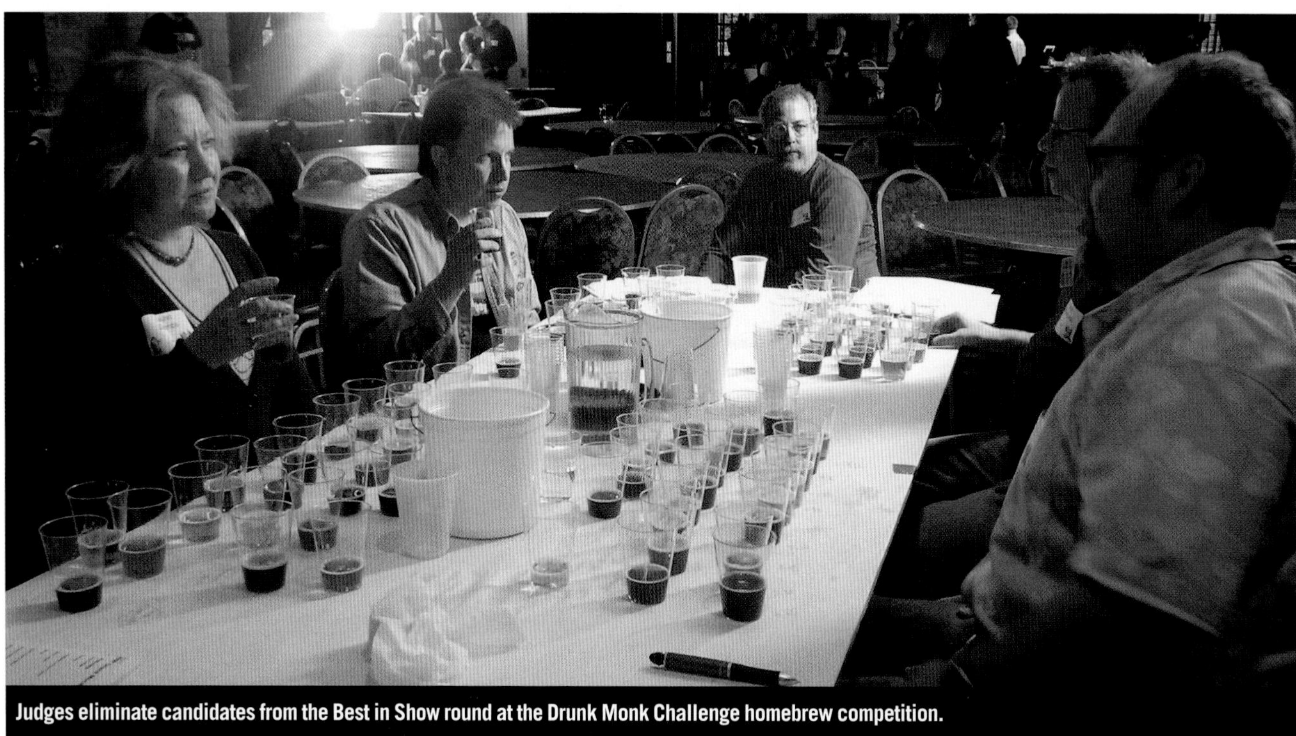

Judges eliminate candidates from the Best in Show round at the Drunk Monk Challenge homebrew competition.

INTERVIEW WITH:
RAY DANIELS: BEER JUDGE AND FOUNDER, CICERONE CERTIFICATION PROGRAM, U.S.

CALL HIM THE MAN WITH A GOLDEN TONGUE. RAY HAS BEEN TASTING AND JUDGING BEER FOR MORE THAN TWO DECADES ON AN INTERNATIONAL STAGE AND NOW LEADS THE CICERONE CERTIFICATION PROGRAM, AN INDUSTRYWIDE SCHOOL TO RID THE WORLD OF IGNORANT BARTENDERS AND DIRTY GLASSES.

FIRST OFF, WHAT'S THE CORRECT PRONUNCIATION OF CICERONE?

Sis-er-own. In short hand, it's a beer sommelier. They're a learned and knowledgeable guide to the world of beer. It's taken from a word of latin root and the word's been used for 400 years as "a guide."

WHO ARE CICERONES?

The program is oriented toward the beer business, running from retailers to distributors to brewers—people involved in selling or serving beer. We have 1,600 Certified Beer Servers—that's the first level of our program. The key emphasis at that level is on keeping and serving beer with an introduction to basic styles.

WHAT ARE THE LEVELS OF THE CICERONE PROGRAM?

After Certified Beer Server is Certified Cicerone. And the third level is Master Cicerone. In the first level, it's just a knowledge test. At the Cicerone level, tasting is part of the exam with twelve beer samples. And then at the Master level, there's an examination by an expert panel and more tasting.

ISN'T THERE ONLY ONE MASTER CICERONE SO FAR?

We've only given the exam once and it's eight hours long. We look forward to having more soon.

TM

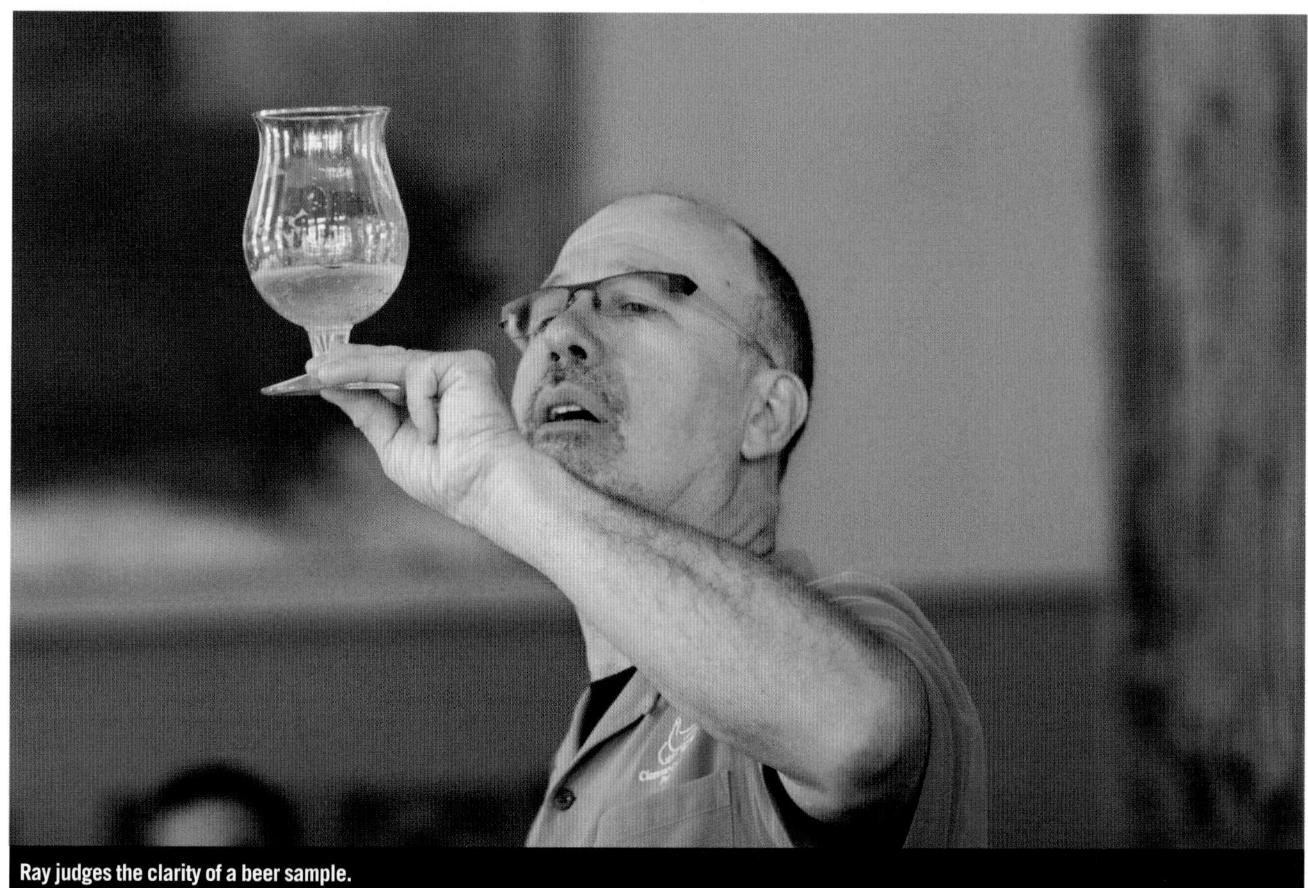

Ray judges the clarity of a beer sample.

YOU'RE ALSO A LEADING BEER JUDGE.

I got my start in judging as a BJCP (Beer Judge Certification Program) judge and do a lot of judging on the professional level now at the Great American Beer Festival and World Beer Cup.

WHAT'S THE DIFFERENCE BETWEEN A BJCP JUDGE AND A PROFESSIONAL?

There are some definite differences in approach. The homebrew judging provides a score and feedback on how to improve their beer regardless of whether they won a medal. Professional judging is oriented to rapidly getting toward the winning beers.

Typically, you judge about twice as many beers as a professional, about twenty-five over a three-hour session. You start with a flight of six to thirteen beers and go through and taste them all at once. You fill out a score sheet, though there's no actual score, to tell the brewer what we tasted and what we liked and didn't like.

From there, we start the discussion process and we'll have two or three everyone agrees won't move on. Typically it's because of a huge flaw like diacetyl or acetaldehyde.

WHAT DO YOU HAVE ON THE TABLE TO CLEANSE YOUR PALATE BETWEEN TASTINGS?

We have low- or no-salt crackers. Unsalted matzo is often the best thing, with lots of water.

Judge, author, and beer educator Ray Daniels

BEER JUDGE CERTIFICATION PROGRAM

Founded in 1985, the BJCP is a nonprofit organization designed to promote the appreciation of beer through establishing beer style standards, training judges, and organizing competitions. Any beer lover can become a BJCP judge but must pass a rigorous, three-hour exam split between essay and tasting sections.

Full Sail Brewing's Brewmaster, Jamie Emmerson, tests a batch of beer for contamination.

You know if there's nothing objectionable in the flavor, I can chug down a beer that's not at the peak of freshness, but to give me a dirty glass or a flat beer, those things are pretty hard to get by.

DO YOU HAVE A PROCESS OR CHECKLIST FOR TASTING A BEER?

I go through every beer in front of me and take notes on aroma before I taste a thing. This gives a cleaner approach to each individual sample with no beer on my palate. So it may help to reduce biases. If you have a beer that's extremely bitter, it could alter your perception of the next beer. It may make the bitterness seem lower.

When you taste, there's a beginning, middle, and end to every beer. And you want to pay attention to all the things going on and pick out what is unexpected. Try to identify that as a starting point. At the end, put your critical mind-set aside, take a sip and ask yourself if you ordered this style of beer at a bar and were presented this, how would you feel?

HOW DOES SOMEONE BECOME A BETTER TASTER?

There are training programs like the BJCP classes. We do sensory training through the Cicerone program for basic off-flavors, but really tasting evolves a taster. I teach a Master of Beer Styles class with Randy Mosher. You get the off-flavors on the first day and then you spend the next three days tasting sixty to eighty examples of commercial beers to develop that library of classic-style flavors by tasting.

WHAT TURNED YOU ON TO GOOD BEER?

As a beer drinker, I was interested in flavor and got into homebrewing. By my third batch, I really felt like I'd made beer better than anything I could pay money for. There was no turning back after that batch. It was a pale ale with grains that I toasted and finishing aroma hops. Back in 1989, that was pretty radical.

WHAT ARE THE MOST COMMON FLAWS YOU SEE IN BEER?

There's a whole collection of off-flavors and many come down to sanitation, boiling, and management of fermentation. I find increasingly that people who have the sanitation and boiling basics down don't give the yeast enough time to finish the job. Proper secondary fermentation is important; otherwise, you'll get diacetyl and acetaldehyde in the finished beer. Both are signs of improperly matured beer.

ARE THERE ANY STYLES THAT ARE HARDER TO JUDGE? ANY THAT MAKE YOU CRINGE?

Yeah, for some styles judging twenty-five samples can be a challenge—intensely flavored beers like stouts and robust porters really tend to push palate fatigue quickly. I think really strong beers over 7 or 8 percent can be a challenge. Most judges don't spit, but it's something I've begun to do with stronger beers. It's just too hard to maintain your concentration.

BUT SOME FOLKS MAINTAIN YOU NEED TO TAKE THE BITTERNESS ON THE BACK OF YOUR TONGUE.

That's not entirely valid. The whole tongue map that shows bitterness on the back of your tongue has been repudiated. You do notice bitterness more in the aftertaste, but it's not necessarily on the back of the tongue. But normally I take two or three sips of beer for the evaluation process. So one I'd swallow, and the others I'd use the spittoon.

YOU TRAIN BARTENDERS. IF YOU COULD FIX ONE SERVING PROBLEM THE WORLD OVER, WHAT WOULD IT BE?

The most unforgivable sin is dirty glasses. Any time a beer is served and there are bubbles clinging to the side of a glass, below the top of the beer, that's a clear sign of a dirty glass. Some sort of schmutz is stuck to glass, didn't get cleaned out, and is giving those bubbles a place to collect. Whatever it is, I don't want to drink it.

THAT'S DISGUSTING.

Typically you'll see a band 2 or 3 inches (5 or 7.5 cm) from the bottom of the glass coated with bubbles. Whatever drink was in that glass last night dried and didn't get washed out.

You know, if there's nothing objectionable in the flavor, I can chug down a beer that's not at the peak of freshness, but to give me a dirty glass or a flat beer, those things are pretty hard to get by.

GOOD BEER IS EASY. GREAT BEER IS AN ENDLESS PURSUIT. CONVERTING SUGAR TO ALCOHOL IS SIMPLE ENOUGH, BUT TO EMULATE THE BEST BREWERIES, HOMEBREWERS NEED TO TAKE A CLOSER LOOK AT THEIR INGREDIENTS AND PROCESS.

CHAPTER 15: MAKING BEAUTIFUL BEER

Dumping caustic cleaner from the fermenter before pumping in wort at Epic Brewing Company

INTRODUCTION TO BETTER BEER

The quality of your beer is largely dependent upon two points. First there's the character of your ingredients, which results from their variety and freshness. Then there's how you control the brewing processes around your ingredients. Although homebrewers don't have access to the same technology as professionals, many theories are easily adapted and the ingredients available are largely the same.

In this chapter you'll learn about:

- **Selecting barley and hops**
- **Cleaning and sanitation**
- **Thermal stress**
- **Oxidation**
- **Trace metals in beer**

A combine sets to work harvesting on Sierra Nevada's 30-plus acres of barley at the brewery.

BETTER INGREDIENTS, BETTER BEER

MALT

Barley and other brewing grains remain stable for both flavor and diastatic power if kept dry and uncrushed. To be safe, always taste your grains before buying or brewing to ensure there are no stale or off-flavors.

The greatest worry for homebrewers isn't old grains, but old malt extract. Generally speaking, dried malt extract stays fresh up to a year, while liquid malt extract tends to deteriorate after six months. Old extract tends to darken in color and adds an unmistakable cider flavor to your beer.

HOPS

Hops help preserve beer, but they also lose their alpha acids quickly if they are not stored properly. In fact, hops begin to break down immediately after harvesting, giving wet-hopped ales an extra kick that is lost during drying and aging.

Hops distributors use humidity-controlled cold storage to minimize deterioration. If left at room temperature for six months, hops, depending on the variety, will lose anywhere between 20 and 65 percent of their alpha acids.

A homebrewer pours his yeast starter in after aerating the wort.

Immediately after harvest, hops are packaged with nitrogen to prevent oxidation. You can check hops for oxidation by smelling for cheesy aromas. Typically, you can use mildly oxidized hops for bittering as the off-flavors will boil away. If you don't use all your hops and need to store them, pack them tightly in a plastic resealable bag and store them in your freezer. A vacuum sealer, however, is ideal. It's worth noting that a small amount of oxidation does improve some hops. It can, for example, increase the floral quality in Cascade hops.

PELLET VS. WHOLE-FLOWER HOPS

There is a certain romance to using minimally processed whole-flower hops in your beer. Sierra Nevada has notably brewed with nothing but whole-flower hops for decades, but most of the great American IPAs are made with pellets and some even use hop oil extract, as we learned from Nick Floyd (see chapter 3).

Still, there is no doubt that whole-flower hops make excellent beer. If you brew with whole-flower hops, be prepared for at least 10 percent lower alpha acid–utilization and a lot more vegetable matter to filter out of your kettle.

YEAST

The magical *Saccharomyces cerversiae* cells are resilient little buggers, but they have their limits. Dry yeast stays healthy in packets for about a year, while White Labs vials and Wyeast smack packs are fresh and fully viable for four months before beginning to lose a significant number of yeast cells. Using a yeast starter to set them up for a fast and healthy fermentation is one of the easiest steps to prevent infection as it outcompetes rival yeast and bacteria for sugar. See page 114 for yeast starter instructions.

CLEANING AND SANITATION

Don't confuse the two as the same step; they have separate functions in giving you the best beer possible. Yes, good sanitary practices ensure no nasty creatures start growing in your beer, but cleanliness removes the grime and undesirable aromas from your equipment.

Cleaning is doubly important for plastic fermenters. While they are food grade, they're easily scratched, giving bacteria a convenient place to hide from sanitizer and breed. Plastic buckets are also porous and can leach and carry over flavors from the previous batch. Dish soap is a simple cleaner, but it can leave a lingering aroma, and its residue will kill head retention. A dedicated brewing cleaner such as Five Star PBW (powdered brewery wash) is ideal and has a low environmental impact.

THERMAL STRESS

A longer, bigger boil isn't always better. Brewing research shows that exposing the wort to excessive thermal stress can slightly degrade the flavor and stability of a beer. That means that it's ideal to minimize your wort's exposure to heat.

A sixty-minute boil is a good compromise that ensures DMS and other undesirable flavors are blown off, without subjecting the wort to undue stress. Also try to reduce the time it takes to heat and cool your wort. Think of your wort like any other food: The longer and hotter it's cooked, the less flavor you have in the end.

OXIDATION AND AERATION

Oxygen provides vital fuel for yeast growth, but in all other instances, it's a sworn enemy of beer. Before wort even hits the kettle, brewers work to reduce oxygen exposure in the grain mill and by removing dissolved oxygen from brewing water. This is called hot-side aeration, and in your brewhouse, boiling your water premash will drive off much of the oxygen while also removing chlorine. Also minimize splashing and aeration of your wort before the kettle.

On the cold side (postboil), any oxygen picked up after the initial fermentation can damage the beer and bring on a papery, cardboard character. Simple measures, such as not splashing your beer when transferring containers and, if possible, purging containers of oxygen with CO_2, prevent introducing oxygen to the beer.

TRACE METALS

Brewing minerals and chemicals such as sulfate and chlorine get more attention in the brewing water, but copper and iron can also wreak havoc. Both bring a harsh metallic flavor, while copper slows mash enzymes, stunts yeast growth, and can cause gushing carbonation in a bottle or keg.

Thankfully, copper usually isn't a threat to homebrewers unless they have bright unoxidized copper equipment. To be safe, avoid contact between your beer and copper at any stage after the boil. Iron is more prevalent and finds its way into your beer primarily through new stainless steel equipment or the use of diatomaceous earth water filters. Cleaning new stainless equipment will help remove that initial iron, and using a carbon filter, instead of diatomaceous earth, removes the risk of additional iron.

While a rolling boil removes DMS, backing off your heat can improve flavor.

Bottling is an easy place for oxygen to sneak into beer for professionals and homebrewers alike.

In 1979, Ken began by literally building his brewery by hand.

INTERVIEW WITH: KEN GROSSMAN: OWNER, SIERRA NEVADA BREWING CO., CHICO, CALIFORNIA, U.S.

WITH A LEGENDARY CRAFT BEER TO HIS NAME, AN OWNER COULD BE COMPLACENT AND COAST, WATCHING THE PROFITS ROLL IN. BUT KEN IS A BEER GEEK FIRST AND FOREMOST. AFTER MORE THAN THREE DECADES IN THE BUSINESS, HE'S STILL RELENTLESSLY CHASING A BETTER BEER.

WHAT WERE THE BIGGEST CHALLENGES WHEN YOU FIRST OPENED IN 1980?

There wasn't a place to buy brewing equipment on the budget or scale we had. I couldn't have afforded something from Germany or England. But I was lucky that UC-Davis was down the road, and they had a pretty extensive brewing library. I went back into books from the '40s, '50s, and '60s, and saw how technology was handled in simpler times.

A lot of the articles I read and copied were on older methods of brewing. We tried to mimic simplified brewing systems with nonpressurized fermentation tanks or heated mash tuns that we now have the luxury of owning.

BUT HOW DID YOU HANDLE THE EQUIPMENT?

I built my first malt mill myself. We built a mash tun out of an old cheese vat I found, and I milled a false bottom myself. I used a lot of fundamental, but simplistic, equipment designs, but it was enough to get us into business.

BUILDING YOUR OWN MALT MILL SEEMS INCOMPREHENSIBLE.

I purchased well casing pipes, welded in end plates, put bearings together, and pieced together a functioning, but crude, malt mill that got us started. Those kind of skills were something I thought I needed, so I went back to junior college and took many classes in fabrication, machining, refrigeration, and so on.

It took a year and a half to put all the pieces together to make our first batch of beer, the building included. I did the carpentry, Sheetrock, painting, and all the plumbing and electrical.

I THINK SIERRA NEVADA HAS A REPUTATION FOR BEING THE BEST EXAMPLE OF THE ART AND TECHNICAL.

A lot of the small brewers that opened in the years before and after us are all gone. And part of their downfall was a lack of consistency, quality control, and getting a handle on brewing science. It's certainly an art, but there's science involved.

AND YOU'VE BEEN HEAD OF THE TECHNICAL COMMITTEE FOR THE BREWERS ASSOCIATION.

It was great; my passion is the science of making beer. I'm boring and read brewing journals in the evening.

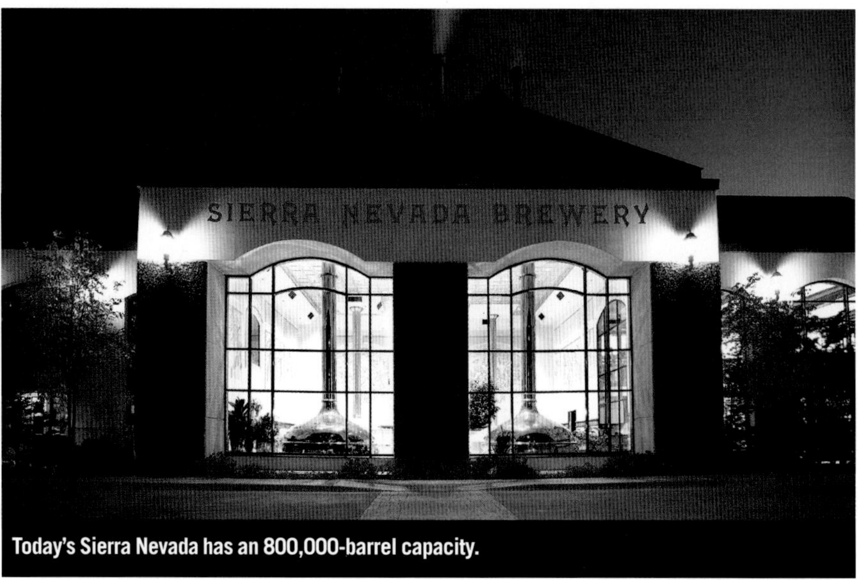

Today's Sierra Nevada has an 800,000-barrel capacity.

SO HOW DID THAT SCIENCE MANIFEST ITSELF?

We studied iron pickup in beer kegs and from water. A little bit of iron is not detectable by most palates, but 40 or 50 parts per billion of iron from natural sources or kegs severely impacts the flavor stability of beer. The consumer will experience a less-than-ideal beer down the road. It's those subtle things that contribute to the overall long-term enjoyment of the product.

In 2007, Sierra Nevada switched from twist-off to pry-off caps for better protection against oxygen.

WHAT SORT OF OTHER THINGS HAVE YOU FOUND IMPROVE FLAVOR STABILITY?

We blanket our mill with nitrogen, de-aereate our brewing water, and we invest in analytical equipment that can look at ppb or lower of iron or other minerals. Not one of these things makes a huge impact by itself, but all these little bits can improve the consumers' experience. That's a core value: We always know we can do a little better here or there.

THAT MAKES ME THINK OF YOUR SWITCH TO PRY-OFF BOTTLE CAPS.

We've done a lot of research on bottle cap liner materials and are still working with European manufactures to find the Holy Grail of bottle cap liners. That'll have benefits for us as well as the rest of the industry. Bottle caps are an inherent detractor from beer flavor stability.

We studied leaving twist-offs for many years. There was certainly the convenience factor, and hundreds of our customers voiced their discontent with our switching over. But we were not able to find a material that would work in a twist-off application as well as the best materials in a pry-off. The twist-off bottle caps have a mineral oil lubricant that allows the plastic to spin off, but it also lets more oxygen in.

WHAT ADVICE WOULD YOU GIVE HOMEBREWERS ON HOW TO IMPROVE THEIR CONSISTENCY?

Adequate wort aeration is one thing too many homebrewers don't get. Getting enough oxygen into the wort to get a quick fermentation and then getting active yeast in a state that it will start rapidly fermenting.

YOU GROW SOME OF YOUR OWN HOPS AND BARLEY. IT'S AN AWESOME WAY TO HELP PEOPLE UNDERSTAND THE CONNECTION BETWEEN SOIL AND WHAT WE ENJOY IN A PINT GLASS. DID ANYTHING DRIVE YOUR DECISION?

Actually, I have memories of moving to Chico in 1972. I was homebrewing and driving up through the Sacramento Valley when there were still hop fields along Highway 99. Then I made my first pilgrimage to Yakima in 1975. When I was starting my homebrew shop, I picked up a hundred brewers' cuts to stock my homebrew shop with. Those are the 1-pound (455 g) bricks normally sent to brewers for selection.

I was always very into hops, so I thought it'd be great to show people what the raw materials look like. We got into it around 2004 and got a hop-picking machine from Germany. Then we started growing barley because we wanted to do an estate beer and had some open property. We have a little rail yard near the brewery to bring in malt [that has] 35 acres (0.1 km^2) of agricultural land with water rights, so we thought it's a perfect place to grow barley.

HOW DOES IT GROW?

Very well. We have great crops and do it all organically. One of our maltsters came here and said it's the best organic field he's ever seen. We're still learning, trying to pump enough nitrogen into the soil organically. We have cover crops, fish emulsion, and whatnot. It's challenging.

LET'S TALK ABOUT THE TECHNICAL SIDE OF SUSTAINABILITY.

Going back to innovating, we followed sustainable practices because we didn't have any extra resources to waste. We started out with a bottle washer, and I used to go behind Mexican restaurants to dig out Dos Equis and Superior bottles because they were close enough to our bottle.

AND HOW'S THAT SPIRIT CARRIED ON TODAY?

Today, we're a very public entity in our community. We acknowledge the fact that brewing is a resource-heavy industry for equipment, barley, transportation, use of water, and discharge of waste water. All those things are in my face, and we try to figure out how to be efficient without compromising quality.

Not all our products have great return on investment, but sometimes it's the right thing to do and it helps with the company's mind-set to occasionally acknowledge we're doing something for the right reason, not because it's going to save us money. We have a garden for the restaurant and just put in a composting system that can take up to 2.5 tons (2,270 kg) per day of food waste and produce compost in twelve to fourteen days.

SO YOU USE IT ALL?

We plan on it. We have a two-acre (8,100 m^2) garden that we're expanding plus a greenhouse. We want to raise the majority of our produce for the restaurant. After that, our hop and barley fields can take all of it.

Not all our products have great return on investment, but sometimes it's the right thing to do and it helps with the company's mindset to occasionally acknowledge we're doing something for the right reason, not because it's going to save us money. We have a garden for the restaurant and just put in a composting system that can take up to 2.5 tons per day of food waste and produce compost in twelve to fourteen days.

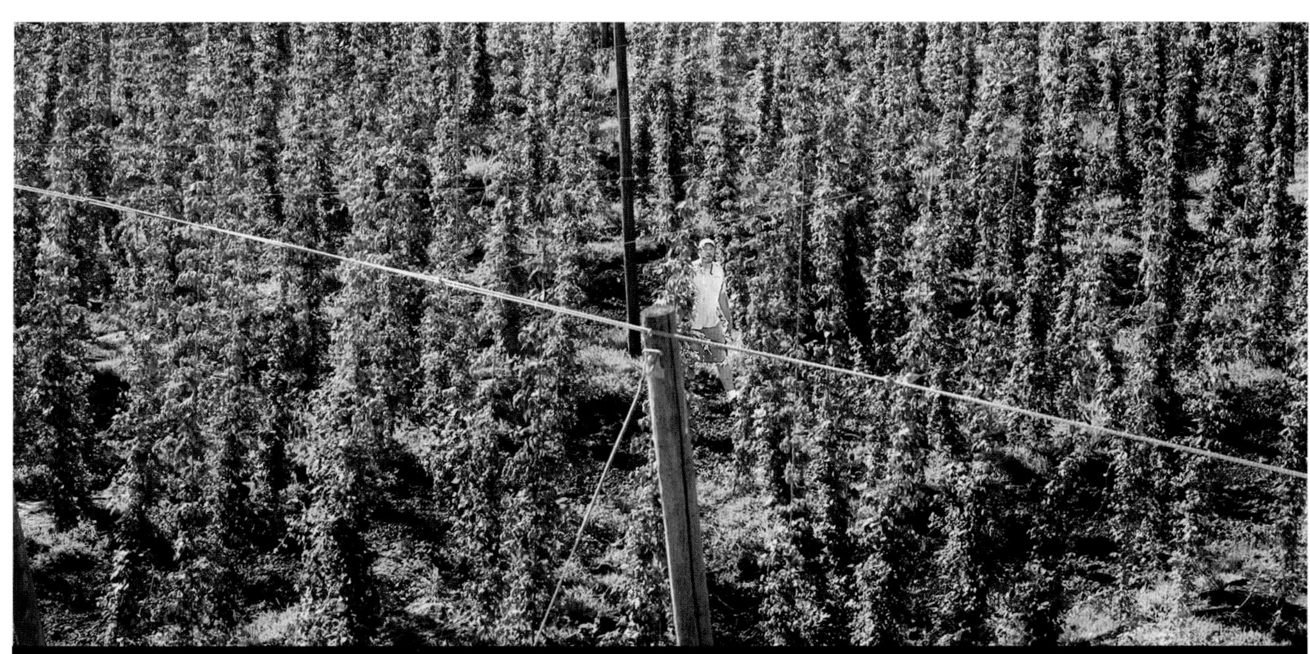

The brewery farms its own barley and hops on-site with hopes to eventually malt their own grains.

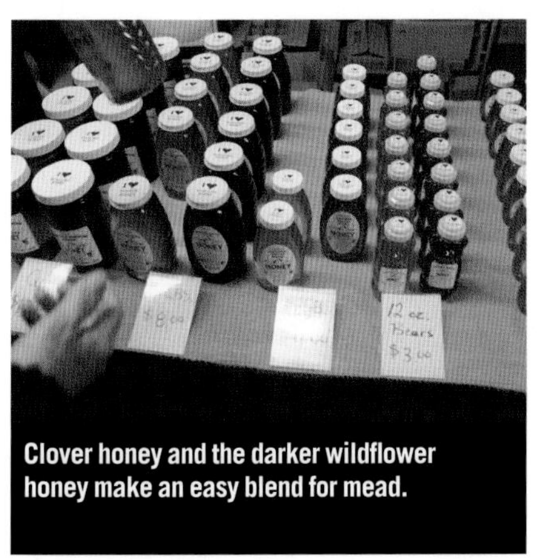

Clover honey and the darker wildflower honey make an easy blend for mead.

BEER HISTORIANS LIKE TO WAX POETIC ON THEIR BEVERAGE HAVING BEEN THE CATALYST FOR EARLY CIVILIZATION, BUT MEAD'S HISTORY TRACES BACK TENS OF THOUSANDS OF YEARS EARLIER AND IS LIKELY OUR EARLIEST FERMENTED DRINK. HONEY DISSOLVED IN WATER CAN'T HELP BUT FERMENT, AND ON A BASIC LEVEL, THAT'S ALL YOU HAVE TO DO—WATER IT DOWN AND WAIT.

CHAPTER 16: MEAD

Often mead recipes will look like a beer recipe: A base honey comprises about 80 percent of the sugar, with one or two other honeys added to complement the base flavor, like the malts in beer. Unlike specialty malts, though, most of the honeys you'd use in small doses could also be used for the base.

In this chapter, you'll learn about:

- **Honey varieties**
- **Mead brewing**
- **Mead yeasts and fermentation**
- **Conditioning mead**

Just as beer has its barley and hop fields, honey has hives.

SELECTING HONEY FOR BREWING

Brewing malts and hops are relatively standard from region to region. Honey, however, draws its character from the flora bees pollinate. An orange blossom honey will be citrusy as a result, and a desert honey will have a more earthy, spicy character.

Although that means there are few flavor standards for honey varieties, as with picking hops or grape varieties, as long as you have a quality product, there are no bad options. We recommend buying locally made honey, which can seem expensive, but simply tastes better and adds true local flavor to your mead.

In general, darker honeys have a richer, more nuanced flavor. Clover honey, which is stocked in every grocery store, is more basic and generic. Wildflower, which is highly dependent on its origin, and orange blossom honey are both reliable, easy-to-find options to begin making mead.

PREPARING YOUR HONEY

Mead makers should warm their honey in a hot box over a day or two before adding it to the brewing water. This dissolves any crystallization (caused by long storage) and makes mixing the honey in considerably easier. Cold honey added to heated water will sink to the bottom of the kettle, splashing the hot water and scorching the bottom of your pot. You can simulate a hot box by giving your container of honey a hot water bath in a tub of hot water from the tap. Ideally, the honey will slowly reach 110°F (43°C), at which point it's ready to mix. Add honey as you would liquid malt extract, warm and with vigorous stirring.

YEAST

Most wine yeast strains will make fine mead under the right conditions, so choose one based on the fermentation temperature, honey strength, and desired sweetness or dryness. Taking a white wine yeast with a lower alcohol tolerance will leave a fair amount of residual sugar in a mead with more gravity than the yeast can process. Likewise, a strong champagne yeast will power through lower-gravity meads, leaving them bone-dry.

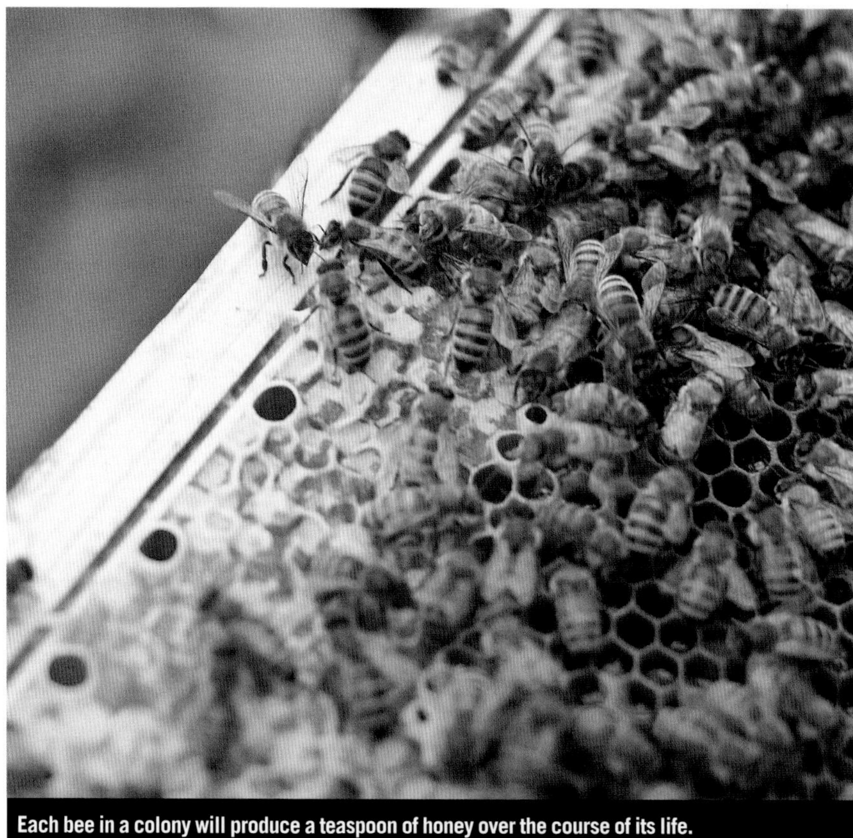

Each bee in a colony will produce a teaspoon of honey over the course of its life.

HONEY TO MEAD

Step 1: Mix the honey and water. You should boil water, not honey. Actually, it doesn't even need to be boiled. Bring your water to 180°F (82°C) and then turn off the heat. Once the temperature reaches 160°F (71°C), add your honey and let it sit for twenty minutes to pasteurize the must (unfermented mead) before cooling. Honey holds a lot of delicate aromas, so the less exposure to heat it has, the better you'll preserve the flavors and aromas.

Step 2: Rehydrate your yeast by mixing it into a small amount of warm water (unless you're using liquid yeast) as your must cools. You may also add a rehydration nutrient (different from fermentation-phase nutrients below) such as Go-Ferm with 1.25 grams for every gram of yeast.

Step 3: Aerate the liquid like you would wort. The yeast cells still need oxygen to work. Take your gravity reading, pitch your yeast, and wait for the first nutrient addition.

YEAST NUTRITION

Honey is relatively pure and sterile compared to most fruits or grains that are fermented. While this takes some stress off sanitation, it also means that beyond sugar, none of the necessary yeast nutrients, such as nitrogen, which you'd find on barley are present. Without small amounts of nitrogen, one of the most important nutrients, yeast won't convert the sugar to alcohol.

Step 1: Add 1 teaspoon (4 g) of yeast nutrient (available at homebrew shops) near the end of the wort boil. Don't add all the nutrient immediately because yeast would burn through it, speeding fermentation when you actually want a steady stream of sugar conversion from yeast for better flavor.

Step 2: Mead needs a number of nutritional boosts throughout fermentation. Add 1 gram per gallon (0.3 g per liter) of the nutrient, rehydrated, to the fermenter after the initial lag time (six to twelve hours before visual activity). Then add half that amount once a third of the mead's sugar has been fermented. This promotes a slower fermentation than adding the nutrient immediately, but the yeast will remain healthy and active longer. Of course, before you add any nutrient, check the dosage instructions and the yeast's nutrition needs. Some strains need more nitrogen than other.

Step 3: Aerate again. It's common practice for some mead makers to aerate after fermentation has begun. Brewing will occasionally perform the same process for high-gravity beers, and the act further fuels the yeast while removing yeast-inhibiting CO_2. Of course, oxidation becomes a worry whenever oxygen is introduced after yeast inoculation. If you feel your mead could benefit from an extra kick of oxygen, try aerating once after the first or second day of fermentation.

CONDITIONING

Mead is slow. There's no way around it, so think of the beverage-to-be as an investment in your cellar like a great barleywine or imperial stout. Eight to twelve months is a typical maturation time for a traditional mead weighing in around 8 percent alcohol. Once you reach 12 percent and beyond, you can expect up to two years, maybe more, for the mead to mellow. A high residual sugar level will also increase aging time by as much as a year. The ideal conditioning temperature for a dry mead is around 60°F (16°C), but for a sweeter mead you can arrest fermentation by dropping the conditioning temperature to around 42°F (6°C).

OXIDATION

Long conditioning times can turn an unbalanced mead to a near work of art, but the longer it sits and the more it's transferred, the more susceptible it becomes to oxidation. You might already recognize the signs of oxidation if you've had a vintage beer. At best, it creates a sherrylike character as ethyl alcohol breaks down to the fruity-tasting acetaldehyde. However, as the process continues, the oxidation flavors nose-dive into a realm of newspaper and nail polish remover.

Three steps help prevent oxidation:
Step 1: Age with minimal head space in your carboy. As yeast goes dormant and less CO_2 is produced, it loses the ability to displace oxygen in the area above the mead.

Step 2: Store the mead cooler than you'd ferment it. This simply slows reaction.

Step 3: Adding Campden tablets, potassium (or sodium) metabisulphite, will bind oxygen to create sulfate and remove the free oxygen.

TYPES OF MEAD

Few mead makers actually focus on simple batches of fermented honey. Instead, there's a rich history of styles, like in beer, calling in various types of ingredients for drastically different drinks.

BRAGGOT

This beer and mead hybrid is loosely defined as a mead that has malt and/or hops in the process. On one hand, you could make a braggot that pulls half its sugar from an amber ale recipe. You could also dry-hop a mead with floral hops, such as Centennial, to complement a floral honey. If you go this route, add up to 2 ounces of hops per gallon (15 g per liter), depending on how happy you want to make fellow hopheads. Other brewing spices are commonly used, added to the kettle while the must is hot.

A typical recipe will have a fairly even split of malt and honey, but keep in mind that barley has a richer character than most honey and can easily overpower and mask a wonderfully complex variety. Honey, per pound, contains slightly more sugar than base malt but ferments completely, whereas barley conversion relies on mash efficiency. To balance malt and honey sugar, use 1.5 pounds of grain for every 1 pound of honey (or 1.5 kg grain for every 1 kg honey).

Brewed with "more honey than water," Półtoraks like the Miód Pitny Półtorak Jadwiga drink like dessert wines.

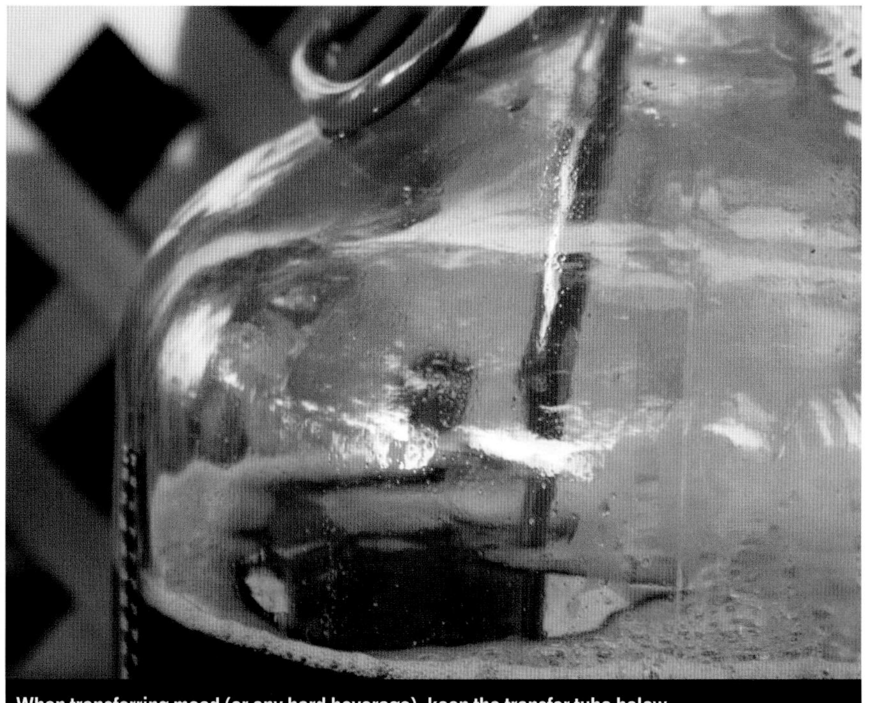
When transferring mead (or any hard beverage), keep the transfer tube below the top of the liquid to avoid splashing.

FRUIT MEAD (MELOMEL)

There are generally even fewer rules to adding fruit to mead than there is with beer. A basic mead makes a great platform for interesting or particularly delicious fruit.

To let fruit, or any flavoring, stand on its own, use a milder honey, such as clover in your mead.

As little as 8 ounces (225 g) of fruit in a 5-gallon (19 L) batch will make a large flavor impact on mild mead. Larger additions, such as 1 pound per gallon (120 g per liter), would be appropriate for sweeter, high-alcohol (12 percent and higher) meads.

CYSER

A meeting of cider and mead, cyser often has the zest and fruit of a white wine, but with a distinct honey character. Like pyment (below), the two components are fermented together and conditioned like a mead. A common blend is 2 pounds of honey per gallon (240 g per liter) of cider. With no added water, this yields a starting gravity near 1.100.

POLISH MEAD

Polish meads stand out for their simplistic, traditional recipes and colorful herbal character. Polish mead makers often age their miód in oak with local herbs for several years and use mostly acacia honey with some buckwheat honey. The varieties are broken down into four styles defined by their water content.

Name	Water-to-Honey Ratio	Approximate Starting Gravity	Approximate Final Gravity	Strength	Character
Czwórniak	3-to-1	1.1	1.02	9 to 11	The lightest of the meads is regarded and enjoyed like a dry white table wine. It also can be added to hot tea or poured over ice cubes in the summer.
Trojniak	2-to-1	1.140	1.04	12 to 15	This registers semisweet, is often aged for a few months in oak, and may have a fruit or herb flavor added.
Dwójniak	1-to-1	1.210	1.09	15 to 18	Sweet and strong, this mead approaches port after several years of aging.
Póltorak	1-to-2	1.250	1.12	15 to 18	The strength increases, leaving it around 16 percent with enough residual sugar to make this a fine dessert mead. It can be and is aged for decades.

If you want to try replicating these sugary wonders, try a small batch with honey, especially acacia honey from Poland, from a European food supplier. (Locust honey, which is widely available in the United States, is similar).

Fruit versions of these Polish meads will swap a third of the water for juice, and herbs are added to the boil (these are boiled, not just heated) and conditioning tank. Use a high-attenuating, alcohol-resistant wine or mead strain. Otherwise, follow the normal mead process and have a little extra patience for behemoths like these to mellow.

PYMENT

This variation of melomel is distinct for its use of wine grapes. Also, although fruit additions are regularly added to (but not limited to) conditioning tanks, the grape juice is fermented along with the honey.

A good starting point for making pyment is to use a sugar content blend of 75 percent honey and 25 percent of your favorite grape varietal. Most homebrewing stores stock wine ingredients, such as grape juice concentrates or, if you're lucky, frozen grapes.

Pyment can be further dissected and becomes hippocras if spices are added. Historically, hippocras referred to a dry wine sweetened with honey and flavored with herbs, such as ginger and cinnamon, but today it is considered a type of mead. The flavoring doesn't need to be anything special, as normal metheglin spices make a fantastic hippocras mead.

METHEGLIN

Metheglin is spiced or herb mead. The most popular infusions are similar to beer, with Belgian and winter spices such as cinnamon, vanilla, ginger, and orange peel commonly used. This style of mead is an opportunity to inject your favorite culinary flavors; nothing is off-limits. If someone can brew a garlic metheglin (and they have), don't be afraid to try to make a chili-pepper mead (Capsicumel) with a half pound (225 g) of jalapeños.

For a less dramatic start in metheglin, try a vanilla-cinnamon mead: Add the contents of three vanilla beans and three cinnamon sticks to a 5-gallon (19 L) batch after primary fermentation. Taste the mead after a week, and when you're satisfied with the infusion, rack the mead into another carboy to separate it from the spices.

ACID AND TANNIN

Honey naturally lacks the acids in most fruit, but to get more of a dry, winelike mouthfeel, some mead makers will add grape tannin and an acid blend. If you've found after conditioning that your mead lacks mouthfeel, or seems watery, start with ½ teaspoon (2 g) of tannin and/or acid, mixed in water, for a 5-gallon (19 L) batch. If after a few days, that addition does not produce enough character, add more and wait again. Be patient: As with a strong spice, you can ruin a batch by adding these overzealously.

Metheglins only need a spice; any will do.

I would first of all advise someone [who wants to make mead to] understand how to make wine or ale first. Get to know the process, then experiment with different yeasts and honeys.

INTERVIEW WITH:
BOB LIPTROT: OWNER, TUGWELL CREEK MEADERY, SOOKE, BRITISH COLUMBIA, CANADA

UNLIKE MOST BREWERS, BOB MAKES HIS BEVERAGE FROM THE SAME RAW MATERIALS HE HELPED CREATE EARLIER IN THE YEAR: HE IS ALSO A BEEKEEPER. OF COURSE, HIS BEES DO A GOOD SHARE OF THE LEGWORK IN CREATING HONEY, BUT BOB'S ATTENTION TO DETAIL AND LIFELONG INFATUATION WITH BEES CREATES AN EXCEPTIONAL MEAD.

HOW DOES ONE CHOOSE TO GET INTO BEEKEEPING?

I started beekeeping as free child labor when I was six years old. My parents literally lined me up with beekeeping equipment and told me to get the colonies ready for next season. Painting, scraping boxes, all the light-duty stuff. From there, I just took an interest in sticking my head into hives and seeing what the bees were up to.

NOVICES MIGHT THINK, "MY GOD, I CAN'T GET NEAR."

That's one reaction we get quite often. The other reaction is they want to just jump in without protection. They think of bees as benevolent and friendly, but bees can have bad days as well. You've got to get to know the livestock, as it were.

DO BEES HAVE PREDICTABLE TEMPERAMENTS?

Yes, if we're talking about the standard European honeybee, which we use for most of beekeeping. But it depends on the breed. What we've done as beekeepers over the millennia is breed for certain characteristics like survival, honey foraging, and attitude. Beekeepers don't want to work with bees that want to sting them.

YOU SAID EUROPEAN HONEYBEES, BUT WHAT ABOUT YOUR NATIVE NORTH AMERICAN HONEYBEES?

The European honeybee is a European-Western Asiatic bee. They probably arrived with the early European settlers. There are upwards of 19,000 native species in North America, so they're not uncommon. Unfortunately, none of those bees produce a large quantity of honey, though a lot of them are good pollinators. When it comes to honey quantities, the European honeybee is on top of the pile.

SO WHAT DO YOU KNOW ABOUT NATIVE NORTH AMERICAN INTERACTIONS WITH OTHER BEES?

There's a lot to be studied, particularly since we're moving bees around the planet with regularity now. With them, we transport pests and pathogens, and some bee populations are undoubtedly [more] susceptible. There are proven cases of the bumblebee industry importing bees from China and transferring various nosema diseases into native bee populations and decimating them.

THERE'S BEEN A LOT OF TALK ABOUT HONEYBEE DIE-OFF.

It's nowhere near being stabilized and is probably going to get worse before it gets better. We know a little more about it than we did when it started around 2005. It's undoubtedly the result of a lot of factors, largely things like climate change, nutritional stress, pesticides, and breeding.

We're [studying] further pesticides, which are highly toxic to bees. It's not being treated seriously by researchers [who are] bringing it to market. Europe has banned some pesticides that [North America] promotes. What's most disturbing is that we're not only seeing large losses in our bee populations, but also other natural pollinators, like hummingbirds, bats, moths, and butterflies.

It's a nonsustainable, spiraling problem: Farmers have to use more pesticides every year to save the year's crop. Are you going to watch your crop get eaten, or spray more pesticides?

SO IT IGNORES DOMINO EFFECTS DOWN THE ROAD. CAN YOU EXPLAIN NUTRITIONAL DISTRESS?

Bees exploited to pollinate large agricultural sectors are put out into 10,000 hectare (25,000 acre) areas of sunflowers, for example, that have very poor nutrition. The average bee only flies up to six miles (10 km), so essentially they're getting one type of food their entire life. That bee and their colony is forced into nutritional deficit by having one type of food, and that causes a lot of stress in organisms and the whole colony. It's like having to live entirely on potatoes.

WALK US THROUGH THE BASICS OF MAKING MEAD, WITH A FOCUS ON MAKING MEAD AT HOME.

I would first of all advise someone [who wants to make mead to] understand how to make wine or ale first. There are some fairly nice meads made in an ale style, a honey and malt mix. Get to know the process, then experiment with different yeasts and honeys. One of the most interesting aspects [of mead] is using different types of honey, like you'd use different types of grapes [in winemaking]. Some honey produces very good mead and some honey produces very poor mead.

YOU MENTION WINE- AND BEER-STYLE MEADS. PLEASE DESCRIBE THE DIFFERENCE.

Wine-style [meads have] higher attenuation and greater acidity, and their yeasts are commonly from the wine industry, derived from root or stem yeast. The ale yeast are derived from grain crops. They're not always, but [they] generally have a lower tolerance for alcohol. Get an idea for what you want to do, then use the appropriate fermentation techniques, instead of trying to hybridize, like using a champagne yeast with ale techniques.

WHAT'S THE DIFFERENCE BETWEEN STORE-BOUGHT HONEY AND HONEY FROM A FARMERS' MARKET?

If you go buying your honey at [a major discount retailer], you could be buying just a percentage of honey and it might have all sorts of crap in it. Some cheap honey is inexpensive because it's mixed with cheap imported honey.

When you buy a kilo of honey on the cheap, you get a different result than getting a kilo of honey from a beekeeper down the street and being charged more. It's like using grapes. You can be the greatest winemaker in the world, but if someone throws a bin of crappy grapes at you, you're going to produce an inferior product.

DO YOU HAVE ANY ADVICE FOR WHEN TO ADD FRUIT AND SPICE?

It depends if it is fresh or not. It really comes down to experimenting and how much you want in flavor, too. It is very much a personal thing. Because mead making is such an old fermentation process, every society has been messing with it and you find many different ways of producing it.

A friend of mine makes t'ej, the national drink of Ethiopia. They use gesho, a hops-like herb that's related to cannabis. It smells like a cross between low-grade hops and real bad pot, but they add to the boil.

DOES THIS PLANT BRING BITTERNESS?

Yeah, it's similar to hopping a beer or mead and has a preservative nature.

CAN YOU DESCRIBE THE FLAVOR PROFILE?

It's a cross between sweet wine and a sparkling ale. It has a bitter taste leaning towards a flat IPA with a little more alcohol in it, but the finish is still quite sweet.

SPOTLIGHT: THE HISTORY OF MEAD

Most people who study the historical aspect of fermentation believe it was one of the first—that or palm resin wines. Some of the earliest records are rock wall painting in southern Spain, northern Libya, and Morocco, depicting people mixing honey with water to no doubt make alcohol. The beverage is 13,000 or 14,000 years old. Bob Liptrot asserts, "It certainly predates anything Egyptians were doing or anything from most of Europe."

Mead probably started as a simple substance of diluted honey in water. Liptrot adds, "Our ancestors in neolithic and paleolithic periods probably found they could source it by getting a few bee stings and running like hell back to the safety of their camp. They let it ferment and probably discovered religion around the same time if they drank enough."

They basically started with crude mead: honey water with maybe a bit of fruit they managed to forage. When you think about the big picture of mead production, the meads that are produced in a brewing style are largely a function of modern agriculture from the past 5,000 years or so.

The two main historical styles of mead that brewers tend to be interested in are metheglins and melomels. Metheglins are spiced or herbacous types of mead and melomels are fruit- or berry-based meads.

36952

THERE ARE FEW FRUITS AS UBIQUITOUS AND PROLIFIC AS THE APPLE. FROM THE VALLEYS OF ASIA, ACROSS THE ROLLING HILLS OF EUROPE, AND SCATTERED FROM COAST TO COAST IN NORTH AMERICA, THE FRUIT HAS PLANTED ITS SEED, AND CIDER HAS ALWAYS FOLLOWED. LIKE BEER, HARD CIDER TRACES ITS ROOTS BACK FURTHER THAN RECORDED HISTORY, WHILE ALSO UNDERGOING A MODERN REVIVAL. HEIRLOOM CIDER APPLE VARIETIES ARE BEING REPLANTED, AND SMALL-SCALE ARTISANS BREW RICH, COMPLEX ELIXIRS THAT EXPOSE THE MASS-PRODUCED CIDERS FOR THE FRAUDS THEY ARE. AND AGAIN, LIKE BEER, GREAT CIDER STARTS WITH GREAT INGREDIENTS.

CHAPTER 17: HARD CIDER

INTRODUCTION TO HARD CIDER

Take the juice from apples, ferment out the sugar, and you have hard, alcoholic cider. Compared to beer, the ingredients are fewer, with just cider and yeast for a basic batch, and the process is shorter. Of course, like with all brewing, you can make cider as complex and time-consuming as you wish.

In this chapter, you'll learn about:

- **Apple and cider sources**
- **Types of cider apples**
- **Pulping and pressing cider**
- **Fermenting and conditioning cider**

LOCAL CIDER

You cannot make great hard cider from store-bought apple cider. Even if high-quality apples are used, these ciders are typically pasteurized. This process makes the cider sanitary, but it also saps flavor and aroma while killing enzymes and other nutrients your yeast needs. That's to say nothing of the preservatives that are in store-bought ciders for improved shelf life, which will further inhibit yeast growth.

If you're not pressing your own apples, find a small, preferably local, orchard that deliberately chooses their apples to improve the quality of their cider. Lesser cider producers will simply use whatever is left over and available. Some rare orchards in the Pacific Northwest go so far as to create heirloom cider juices designed for fermentation.

Cider apples are pressed and used within weeks of picking while dessert apples are often picked early and stored cold year-round.

GROCERY STORE APPLES

If you do not have access to a local orchard, you can make cider with in-season apples from the grocery store. Eating, or dessert, apples can make a fine cider, but because of their higher water content (compared to cider apples), the end product will be lighter in alcohol and character.

The key to good apples is finding ones picked fresh and in season. The best apples are high in sugar and acid content. Eating apples can be split into two camps, the acidic and tart "sharps," and "sweets." A 50-50 mix of sweets and sharps will make a balanced blend for your cider, but the best route is to press two ciders—one with sweets, one with sharps—and then blend to taste before fermenting.

Sharps	Sweets
Granny Smith	Fuji
Pippin	Red Delicious
Braeburn	Golden Delicious
Jonathan	Jazz

LOCAL ORCHARD APPLES

For the best apples, think local. Visit farmers' markets and talk to apple growers; the smaller orchards selling direct to consumers will have the most interesting apple breeds. If you don't have access to local growers, contact a state extension office to connect with farmers.

APPLE TYPES

The world of apples is broken down into three categories:

- Dessert apples, which are used for eating and baking.
- Cooking apples, which are larger, tarter, and used for baking.
- Cider apples, which hold a much higher sugar content, up to twice as much as a typical dessert apple such as a Red Delicious.

Cider apples are then divided into four types:

SHARPS

These highly acidic apples bring bite to a cider but are lower in sugar content and tannin level. They'll have a pH of 3.2 to 3.6, compared to a dessert apple that sits near a pH of 4.0. These are the backbone of a great cider. Examples include Brown's Apple, Crimson King, and Frederick.

SWEETS

As you can guess, sweets primarily have a high sugar content, while they're low in tannins and acidity. Used alone, they would make a boring cider without any bite or bitterness. Examples include Russet, Sweet Coppin, and Sweet Alford.

BITTERSHARPS

Matching tannins and acid with moderate sugar, these are relatively balanced and have the potential for single-varietal ciders. Examples include Kingston Black, Breakwell's Seedling, and Stoke's Red.

BITTERSWEETS

These apples pair sugar with tannin, so they both sweeten to counter acidity, but retain the bitterness. Examples include Dabinett, Bulmer's Norman, and Michelin.

ACIDITY

The pH of your cider isn't just a good guide for balancing how tart it is; it also helps support your cider while helping kill wild yeast. A pH level between 3.3 and 3.7 is ideal, with wiggle room for personal taste and desired acidity. Of course, if low pH is a concern, you can use tannin-rich bittersweet apples to add bite without the acid of sharps.

BASIC CIDER RECIPES

If you're going to press your own apples, there are two basic recipes for store-bought apples and cider apples. With a basic screw press, expect to use 17 pounds of apples for every gallon (2 kg for every liter) of cider. Assume a 5-gallon (19 L) batch for these recipes.

If using apples from a store or orchard, use 42.5 pounds (19 kg) of a sweet dessert apple, such as a Fuji, and 42.5 pounds (19 kg) of a sharp dessert apple, such as a Granny Smith.

If you can get cider apples, use 34 pounds (15.4 kg) of a bittersweet, such as Dabinet, 25.5 pounds (11.6 kg) of a sharp or bittersharp apple, such as a Kingston Black, and 25.5 pounds (11.6 kg) of a sweet apple, such as a Russet.

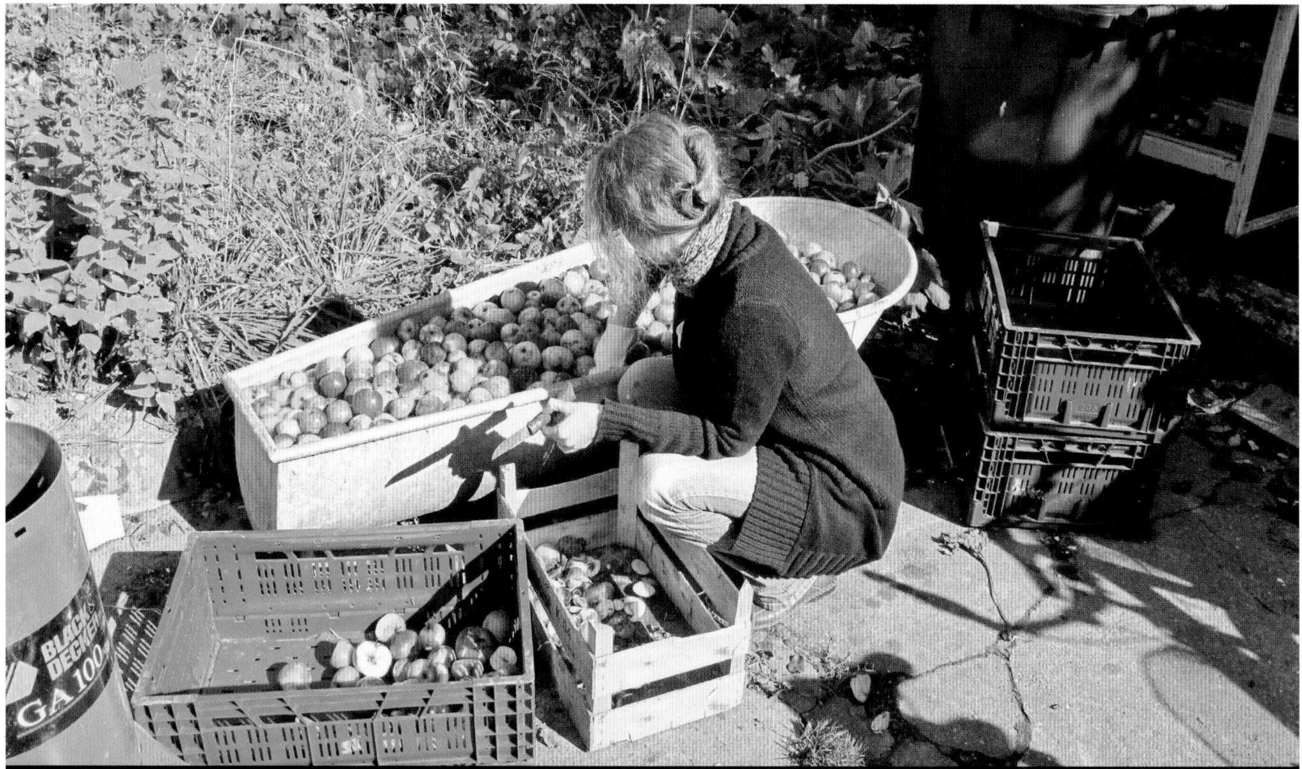

A few bad apples can ruin a cider. Check every apple for rot. If you're working with a large batch of apples, a simple way to separate rotting apples is to dump them into water. Fresh apples will float and rotting apples will sink.

PICKING AND PREPARING APPLES FOR MAKING CIDER

If you can pick your own apples from an orchard, or even from a store, the ideal cider apple is fresh but firm. Overripe, soft apples turn to slime once crushed and halt cider flow when you're pressing out juice. Even worse are rotting apples, which can introduce *Acetobacter,* the bacteria that produces vinegar, to your cider.

Once you have nothing but firm, ripe apples, wash and clean the fruit to remove any dirt, rocks, or twigs. Small stems are fine and there's no need to core or peel the apples. The miniscule amount of arsenic in apple seeds poses no harm to you or your cider, and the skin contains flavor and tannins.

PULPING AND PRESSING CIDER

Unlike barley grains, the finer you pulp and crush your apples, the easier it will be to extract juice. (Commercial cider brewers will essentially press thick applesauce.) If there are soft apples that gum up your pulp, adding rice hulls will create channels for the juice to flow out, much like you'd remedy a stuck wheat beer lauter. In cider brewing, the juice character is lighter than most beers, so use rice hulls sparingly to avoid contaminating the cider flavor.

If you have access to a hydraulic cider press, expect to get 60 to 70 percent extraction from your fruit. That means if you have 13 pounds (5.9 kg) of apples, you can press out 8.5 pounds (3.9 kg) (about a gallon, or 3.8 L) of juice. The traditional (and more affordable) screw presses can hit about 50 percent extraction with a fair amount of muscle to compress the pulp.

CIDER YEAST AND FERMENTATION

Apples bring their own wild yeast, but they are difficult to control and can create funky nonapple flavors most people find undesirable. Instead, adding a small amount (¼ teaspoon per 5 gallons, or 52 mg per liter) of potassium metabisulfite, also called sulfites, will kill wild yeast while still allowing your chosen yeast strain to shine. With sulfites, boiling is unnecessary. In fact, heating the cider is discouraged as the heat burns off delicate aromas and flavors.

Champagne yeast is a favorite choice for its predictable and powerful fermentations. A white wine or cider yeast will also perform well and leave slightly more residual sugar. All these strains are relatively aggressive, so to ensure your cider's character isn't wiped out, ferment at cooler temperatures (50°F to 60°F, or 10°C to 16°C) for up to six weeks before transferring to a conditioning vessel.

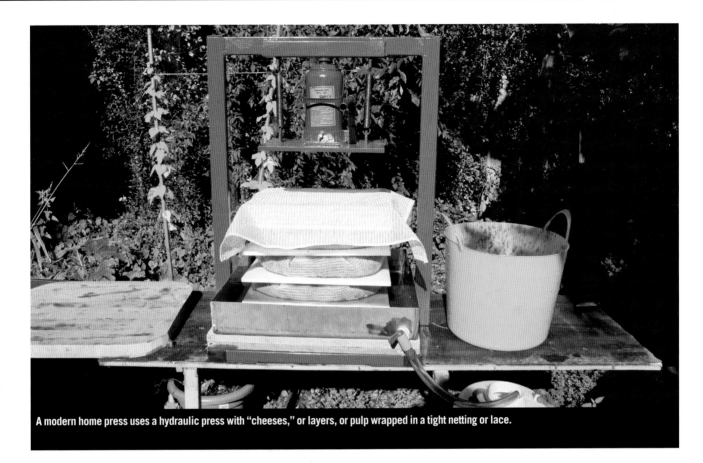

A modern home press uses a hydraulic press with "cheeses," or layers, or pulp wrapped in a tight netting or lace.

CONDITIONING AND BLENDING

Ciders require at least a month's conditioning after primary fermentation, with more time needed for stronger and drier batches. Six months for an 8 percent or stronger cider is completely reasonable, if it's not yet deemed satisfactory.

A strong fermentation will yield a finished cider with a gravity as low at 1.000. To help balance and add sweetness, backsweetening with a small amount of fresh cider or other juice is customary. How much to add comes down to personal taste, but for a rough guide, blending in enough juice to raise the gravity to 1.005 will be a semidry cider and 1.010 will be medium-sweet.

Once your cider reaches your fermenter, the process is pleasantly familiar to beer brewing.

Wandering Aengus's James Kohn is a champion of traditional ciders.

INTERVIEW WITH: JAMES KOHN: MARKETING DIRECTOR, WANDERING AENGUS CIDERWORKS, SALEM, OREGON, U.S.

ALONG WITH WANDERING AENGUS FOUNDERS NICK GUNN AND MIMI CASTEEL, JAMES BUILT ONE OF THE CIDER WORLD'S BEST EQUIVALENTS TO A CRAFT BREWERY. INSTEAD OF PRODUCING A SWEET, INOFFENSIVE APPLE WINE, THE WANDERING AENGUS CREW BLENDS TRADITIONAL METHODS AND RARE APPLES WITH THE SAME INNOVATIVE SPIRIT OF CRAFT BEER.

FIRST OFF, WHAT IS A WANDERING AENGUS?

It's from a poem by William Butler Yeats, called the "Song of Wandering Aengus." It describes a guy who has his fire in his head, an idea or lust. He heads out in the middle of the night to occupy himself and goes fishing. He catches a silver trout and, of course, the trout turns into a lovely woman who runs away. And he spends a lifetime chasing after her and lamenting the fact that he can't find her.

WHAT'S THE CONNECTION TO CIDER?

That's what we [based] the company on, having a passion and trying to execute it. Of course, we're trying to avoid the lamenting part.

SO WHAT MAKES GOOD CIDER?

This is a huge debate in cider land. There are basically two ways to make cider, two sets of ingredients. You can make an apple wine base. You get apples, juice, add sugar, and chaptalize it to a make a higher alcohol base. It's called apple wine and has more than 10 percent alcohol.

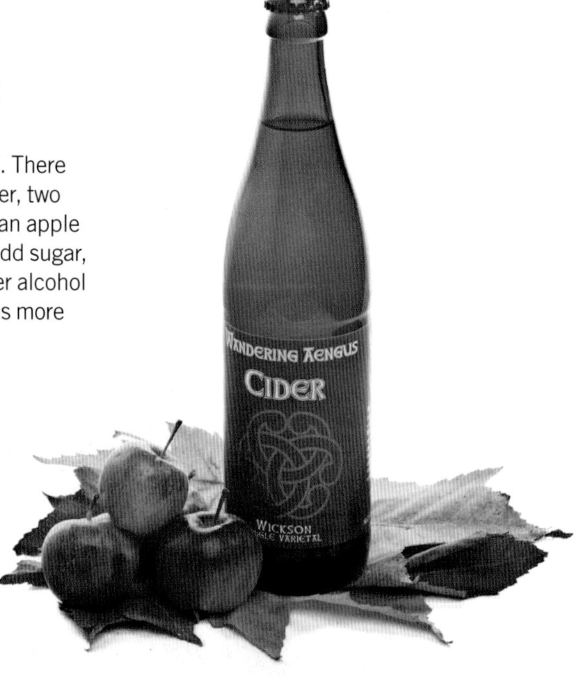

The Wandering Aengus Wickson is a single-variety cider with Oregon-grown Wickson crab apples.

WANDERING

CHAPTALIZE?

Yeah, it's actually a Roman technique. Wineries use it by adding sugar to wine or juice to increase starting gravity and potential alcohol. And the reason for vintners is because if a pinot is supposed to be 13 percent and if the grapes are set for 11, you're going to have something that doesn't necessarily taste like a Pinot and you'll have stability problems because the alcohol isn't strong enough for a nice, stable shelf life.

BUT IN CIDER?

It's more of an English way of making cider. A lot of larger producers chaptalize because it's more economical. Some homebrewers do it. When you chaptalize the juice, you get a more stable thing. On the producers' side, you can sit on product for a while, then bottle out as needed. From an economic standpoint, and I don't want this to sound bad, but if you water down a higher alcohol beverage, you get better efficiency and have more consistency over time. Sometimes the apples don't yield the same amount of alcohol content.

I'M GETTING A HINT THAT DOING IT THE APPLE WINE WAY AND YOUR PHILOSOPHY DON'T MATCH.

No, then there's the way we do it. We don't have a name for it, and this is also the way for most of the homebrewers. You get apples, press them, and add a tiny bit of sugar to help prime it for fermentation.

SO THE PRIMING IS JUST TO KICK-START FERMENTATION?

Yes, then there'll be alternatives once you're done fermenting for how you deal with residual sugars. There's debate for traditional cider makers how to get some residual sugars at end. We ferment bone-dry; we start at 1.060, higher than most because our apples are very special. Then we get to a final gravity of 1.000 or lower.

Some of the juice we put in a freezer. But after six to eight weeks, depending on what we start with, the nitrogen content, and some other variables, we'll rack the fermented cider the sediment off yeast. Then we age another two to six months depending on the cider.

WHY DO YOU AGE THAT LONG?

For one, it calms down the malic acid content, which is the main flavor constituent. If you were to think of hops with the alpha acids being your bitterness, the malic acid is our equivalent.

SO THE TART ASSOCIATED WITH APPLES?

Yes, and the more time you give the aging process, the calmer it gets. Also it clarifies the cider so we don't need to filter it as much. If it's our oaked, dry cider, it does not need to be backsweetened. With our two main ciders, Bloom and Wanderlust, we bring back that frozen juice and add it for the sweetness.

HOW MUCH ARE WE TALKING ABOUT?

It could be 5 percent, or if someone wants to go crazy, 20 percent, but it tastes like juice at that point. That's the way we do it, but some will add cane sugar to backsweeten it.

ARE THERE OTHER OPTIONS?

Some producers, instead of letting the cider go straight to dry, they'll crash cool it to around freezing, or crash cool and filter, or just filter to remove yeast and leave the residual sugars.

The reason we don't use dessert apples is they aren't picked at the right time. With Wandering Aegnus, we're using the right apples picked at the right time.

Cofounder Nick Gunn and James Kohn pose with their range of hard ciders, including a pommeau, which is a distilled cider.

WHY DON'T YOU JUST DO THAT?

We found in the past it's really hard to stop our champagne yeast. It has to be almost frozen for them to stop. Also, it doesn't have the same quality as if we ferment it dry and add something back. It doesn't have that finished quality that our aged ciders have.

YOU MENTIONED USING SPECIAL APPLES.

There's a big division between our apple for Anthem and our Wandering Aengus cider. Anthem is draft cider that's less focused, for a broader appeal. It's based on commodity fruit—basically grocery store apples available year-round.

Wandering Aengus is based on the opposite. Its apples are highly rare, almost nobody grows them, and they're highly specific to cider. The reason we don't use dessert apples is they aren't picked at the right time. With Wandering Aegnus, we're using the right apples picked at the right time. Eating apples are picked way before they're ripe so they store better.

SO YOU PICK AND USE YOUR APPLES WHEN THEY'RE RIPE?

We want everything to be ripe, but you also need to have some a little bit past the ripeness point. Once we pick them, depending on flavor and how much time we have, we also let the apples sweat for a week to release water content. We're measuring the acid and the sugar development and taste for flavor development. For some of our apples, that takes until November. Some you can let hang on the tree until winter.

WHAT ELSE ARE YOU LOOKING FOR WHEN YOU PICK YOUR APPLES?

You want to pick dessert apples that look stressed. When they're underwatered and underfertilized, you have a higher sugar content. Healthier-looking apples will make fine cider, but it will be more watery.

Small, bittersweet cider apples at harvest time.

IS THERE ANY CIDER-SPECIFIC EQUIPMENT HOMEBREWERS SHOULD PURCHASE?

For cider, pH is really important. The pH strips are kind of silly and don't work well, so get a pocket pH meter you can dip in a solution of juice and test. You want the pH around 3.5, between 3.3 to 3.7. Then you're going to ferment a good shelf-stable cider. Below that tastes like battery acid.

ANY OTHER ADVICE FOR HOMEBREWERS?

The biggest thing for homebrewers is sanitation. You're 75 percent of the way to good cider with good practices. The other thing is good use of sulfites, not more than you need to get clean fermentation from yeast. I also always recommend champagne yeast—it's bulletproof. And then there's temperature. Fermenting in a hot part of your house gives you a fast, out-of-control fermentation with a lot of very harsh dry fusel alcohols.

You want the pH around 3.5, between 3.3 to 3.7. Then you're going to ferment a good shelf-stable cider. Below that tastes like battery acid.

DEFYING GRAVITY

Fermented beverages can dip below 1.000, the gravity of water, when nearly all the sugar is fermented out because alcohol has a lower gravity (0.786).

Green Mountain Orchards in Putney, Vermont, is a fourth-generation family-run New England orchard.

BELIEVING ALL THE WORLD'S CIDERS ARE SIMPLY SPARKLING SEMISWEET BEVERAGES WOULD BE LIKE ASSUMING ALL BEERS WERE FIZZY PALE LAGERS. EVEN FOR HOMEBREWERS, HARD CIDER IS OFTEN LIMITED TO A MIXTURE OF DEXTROSE, APPLE JUICE, AND WINE YEAST. BUT THIS ANCIENT BEVERAGE HAS AN ARRAY OF FLAVOR EXPERIENCES, FROM TART, WILD, AND CITRUSY, TO BALANCED AND QUAFFABLE, IF YOU'RE WILLING TO TAKE ON OR ADAPT HISTORIC CIDER BREWING PRACTICES AND STYLES.

CHAPTER 18: TRADITIONAL CIDER

INTRODUCTION TO TRADITIONAL CIDER

It would be no more fair to describe only straightforward, apples-to-alcohol cider than it would be to only teach how to brew pale ales. Think of traditional ciders along the same lines as Belgian ales or German lagers; they are regional styles based on growing environment and local taste. These ciders also steadfastly follow age-old brewing techniques, which help define their flavor.

In this chapter, you'll learn about:

- **American cider**
- **British cider**
- **French cider**
- **Spanish cider**
- **Keeving**

AMERICAN CIDER

Unbound by tradition, American cider producers brew everything from sweet, juicy fruit ciders to dry, complex farmhouse styles.

COMMON CIDER

Your most basic cider is sterile compared to wild European styles, but it is a simple refreshing beverage. Use a mix of dessert and cider apples (usually with more cider apples) to create a sweet cider balanced by mild acidity.

NEW ENGLAND CIDER

High in tannins and alcohol, New England cider doesn't have stylistic limitations, so much as options. Beyond using apples grown in the region, New England ciders often use flavorful adjuncts, such as brown sugar and golden raisins, to boost the strength in a process called chaptalization. (For more on chaptalization, see chapter 17.) Oak barrel aging is appropriate, and the ciders typically finish dry.

NEW WORLD CIDER

Cider makers in the United States are more concerned with complex, enjoyable ciders than mimicking traditions or the commonly accepted sweet, sugary drinks. These ciders typically use a blend of locally sourced apples, which create regional flavor, as varieties of cider apples will develop a unique character depending on an area's soil and climate. In beer terms, this is like a clean American-style beer that lets ingredients speak for themselves without character from yeast. (See chapter 17 for more on craft cider process.)

Sheppy's Cider in Taunton, UK, brews farmhouse ciders and single-varietal batches with apples including bittersweet Dabinett and bittersharp Kingston Black.

A West Country cider, Thatchers Old Rascal is aged in oak vats and uses Dabinett and Redstreak apples.

ENGLISH CIDER

The British lead the world in cider production, but the mass appeal they have means that the farmhouse traditions of West Country ciders have been preserved. However, the market is also flooded with overly sweet alcopops bearing a cider label.

MASS-PRODUCED

"White cider" is Britain's malt liquor of the cider world, if you're generous enough to call it cider. It's cheap, alcoholic, and derives most of its alcohol from adjunct sugars. The less-offensive industrial ciders use apple concentrate and sugar to brew high-alcohol cider, which is then watered down to around 5 percent alcohol.

FARMHOUSE CIDER

With its roots in southwestern England, this real cider blends vintage and heirloom cider apples for a dry, bitter drink. Often hazy and served flat from casks, cider makers may use up to 10 percent sugar in a recipe and condition the cider in oak barrels. There's a degree of variation, with many cider producers making clear and sparkling products, but their common line is British cider apples.

Wine or cider yeast is appropriate, and, as with American ciders, brewers control for wild yeast with potassium metabisulphite. A cool fermentation (60°F or 16°C) over four to six weeks is normal, letting the gravity hit about 1.005 before you transfer to a secondary tank for several months of conditioning.

FRENCH CIDER

The Norman ciders of France have much in common with the lambics of Belgium. Not only are they brewed by families with a history in the business, but they use wild yeast fermentation and long conditioning times to produce a tart, acidic brew.

The Normans go a step further, however, using distinctive local apples specific to their region. These small, nearly golf ball–sized fruit are distantly similar to English cider apples, but they can be the same or indistinguishable in character from the British apples thanks to different soil and weather. If you can get your hands on French cider apples, a common blend is 40 percent bittersweet, 30 percent acidic (or sharp), and 30 percent sweet apples.

KEEVING

This step is used by traditional English cider makers as well, though the French name for keeving is an ugly word in English: *defecation*. This age-old process stunts yeast growth and clarifies cider by removing the pectin. First, after pulping the apples, the fruit sits in cold storage (about 40°F, or 4°C) for a day. This process, maceration, oxidizes the fruit to bring color while the pectin is pulled into the juice.

After pressing, the juice remains cold and wild fermentation slowly starts up. After a week, pectin will have formed into gel, and bubbles from the initial fermentation will have pushed it to the top of the fermenter. Calcium brewing salts, such as calcium chloride or calcium carbonate, may be used to enhance pectin coagulation. The gel, called the brown cap, is separated from the cider, pulling out yeast and nutrients, which will naturally slow the fermentation.

While craft brewers want to support a fast, vigorous, and healthy fermentation, this process creates a depleted, months-long

Spanish Basque cider, or sidra, country

fermentation that these cider makers prefer. Aside from the belief that a slow fermentation creates more complex character, the yeast will also sputter out with residual sugar in the cider, leaving it sweet with a final gravity around 1.010 to 1.015.

FERMENTATION AND CONDITIONING

You might assume that any drink expected to ferment for three or four months could be easily forgotten until it's time to rack, but pacing is a key to traditional French cider. The producers will watch the progress, wanting the gravity to drop no more than two points (0.002) per week. If a batch ferments too quickly, rack (and if possible filter) the cider to remove a portion of the yeast and arrest progress.

When the gravity reaches about 1.016, cider makers bottle, though to avoid exploding bottles at home, 1.010 is a safer target. No sugar or fresh cider is added back to the bottle, but after filtering the cider, a small wild yeast or champagne culture is added, depending on whether the goal was a funkier or a clean cider.

SPANISH CIDER

With homes in the principality of Asturias and parts of Basque Country, Spanish cider (sidra) uses a blend of cider apples and weighs in at a typical strength (4.5 to 6 percent alcohol). Sidra, however, is easily distinguished by its lack of carbonation and serving style. To mimic the dissolved CO_2 found in sparkling ciders, a sidra bottle is held overhead and poured onto the side of a glass held several feet below. This aerates the sidra, much like a sparkler nozzle on a beer engine froths up a cask ale.

The brewing process uses naturally occurring (wild) yeast, like French cider. But Spanish producers let the cider ferment out dry instead of slowing the yeast. To compensate for the resulting acidity, a malolactic conversion follows the initial two- to six-week fermentation.

This converts malic acid into lactic acid, which like with wine, creates a sweeter drink with a fuller mouthfeel. Malolactic fermentation will occur naturally in an unpasteurized cider, but adding a ¼ teaspoon of potassium metabisulphite per 5 gallons (52 mg per liter) to prevent wild yeast will require the addition of malolactic culture.

FERMENTATION STEPS

- **Control for wild yeast and other bacterial growth, a ¼ teaspoon of potassium (or sodium) metabisulphite, sold as Camden tablets, is added for every 5 gallons (0.3 g per liter) of juice.**
- **Use a white wine or champagne yeast to ferment the cider for a month at 60°F (16°C).**
- **After racking to a secondary fermenter, condition for an additional one to two months.**
- **When it's time to bottle and sweeten, adding 2½ teaspoons of potassium sorbate for every 5 gallons (0.5 g per liter) will prevent renewed yeast growth but require forced carbonation.**

To mimic the character of an oak barrel, add 1 ounce (28 g) of sterilized oak chips when the cider is nearly ready for bottling. Check the flavor weekly and bottle when you're satisfied with the wood character.

Jérôme began working on the family's ciders in 2002.

INTERVIEW WITH:
JÉRÔME DUPONT: CO-OWNER, DOMAINE FAMILIAL LOUIS DUPONT, VICTOT-PONTFOL, FRANCE

JÉRÔME WAS BORN INTO THE APPLE BUSINESS, OR RATHER THE BUSINESS OF TURNING APPLES INTO ALCOHOL. THOUGH THE DUPONT FAMILY (NO RELATION TO BELGIUM'S BRASSERIE DUPONT) HAD LONG EARNED ITS LIVING WITH CALVADOS, HE FOLLOWED HIS FATHER'S DEVIATION INTO TRADITIONAL FRENCH CIDERS, TAMING AND NEARLY PERFECTING A WILD AND UNPREDICTABLE STYLE.

Normandy's stronger drink, Calvados, is distilled from hard cider and relies on the same local apples.

YOUR FAMILY HAS MADE CALVADOS, AN APPLE BRANDY, FOR CENTURIES.

The family tradition was calvados, starting with my great-grandfather. But to tell the truth, cider has always been in the family too: My father, grandfather, and great-grandfather made cider. It was the most accessible drink when there was no potable water. Or it was often made for farm workers to drink. But commercial cider started when my father joined the family business in 1980.

HOW WOULD YOU DESCRIBE THE DIFFERENCES IN YOUR CIDER TO WHAT MOST PEOPLE HAVE TRIED?

You can make quite a link with the commercial beer and craft beer. Most commercial ciders use the big industrial techniques. In terms of flavors, our ciders have an appley flavor and some citrus aromas when they're young. As they're bottle conditioned, the yeast works over time and the cider becomes drier, more citrusy, and more acidic. After several years they have a lot in common with gueuzes and lambics.

SO YOU CAN EXPECT A STRONG ACIDIC CHARACTER AND WHAT WE DESCRIBE AS "FUNKY"?

Of course. Funkiness is something that comes to mind very often; it's very distinctive. Tartness dominates the ciders when you let them age to four or five years old.

WHAT WOULD WE EXPECT ALCOHOL TO BE FOR THIS TYPE OF CIDER?

We produce different styles. But they mostly depend on the vintage because the apples have more or less sugar content year to year. We don't add any sugar, so our cider can be 4.5 to 6.5 percent alcohol.

DO YOU HAVE YOUR OWN ORCHARDS?

Eighty percent of the apples we use come from our orchard and then 20 percent comes from the neighbors, but nothing further than ten miles (16 km) around the domaine. The only apples we use are local to Pays d'Auge in Normandy.

LET'S TALK ABOUT THESE APPLES. WOULD WE EXPECT TO SEE THESE ON THE MARKET FOR EATING?

No, the cider apples from Normandy are very special. The size is more like a golf ball. They have a very thick skin with high polyphenol and tannin content. They have also quite a high sugar content, 160 to 180 grams per liter.

It's always difficult to give a number of the varieties of apples we have in Normandy because if you go from village to village, the same apple is sometimes called different names. But there are three definite styles—acidic, bittersweet, and bitter—that are broadly used.

DO YOU EVER USE A SINGLE VARIETY FOR A CIDER?

Cider producers believe that the more apples in their blend, the more complex it will be. Whether it's true or not, I don't know, but it's very unlike wine where people talk about cépage and grape varieties.

SO WHAT KIND OF BLENDS DO YOU USE?

It's important to have apples of all different styles (sweet, acidic, bittersweet): maybe 40 percent bittersweet, 30 percent acidic, and 30 percent sweet. It changes every year. Is a cider with twenty varieties better than a cider with six well-chosen varieties? That's difficult to debate, but a blend of different styles is very important for final balance.

WHY DO YOU USE SUCH LOCAL APPLES?

We use apples from Pays d'Auge, which is an appellation. There's really a terroir and the apples have been growing here for at least one hundred years.

YOU USE LOCAL APPLES, BUT WHAT ABOUT YOUR YEAST?

We use indigenous yeast in the apples and the air for the beginning of fermentation. It's very common to have fermentation [last] up to three months, and if it goes too quickly, we might filter.

Domaine Dupont uses about a dozen different apple varieties.

Cépage literally means grape varietal or cultivar. In wine, single-grape variety batches are most common, lending to more focus on the attributes and flavors of a single cépage. Though not often found, this would be somewhat similar to a single-hop variety IPA, or a single-apple variety cider.

Jérôme and his father, Etienne, who developed their cider for commercial production.

It's always difficult to give a number of the varieties of apples we have in Normandy because if you go from village to village, the same apple is sometimes called different names. But there are three definite styles—acidic, bittersweet, and bitter—that are broadly used.

WHY SLOW IT DOWN?

If you have a very active fermentation in cider during the first part, once you bottle condition, the yeast will be very active and you risk overcarbonation. The idea is to have a cider that will ferment slowly from day one, so yeast gets used to working slowly. The carbonation process takes two months, and we put the bottles in a temperature-controlled room at 10°C to 12°C (50°F to 54°F). We try to put an amount of yeast back in to continue to fermentation but still leave some sugar.

DESCRIBE YOUR FERMENTATION CONDITIONS.

We use stainless steel tanks, but it's not temperature controlled, so we depend on the weather and external temperature. We like it around 8°C to 12°C (46°F to 54°F)—that's the ideal temperature for yeast. We try to limit aeration to really limit oxidation. The whole keeving and transfer process brings enough oxygen for the whole fermentation process, as we want a very slow fermentation.

WHAT ARE YOU DOING BEFORE FERMENTATION?

The apples are picked, washed, and hand sorted. After the crushing machine, we press the pulp, and the pressure is around two bars. It takes two hours, and we get 60 to 70 percent extract. Just after that, we cool the cider to stop fermentation. After a week, pectin builds up and we rack the cider off the brown cake, warm it, and ferment.

DO YOUR APPLES AND TERROIR HAVE AN ADVANTAGE OVER OTHER CIDERS?

Once we're talking about real cider, it's like beer—you don't compare a brown ale against a pale bitter. They are two different animals to be appreciated. Eating apples will produce a cider with less tannins, less concentration. You might get a nice light cider that will be appreciated in some circumstances. If you use only very bitter apples, you still have quite an interesting cider. Apples have a lot to offer and are underused as far as I'm concerned.

AND THERE'S YEAR-TO-YEAR CROP VARIATION AS WELL?

It is like grapes; some years have more sugar concentration. Our apple trees tend to have high yield one year and low the next.

WHAT YEAST ARE YOU ADDING WHEN YOU BOTTLE?

Because wild yeast can be pretty extreme in flavor, close to bottling we think that the wild *Brett*-type yeast already has a strong character, so we filter and add champagne or white wine yeast to carbonate.

SO WHERE DO YOU SEE CIDER GOING?

What I've seen in the U.S. is quite interesting. It's not huge and as big as beer, but there's more and more cider production there. People educated in biology are going into cider, and I feel this is very positive. Go back twenty or thirty years, especially in Normandy, cider production was an agricultural activity—there wasn't a lot of knowledge. It was a product that was very rustic and not always very well mastered.

BREWER'S GLOSSARY

Adjunct
A fermentable beer ingredient beyond barley. Industrial brewers use adjunct grains, such as rice and corn, along with barley, because they ferment dry and create a lighter-feeling drink.

Ale
A type of beer differentiated from lagers by its yeast strain. Ale yeast ferments best at warmer temperatures (60°F to 75°F [16°C to 24°C]) over a shorter period of time.

All-Grain
The process of using only malted grains to make beer. Often new homebrewers use malt extract in place of grains to simplify the brewing process.

Alpha Acids
The compounds in hops that impart bitterness, flavor, and aroma, depending on when they are added during brewing.

Aroma Hops
All hops have the potential to contribute aroma (along with flavor). Aroma hops refers to hops added in the final 30 minutes of the boil, though hops also contribute aroma during and after fermentation.

Attenuation
A measurement of how much sugar has converted to alcohol. A "high attenuation" beer, including most Belgian ales, will have less sugar remaining post-fermentation.

Barley
A cereal grain and one of the four basic ingredients in beer. Barley's starch is converted to sugar, which provides the fuel for yeast to create alcohol.

Bittering Hops
These hops are added at the beginning of a wort boil to contribute the majority of a beer's bitterness. Certain varieties are bred for higher alpha acids levels, which will contribute more bitterness.

Carboy
A large jug-shaped fermenter, usually glass, with a round, wide body and small top opening.

Cider
Apple cider is made from the pure, unsweetened juice pressed from apples.

Conditioning
After the primary fermentation step in brewing, conditioning refers to aging a beer after removing much of the yeast. This also allows the remaining yeast to develop and improve flavors.

Conversion
The process occuring in a mash tun in which properly heated enzymes turn the starch in barley to sugar.

Diastatic Power
The ability of a malt's enzymes to function. Kilning removes the enzymes so that specialty malts with no power need high-powered pale malts to convert their starch.

Dry-Hop
Adding aroma hops after the boil.

Enzyme
A catalyst that encourages a chemical reaction. In brewing, enzymes on barley malt convert starch to sugar. Two brewing enzymes are alpha amylase and beta amylase.

Ester
A generally fruity flavor and aroma component in beer.

Extract
Dry or liquid sugar derived from brewing grains. These save homebrewers time and require no mashing, but typically can't match the flavor of actual malt.

Fermentation
The process in which yeast converts oxygen and sugar to alcohol and carbon dioxide.

Final Gravity
The gravity of a beverage after fermentation.

Gravity
A measurement of beer or wort density that can be used to calculate potential and actual alcohol content.

Grist
The mix of crushed grains used in a mash tun.

Hardness
A measurement of minerals in water. Harder water has a higher mineral content and accentuates hop character.

Hop Utilization
The amount or percentage of alpha acids wort absorbs during the boil.

Hops
Green cone-shaped flowers that can impart bitterness, flavor, and aroma in beer depending on when they're added to the boil.

International Bittering Unit
A measurement of alpha acids in a beer.

Kettle
A brewing stock pot, or kettle, is primarily used by homebrewers to boil wort.

Lager
A type of beer differentiated from ales by its yeast strain. Lagers ferment at colder temperatures (50°F [10°C] or lower) for longer durations.

Lauter
The step after the mash that creates wort by separating the liquid from grains.

Liquor
Water directly added to a beer during the brewing process.

Malt
Malted grains, usually barley, used to make beer. Malting increases starch content, which will eventually become sugar and then alcohol.

Mash
The first major step in brewing that combines the grist and hot liquor.

Mead
Fermented honey and water mixtures, potentially with fruit and spices added.

Original Gravity
The gravity reading of wort before fermentation.

Oxidation
A common beer spoiler, oxidation creates a cardboard and paper taste.

Pitch
Inoculating wort by adding yeast.

Primary Fermentation
The main driver behind sugar-to-alcohol conversion. Typically lasts one to two weeks.

Rack
Transferring wort or beer from one container to another.

Rest
A temperature at which the grains are held in a mash tun to prompt specific enzymes and reactions. Most homebrewers use a single mash rest to convert starch to sugar.

Secondary Fermentation
Also called conditioning.

Sparge
The act of draining your mash with additional water during the lauter.

Sparge Water
Hot liquor (around 170°F [77°C]) used to sparge and reach a beer's batch size.

Sterilization
Different from cleaning, sterilization is the process of killing microorganisms that will interfere with the brewing process.

Strike Water
Water to be mixed with the grains for your mash.

pH
The acidity of your wort and beer.

Phenol
A spicy flavor and aroma compound found in many wheat beers and in Belgian ales.

Yeast
The microorganism that converts sugar into alcohol.

Wort
Unfermented beer, the sweet liquid drained from a lauter tun.

CONTRIBUTORS

Tomme Arthur
The Lost Abbey
155 Mata Way #104
San Marcos, CA 92069
U.S.
800-918-6816
www.lostabbey.com

Sam Calagione
Dogfish Head Craft Brewery
6 Cannery Village Center
Milton, DE 19968
U.S.
302-684-1000
www.dogfish.com

Bill Covaleski
Victory Brewing Company
420 Acorn Lane
Downingtown, PA 19335
U.S.
610-873-0881
www.victorybeer.com

Vinnie Cilurzo
Russian River Brewing Company
725 4th Street
Santa Rosa, CA 95404
U.S.
707-545-2337
www.russianriverbrewing.com

Ray Daniels
Cicerone Certification Program
Chicago, IL
U.S.
773-769-1300
www.cicerone.org

Hans-Peter Drexler
Weissbierbrauerei G. Schneider & Sohn
Germany
Emil-Ott-Str. 1
93309 Kelheim
Germany
09441 705-0
www.schneider-weisse.de

Jérôme Dupont
Domaine Familial Louis Dupont
Licu Prć
14430 Victot-Pontfol
France
02 31 63 24 24
www.calvados-dupont.com

Nick Floyd
Three Floyds Brewing Company
9750 Indiana Parkway
Munster, IN 46321
U.S.
219-922-3565
www.3floyds.com

Ken Grossman
Sierra Nevada Brewing Company
1075 East 20th Street
Chico, CA 95928
U.S.
530-345-2739
www.sierranevada.com

Eric Harper
Summit Brewing Company
910 Montreal Circle
St Paul, MN 55102
U.S.
651-265-7800
www.summitbrewing.com

John Keeling
Fuller, Smith and Turner
Chiswick Ln S
London W4 2QB
UK
020 8996 2000
www.fullers.co.uk

James Kohn
Wandering Aengus Ciderworks
6130 Bethel Heights Road NW
Salem, OR 97304
U.S.
503-361-2400
www.wanderingaengus.com

Bob Liptrot
Tugwell Creek Meadery
West Coast Road
Sooke, BC V9Z 1C9
Canada
250-642-1956
www.tugwellcreekfarm.com

Mitch Steele
Stone Brewing Co.
1999 Citracado Parkway
Escondido, CA 92029
U.S.
760-471-4999
www.stonebrew.com

Bernie Tonning
Redstone Meadery
4700 Pearl St # 2A
Boulder, CO 80301
U.S.
720-406-1215
www.redstonemeadery.com

Scott Vaccaro
Captain Lawrence Brewing Company
99 Castleton Street
Pleasantville, NY 10570
U.S.
914-741-2337
www.captainlawrencebrewing.com

Jean Van Roy
Brasserie Cantillon
Rue Gheude 56
1070 Anderlecht
Belgium
02 521 49 28
www.cantillon.be

Ted Vivatson
Eel River Brewing Company
1777 Alamar Way
Fortuna, CA 95540
U.S.
707-725-2739
www.eelriverbrewing.com

James Watt
BrewDog Ltd.
Kessock Workshop, Unit 1,
Fraserburgh AB43 8UE
UK
1346 519009
www.brewdog.com

RESOURCES

BOOKS

Calagione, Sam. *Brewing Up a Business: Adventures in Beer from the Founder of Dogfish Head Craft Brewery.* Hoboken, NJ: John Wiley and Sons Inc, 2005.

Calagione, Sam. *Extreme Brewing: An Enthusiast's Guide to Brewing Craft Beer at Home.* Beverly, MA: Quarry Books, 2006.

Daniels, Ray. *Designing Great Beers: The Ultimate Guide to Brewing Classic Beer Styles.* Boulder, CO: Brewers Publications, 2000.

Hieronymus, Stan. *Brew Like a Monk: Trappist, Abbey, and Strong Belgian Ales and How to Brew Them.* Boulder, CO: Brewers Publications, 2005.

Higgins, Patrick. *The Homebrewers' Recipe Guide.* New York, NY: Fireside, 1996.

Mosher, Randy. *Radical Brewing: Recipes, Tales and World-Altering Meditations in a Glass.* Boulder, CO: Brewers Publications, 2004.

Noonan, Gregory. *New Brewing Lager Beer: The Most Comprehensive Book for Home and Microbrewers.* Boulder, CO: Brewers Publications, 2003.

Palmer, John. *How to Brew: Everything You Need To Know To Brew Beer Right The First Time.* Boulder, CO: Brewers Publications, 2006.

Papazian, Charlie. *The Complete Joy of Homebrewing.* New York, NY: HarperResource, 2003.

Schramm, Ken. *The Complete Meadmaker: Home Production of Honey Wine From Your First Batch to Award-winning Fruit and Herb Variations.* Boulder, CO: Brewers Publications, 2003.

Sparrow, Jeff. *Wild Brews: Beer Beyond the Influence of Brewer's Yeast.* Boulder, CO: Brewers Publications, 2005.

Watson, Ben. *Cider, Hard and Sweet: History, Traditions, and Making Your Own.* Woodstock, VT: Countryman Press, 2008.

Wheeler,Graham. *Brew Your Own British Real Ale.* St Albans, England: CAMRA Books, 2010.

White, Chris and Jamil Zainasheff. *Yeast: The Practical Guide to Beer Fermentation.* Boulder, CO: Brewers Publications, 2010.

BREWING PUBLICATIONS

Brew Your Own. Battenkill Communications.
www.byo.com

The New Brewer. Brewers Publications.
www.brewersassociation.org/pages/publications/the-new-brewer

Zymurgy. Brewers Publications.
www.homebrewersassociation.org/pages/zymurgy

ONLINE RESOURCES

BeerAdvocate
Beer ratings and forums
www.beeradvocate.com

Brewing Network Forum
Brewing forums and radio
www.thebrewingnetwork.com/forum

Cicerone
Cicerone certification program
www.cicerone.org

CraftBeer.com
Beer guide from the Brewers Association
www.craftbeer.com

HomeBrewTalk
Homebrewing community and forums
www.homebrewtalk.com

Northern Brewer Homebrew Forum
Popular forums connected to the homebrew retailer
forum.northernbrewer.com

RateBeer
Beer ratings and forums
www.ratebeer.com

ONLINE HOMEBREW SHOPS

Austin Homebrew Supply
Austin, TX
www.austinhomebrew.com

Brooklyn Homebrew
Brooklyn, NY
www.brooklyn-homebrew.com

Homebrew Heaven
Everett, WA
store.homebrewheaven.com

Home Brew Mart
San Diego, CA
www.homebrewmart.com

Keystone Homebrew Supply
Montgomeryville, PA
www.keystonehomebrew.com

Midwest Homebrew Supply
Minneapolis, MN
www.midwestsupplies.com

More Beer!
Concord, CA
www.morebeer.com

Northern Brewer
St. Paul, MN
www.northernbrewer.com

Seven Bridges Cooperative
Santa Cruz, CA
www.breworganic.com

William's Brewing Supply
San Leandro, CA
www.williamsbrewing.com

INDEX

alpha acids, 26, 28
American hops, 35, 41
aroma hops. *See also* bittering hops; hops.
  American, 35, 41
  blending chart, 36
  dry-hopping, 37
  European, 36, 41
  hopbacks, 37
  "hop bursting," 37
  humulene, 37
  introduction, 10, 35
  myrcene, 37
  new varieties, 37
  Nick Floyd on, 38, 40–41
  terroir, 36
Arthur, Tomme, 70, 72–73
Austin, Peter, 85
autosiphons, 11

barrel aging
  aging time, 126–127
  barrel preparation, 123
  barrel size, 122
  introduction, 121
  Scott Vaccaro on, 124, 126–127
  temperature changes, 122
  toasted wood, 122
  wood additives, 122–123
Belgian brewing
  adjunct sugars, 67–68
  fermentation, 69–70, 72, 73
  history, 65
  hops, 66–67
  introduction, 65
  malt selection, 66
  mash, 66
  spices, 69, 73
  sugars, 67–68 , 72
  Tomme Arthur on, 70, 72–73
  yeast, 68–69, 72, 73
better beer
  cleaning and sanitation, 152
  hops, 152, 156–157
  introduction, 151
  Ken Grossman on, 155–157
  malt, 152
  oxidation and aeration, 153
  thermal stress, 153
  trace metals, 153
  yeast, 152
big beers
  aging and conditioning, 114
  champagne fermentation, 114
  freeze-distillation, 118–119
  introduction, 111
  James Watt on, 117–119
  starters, 113
  yeast, 114–115
  yeast pitching rate, 112
bittering hops. *See also* aroma hops; hops.
  alpha acids, 26, 28
  boiling, 25, 26, 32–33
  chart, 28
  cohumulone, 26, 28
  first wort hopping, 27
  history, 25–26
  International Bittering Units (IBUs), 26–27, 33
  introduction, 10, 25
  Vinnie Cilurzo on, 29, 31–33
bottling
  bottle conditioning, 72, 73, 89
  bottling buckets, 11
  caps, 11, 156
  gallon-to-bottle ratio, 13
  lambic brewing, 94
  traditional cider, 179, 183
Brewdog brewery, 117–119
brewing salts, 55, 60, 63
brewing terms
  adjunct sugar, 67
  hop utilization, 63
  hot and soft alcohol, 127
  phenol, 21
  pitch, 45
  Reinheitsgebot, 17
  yeast propagation, 81
brew kettles, 11, 68, 144
Burton-on-Trent, England, 57, 60, 63

Calagione, Sam, 106, 108–109
Cantillon brewery, 97–99
Captain Lawrence Brewing Co., 124, 126–127
charts
  aroma hops, 36
  bittering hops, 28
  brewing salts, 55
  disease-resistant hops, 133
  English ale malts, 83
  fermenting bacteria and yeasts, 92
  flavor troubleshooting, 144
  high-test yeast strains, 115
  International Bittering Units (IBU), 27
  lambic brewing yeast, 93
  mash temperatures, 17
  Polish mead, 162
  water reports, 57
  wheat types, 76
Cicerone Certification Program, 145, 147, 149
cider. *See* hard cider; traditional cider.
Cilurzo, Vinnie, 29, 31–33
cohumulone, 26, 28
conditioning
  big beers, 114
  bottle conditioning, 72, 73, 89
  hard cider, 171
  lager brewing, 44, 45, 51
  mead, 160
  introduction, 13
  traditional cider, 179, 183
Covaleski, Bill, 47–49, 51

Daniels, Ray, 145, 147, 149
decoction mash, 17, 51, 77
diacetyl, 84, 85
Dogfish Head Craft Brewery, 106, 108–109
Domaine Familial Louis Dupont, 180, 182–183
Drexler, Hans-Peter, 78, 80–81
dry-hopping, 37
Dupont, Jérôme, 180, 182–183

Eel River Brewing Company, 134, 136, 139
English ales
diacetyl, 84, 85
fermentation, 84, 88
flaked maize, 84
gruit, 84
hops, 84
introduction, 83
isinglass, 84
John Keeling on, 87–89
malts, 83
yeast, 84, 87, 88
European hops, 36, 41
evaluation
appearance, 142
aroma, 142
introduction, 141
mouthfeel, 143
pouring, 142
Ray Daniels on, 145, 147, 149
tasting technique, 143
troubleshooting, 144

fermentation
Belgian brewing, 69–70, 72, 73
champagne fermentation, 114
cleaning and sanitation, 152
English ales, 84, 88
fruit beers, 101, 102
hard cider, 170, 174, 175
introduction, 11, 13
lagers, 43, 44, 51
lambic brewing, 92, 93, 98
mead, 160, 165
sugar types, 69
traditional cider, 178–179, 182, 183
wheat beer, 81
Floyd, Nick, 38, 40–41
fruit beers
adding fruit, 102, 106, 108
dosing, 102
fermentation, 101, 102
forms of fruit, 102, 106, 108
fruit flavoring, 103
fruit preparation, 101
introduction, 101
lambic brewing, 94
mead, 161, 165
Sam Calagione on, 106, 108–109
sanitation, 101
Fuller, Smith & Turner Brewery, 87–89

Grossman, Ken, 155–157

hard cider. *See also* traditional cider.
acidity, 169, 175
apple preparation, 170
apple selection, 167, 169, 175
apple types, 169
basic recipes, 169
chaptalizing, 172, 174
conditioning and blending, 171
fermentation, 170, 174
introduction, 167
James Kohn on, 172, 174–175
local cider, 167
pulping and pressing, 170
yeast, 170
Harper, Eric, 18, 20, 22–23
high-alcohol beers. See big beers.
hops. *See also* aroma hops; bittering hops.
Belgian brewing, 66–67
better beer, 152, 156–157
disease-resistant varieties, 133
English ales, 84
growing, 132–133
lagers, 45, 49
lambic brewing, 91
noble hops, 45
organic brewing, 130, 132, 136, 139
pellet vs. whole-flower, 152
wheat beer, 77, 80
humulene, 37
hydrometers, 11, 13

inoculation, 13, 93
International Bittering Units (IBUs), 26–27, 33

Keeling, John, 87–89
Kohn, James, 172, 174–175

lagers
Bill Covaleski on, 47–49, 51
conditioning, 44
equipment, 43
fermentation, 43, 44, 51
hops, 49
introduction, 43
malts, 45
yeast, 44

lambic brewing
blending, 94
bottling, 94
fermentation, 92, 93, 98
fruit lambics, 94
hops, 91
ingredient selection, 91
inoculation, 93
introduction, 91
Jean Van Roy on, 97–99
malt, 91
mash, 92–93
yeast, 92, 93
lautering
Eric Harper on, 22
introduction, 15
sparge, 17, 23
tuns, 11, 16
malts, 12, 13
wheat beer, 77, 78, 80
Liptrot, Bob, 163–165
Lost Abbey brewery, 70, 72–73

malts
Belgian brewing, 66
better beer, 152
English ales, 83
introduction, 10
lagers, 45
lambic brewing, 91
mashing and lautering, 12, 13
mash
Belgian brewing, 66
decoction, 17, 51, 77
Eric Harper on, 18, 20, 22–23
grist, 16
introduction, 15
lambic brewing schedule, 92–93
organic brewing, 130
introduction, 12, 13
steps, 16
temperatures, 16, 17, 20, 23
tuns, 11, 16
water-to-grain ratio, 56
wheat beer, 77

mead
acid and tannin, 162
beekeeping, 163–164
Bob Liptrop on, 163–165
conditioning, 160
fermentation, 160, 165
fruit, 165
history, 165
honey preparation, 159
honey selection, 159
introduction, 159
oxidation, 160–161
Polish mead, 162
types, 161–162
yeast, 159–160
myrcene, 37

organic brewing
barley, 130
hops, 130, 132, 136, 139
introduction, 129
Ted Vivatson on, 134, 136, 139
oxidation
better beer, 152, 153
mead, 160–161
midfermentation aeration, 115
taste, 144
wood, 122

quality. *See* better beer.

refractometers, 11, 13
Ringwood Brewery, 85
Russian River Brewing Company, 29, 31–33

Sierra Nevada Brewing Co., 155–157
sour beer. *See* lambic brewing.
sparge, 15, 17, 22, 23
spices
Belgian brewing, 69, 73
chocolate, 104
coffee, 104
mead, 161, 165
peppers, 105
pumpkin and squash, 103
vanilla beans, 105
wheat beer, 77, 81
wood, 122–123

Steele, Mitch, 58, 60, 63
Stone Brewing Co., 58, 60, 63
sugars
adjuncts, 67–68
Belgian brewing, 67–68 , 72
brown sugar, 69
candi sugar, 69
dextrose, 69, 72
hydrometers, 11, 13
invert sugar, 69
refractometers, 11, 13
sucrose, 69
Summit Brewing, 18, 20, 22–23

tasting. *See* evaluation.
Three Floyds Brewing Co., 38, 40–41
traditional cider. *See also* hard cider.
American, 177
English, 178
fermentation, 178–179, 182, 183
French, 178
introduction, 177
Jérôme Dupont on, 180, 182–183
keeving, 178–179
Spanish, 179
yeast, 179, 182, 183
Tugwell Creek Meadery, 163–165

Vaccaro, Scott, 124, 126–127
Van Roy, Jean, 97–99
Victory Brewing Co., 47–49, 51
Vivatson, Ted, 134, 136, 139

Wandering Aengus Ciderworks, 172, 174–175
water
analysis reports, 53, 57, 63
brewing salts, 55, 60, 63
filtering, 54, 58, 63
hard water, 53, 58, 60
introduction, 10, 53
mash ratio, 56
Mitch Steele on, 58, 60, 63
pH levels, 54
soft water, 54, 58, 63
wastewater treatment, 63
Watt, James, 117–119
Weissbrierbrauerei G. Schneider & Sohn, 78, 80–81

wheat beer
adjuncts, 77
fermentation, 81
Hans-Peter Drexler on, 78, 80–81
hops, 77, 80
introduction, 75
lautering, 77, 78, 80
mashing, 77
spices, 77, 81
wheat types, 76
yeast, 76, 77, 80, 81
wort
aeration, 13, 153, 156, 160
boiling, 13
chillers, 11
first wort hopping, 27
hopbacks, 37
lambic brewing, 92, 93
thermal stress, 153

yeast
Belgian brewing, 68–69, 72, 73
better beer, 152
big beers, 112, 114–115
English ales, 84, 87, 88
hard cider, 170
high-test strains, 115
introduction, 10
lager yeast, 44
lambic brewing, 92, 93
mead, 159–160
traditional cider, 179, 182, 183
wheat beer, 76, 77, 80, 81

PHOTO CREDITS

Allagash Brewing Company: page 74
Edwin Bautista: page 48
Matthew Beckler: page 43
Belgian Tourist Office: page 142
bhenak, flickr.com/photos/bhenak: page 44
BillBl, flickr.com/photos/billbliss: page 121
Simon Blackley, flickr.com/photos/sblackley: pages 90, 98 (left), and 98 (right)
David Blaikie on Flickr.com: pages 57 and 114
John Bollwitt (johnbollwitt.com): page 141
Boulevard Brewing Co.: pages 7 and 67
© William Bragg: pages 168, 172, 173, 174, and 175
Brasserie Cantillon Brouwerij: page 96
BrewDog: pages 116, 118 (top), and 119
Matt Brown: page 178 (top)
Blake Burris & Ethan Thompson: page 152
Christopher Carlson: page 27 (right)
Chimay: pages 64, 66, 68 (top), 68 (bottom left), and 68 (bottom right)
Christopher Collins: page 99
Scott Collins: page 42
Lorena Cupcake, flickr.com/photos/juliet-banana: page 40
Jerome Dupont - Domaine Dupont: pages 181, 182, and 183
@epicbeer: pages 34, 37, and 151
Andrei Federov: page 163
Firestone Walker Brewing Co.: pages 12 and 120
Kevin Fleming: pages 11 and 107
Foodcollection RF/Getty Images: page 6 (right)
fotolia.com: page 166
Ben Fredericson: page 80 (right)
Full Sail Brewing Company: page 148
Fuller, Smith & Turner PLC: page 86
Chris Gehlen: page 158
Iain Gillespie: page 178 (bottom)
David M. Goehring: page 160
Simon Götz: page 105
Patrick Greaney: page 94
Green Mountain Orchards, Putney, VT: page 176
Joe Hakim/thehungrydudes.com: page 39
Joe Hall: page 156 (bottom)
Hameisterphoto.com: page 143
Shawn Hargreaves: page 76
Emma Jane Hogbin: page 104
Logan Ingalls: page 16
istockphoto.com: page 6 (center)
Andy Jakeman, flickr.com/andyjakeman: page 84
Johnny Knight Photography & Matt Taplinger: pages 146 and 147
Jonathan Castner Photography: page 122
Marty Jones: page 102
Karsten Juhl: page 45
k4dordy: page 36 (left)
Greg Koch, Stone Brewing Co.: pages 59 and 62
Tim LaBarge: page 129
R. Liptrot, Tugwell Creek Honey Farm & Meadery: page 164
Wendy Mann: page 82
Media Viking: page 87
McMenamins: page 38
Matt Mets: page 103
Brian Mulcahy: pages 85 (top) and 115
New Belgium Brewing: pages 26 and 140
Odell Brewing Company: page 93
Samuel Peters (Leipzig): pages 170 and 171 (top)
Ethan Prater: page 88
Spencer Ritenour: page 162
Andy Roberts: page 179
Bernt Rostad, flickr.com/photos/brostad: pages 35, 41, 61, 70, 77, 89, 92 (right), 95, 106, 110, 112, 108 (left), 108 (right), 118 (bottom), 126 (top), and 161 (top)
Russian River Brewing Company: pages 30 and 32
Schneider: pages 79 and 80 (left)
John Schulz, Studioschulz: pages 71, 72, and 92 (left)
Abbey Scourmount: page 65
Shipyard Brewing Co.: page 85 (bottom)
shutterstock.com: page 6 (left)
Rebecca M. Siegel: pages 55 and 171 (bottom)
Sierra Nevada Brewing Company: pages 150, 154, 156 (top), and 157
DJ Spiess: page 123
Hans Splinter: page 14
Dylan Stark: page 54
Aaron Stearrett: page 113
Stone Brewing Co.: pages 9, 27 (left), 52, 111, and 153 (bottom)
Rhett Sutphin: page 33
Matt Sweeny/Simple Earth Hops, Dodgeville, WI: pages 130, 132, and 133
Kelly Teague: pages 56, 153 (top), and 161 (bottom)
Urban Knaves of Grain: page 144
Marc Vaccaro: pages 125, 126 (bottom), and 127
Abby H. Van Stone: pages 19, 20, 21, 22, 23, and 75
John M. Verive, flickr.com/photos/octopushat: page 60
© Victory Brewing Company: pages 46, 49, and 50
Warminster Maltings Ltd. Traditional Floor Maltings, Wiltshire, UK: pages 83 and 131
Rachael Weseloh: pages 135, 136, 137, 138, and 139
Weyermann® Specialty Malts: page 128
Desiree N. Williams: page 159
Gail Williams: page 31
Ben Winnick: page 69
Ralph Woodall, courtesy of Hopunion, LLC: pages 25 and 36 (right)
Ed Yourdon: page 100

ABOUT THE AUTHORS

Greg Koch is co founder and CEO of Stone Brewing Co. in Escondido, California. Since Greg started the company with his partner Steve Wagner in 1996, Stone has become one of the fastest-growing and highest-rated breweries in the world. Brewing 115,000 barrels in 2010, Stone is the 18th largest craft brewery in the United States, a position it achieved without ever advertising, discounting, giving away freebies, or compromising. Greg passionately believes that environmental and social sustainability goes hand in hand with brewing mind-blowing beer, and he frequently speaks on topics ranging from craft beer to business to food to marketing, bringing a bold, entertaining, and often humorous approach to public speaking engagements. @stonegreg

Matt Allyn is a freelance writer living, drinking, and brewing in Pennsylvania. He's a certified, card carrying beer judge, and has been homebrewing award winning beers for five years. His writing has been published in *Men's Health*, *Draft*, *Runner's World*, and *Bicycling*. And although he doesn't have a favorite beer, he prefers whatever is fresh, seasonal, and in his hand.